The Fullness of Divine Worship

The Fullness of Divine Worship:
The Sacred Liturgy and Its Renewal

Edited by Uwe Michael Lang

The Catholic University of America Press
Washington, D.C.

The paper used in this publication meets the minimum requirements of American National Standards for Information Science—Permanence of Paper for Printed Library materials, ANSI Z39.48-1984.

∞

Library of Congress Cataloging-in-Publication Data

Names: Lang, Uwe Michael, 1972- editor.
Title: The fullness of divine worship : the sacred liturgy and its renewal : essays from Antiphon / edited by Uwe Michael Lang.
Other titles: Antiphon (Mundelein, Ill.)
Description: Washington, D.C. : Catholic University of America Press, 2018. | Includes bibliographical references.
Identifiers: LCCN 2018027150 | ISBN 9780813231396 (pbk. : alk. paper)
Subjects: LCSH: Catholic Church—Liturgy. | Public worship—Catholic Church.
Classification: LCC BX1970 .F85 2018 | DDC 264/.02—dc23
LC record available at https://lccn.loc.gov/2018027150

Contents

Introduction

UWE MICHAEL LANG

This volume contains a selection of essays from the pages of *Antiphon: A Journal for Liturgical Renewal*, the official organ of the Society for Catholic Liturgy. The Society was founded in 1995 by Msgr. M. Francis Mannion as a multidisciplinary association of Catholic scholars, teachers, pastors, and ecclesiastical professionals in the Anglophone world, with the aim of promoting the scholarly study and practical renewal of the sacred liturgy. Since the publication of its first issue in 1996, *Antiphon* has become an important voice in the academic and pastoral debates on liturgy and sacramental theology. As the present editor of the journal, I gratefully acknowledge the work of my predecessors: M. Francis Mannion (1996–2002), Timothy V. Vaverek (2002–2004), Neil J. Roy (2005–2008), Thomas M. Kocik (2009–2011), and Carmina Magnusen Chapp (2011–2012). In 2017, *Antiphon* came under the aegis of the Catholic University of America Press, which now produces and distributes the peer-reviewed journal on behalf of the Society for Catholic Liturgy.

This collection is inspired by the affirmation of the Second Vatican Council, taking its cue from an ancient prayer of the Roman Rite, that in Christ, "the fullness of divine worship was given to us."[1] The Father sent His Son into the world as the "high priest of the good things that have come" (Heb 9:11) and "medi-

---

1 Second Vatican Council, Constitution on the Sacred Liturgy *Sacrosanctum Concilium* (4 December 1963) no. 5. The quotation is from a *super oblata* prayer for the Nativity of the Lord in the *Sacramentarium Veronense (Cod. Bibl. Capit. Veron. LXXXV [80])*, ed. Leo Cunibert Mohlberg, OSB, Leo Eizenhöfer, OSB, and Petrus Siffrin, OSB, Rerum Ecclesiasticarum Documenta, Series Maior, Fontes I, 3rd ed. (Rome: Casa Editrice Herder, 1994) XL, no. 1265 (p. 162): "diuini cultus nobis est indita plenitudo."

ator of a new covenant" (Heb 9:15). The Incarnation reveals Christ's consecration as priest to offer sacrifice and to intercede for his people, and this consecration is perfected in the Paschal Mystery, which is made present above all in the sacrifice of the Eucharist. The sacred liturgy, the visible worship in which we are called to participate in this world, is an exercise of the priesthood of Christ—to be more precise, of *Christus totus*: the whole Christ, the Head and the members of His Mystical Body, which is the Church. Pope Pius XII expressed this lucidly in his encyclical *Mediator Dei*:

> The sacred liturgy is, consequently, the public worship which our Redeemer as Head of the Church renders to the Father, as well as the worship which the community of the faithful renders to its Founder, and through Him to the heavenly Father. It is, in short, the worship rendered by the Mystical Body of Christ in the entirety of its Head and members.[2]

The eternal high priesthood of Christ is represented in the image chosen for the front cover of this book. The splendid mosaic from the apse of San Vitale in Ravenna, dating from the first half of the sixth century, shows the sacrifice of Abel and Melchizedek's offering of bread and wine as mystical anticipations of the Eucharistic sacrifice celebrated on the altar below.

The contributions gathered in this volume cover a variety of topics and offer different perspectives, but they are united by their grounding in the rich history of Christian liturgy, by their theological awareness and reflection, and by the authors' shared concern for the state of divine worship in the Catholic Church today. Alcuin Reid[3] considers the place of positive liturgical law in the

---

2   Pius XII, Encyclical Letter on the Sacred Liturgy *Mediator Dei* (20 November 1947) no. 20. See also *Sacrosanctum Concilium*, no. 7, and *Catechism of the Catholic Church*, 2nd ed. (Washington, DC: United States Catholic Conference, 2000) nos. 1066–1070.

3   "From Rubrics to *Ars Celebrandi*—Liturgical Law in the 21st Century," originally published in *Antiphon* 17 (2013) 139–167.

twenty-first century and explores the theological dimensions of *ars celebrandi*. Ryan J. Marr[4] relates the seminal thought of René Girard to contemporary discussions on the sacrificial character of the Eucharist and on liturgical reform. My article[5] offers a fresh reading of Augustine's conception of sacrifice in *City of God*, Book X, a historically charged text that continues to generate lively interest among theologians and liturgists. Michael P. Foley[6] sheds light on the origins of the rite of peace in the Roman tradition and discusses its significance and practice in contemporary liturgical celebrations. Madeleine Grace, CVI,[7] makes a compelling case from biblical, liturgical and canonical sources to recover the spiritual benefits of Eucharistic fasting. Daniel G. Van Slyke[8] compares and contrasts the current Order for Blessing Water Outside of Mass with its immediate predecessor. Clinton Allen Brand[9] presents the language of the liturgical books approved for the Ordinariates according to the Apostolic Constitution *Anglicanorum Coetibus* as an idiom of worship that resonates with Anglophone culture and provides an opportunity for evangelization.

While these contributions have been carefully edited and their style of referencing has been harmonized, no changes to their contents have been made. The reader will find that the essays I have selected after careful search through past years of *Antiphon* stand the test of time and remain as relevant to liturgical scholarship and practice as they were at their first publication.

---

4   "René Girard and the Holy Sacrifice of the Mass: Re-Assessing the Twentieth-Century Liturgical Reform," originally published in *Antiphon* 20 (2016) 191–212.

5   "Augustine's Conception of Sacrifice in *City of God*, Book X, and the Eucharistic Sacrifice," originally published in *Antiphon* 19 (2015) 29–51.

6   "The Whence and Whither of the Kiss of Peace in the Roman Rite," originally published in *Antiphon* 14 (2010) 45–94.

7   "Eucharistic Fasting: A Review of Its Practice and Evaluation of Its Benefit," originally published in *Antiphon* 17 (2013) 225–246.

8   "The Order for Blessing Water: Past and Present," originally published in *Antiphon* 8 (2003) 12–23.

9   "Very Members Incorporate: Reflections on the Sacral Language of *Divine Worship*," originally published in *Antiphon* 19 (2015) 132–154.

Thanks are due above all to Trevor Lipscombe of the Catholic University of America Press for initiating this publication and seeing it through. I am also grateful to Br. Joseph Rodrigues for his most valuable assistance in preparing the typescript.

List of Abbreviations

CCCM   Corpus Christianorum. Continuatio Mediaevalis
        (Turnhout: Brepols, 1966–)

CCSL   Corpus Christianorum. Series Latina (Turnhout:
        Brepols, 1953–)

CSEL   Corpus Scriptorum Ecclesiasticorum Latinorum
        (Wien: Geroldi, then Tempksy, 1866–)

PG   Patrologiae Cursus Completus, accurante J.-P. Migne,
        Series Graeca, 166 vol. (Paris: Petit-Montrouge,
        1857–1883)

PL   Patrologiae Cursus Completus, accurante J.-P. Migne,
        Series Latina, 221 vol. (Paris: J.-P. Migne, 1844–1865)

SC   Sources Chrétiennes (Paris: Cerf, 1941–)

From Rubrics to *Ars Celebrandi*— Liturgical Law in the Twenty-First Century

ALCUIN REID

INTRODUCTION

During the 1970s and 1980s rubrics—even modern ones—were widely disregarded if not dismissed as irrelevant. They were years when the General Instruction of the Roman Missal was too often treated simply as a set of guidelines and the Missal itself as a mere planning resource. Liturgical law was not taken seriously and grave liturgical abuses took place, even in seminaries. Bishops were not infrequently "surprised" by occurrences in liturgies over which they presided.

Today the abuses of the immediate post-conciliar decades seem largely—though not entirely—to have ceased. The problem now is more one of ignorance of liturgical law and of a *laissez-faire* attitude to ritual which evacuates liturgical rites of the sacred and to a lesser or greater extent renders each parish or community's celebration not the celebration of the liturgy of the Church as the Church has given it us, but a celebration of "what we do here."

Thus a subjectivization of the Church's liturgy endures and in some places has taken root. It gives rise to the question: Does positive liturgical law have a place in the life of the Church of the twenty-first century? Or is such law devoid of meaning and authority? Are there reasons for taking rubrics seriously?[1]

---

1   I am assuming that for celebrations of the *usus antiquior* the answer is self-evident; see Pontifical Commission *Ecclesia Dei*, Instruction on the Application of the

THE NATURE OF LITURGICAL LAW

What is liturgical law? The clearest definition may be found in the 1954 doctoral dissertation of Msgr. Frederick R. McManus (1923–2005): "The ordering and regulation of the Sacred Liturgy make up liturgical law."[2] McManus sees liturgical law as having divine origin in the dominical command: *Hoc facite in meam commemorationem* (see Lk 22:19; 1 Cor 11:23), and in the authority given by Christ to the Church (see Mt 28:18-20). He regards it as part of the *potestas ministerii* of the Church.[3]

Historically, this *potestas* was exercised at a local level; bishops or their chapters gave assent to the modification of liturgical rites and texts as necessary.[4] At times secular princes—who were by no means "secular" in the sense of the separation of church and state as we understand today—intervened in liturgical regulation, the most notable example of whom was the Emperor Charlemagne (c. 742–814), in what has become known as "the Carolingian reform" at the end of the eighth century.[5]

The disputes and denials of the Protestant Reformation and the decadence that had given rise to them led the Council of Trent to underline the local bishop's duty to correct sundry errors and to supervise liturgical observances.[6] Interestingly, in its seventh

---

Apostolic Letter *Summorum Pontificum* Given Motu Proprio *Universae Ecclesiae* (30 April 2011), no. 28.

2   Frederick R. McManus, *The Congregation of Sacred Rites* (Washington, DC: Catholic University of America Press, 1954) 5.

3   See ibid., 6–7.

4   Examples of pre-Reformation liturgical regulation of local liturgical books may be found in: Archdale A. King, *Liturgies of the Primatial Sees* (London: Longmans, 1957).

5   See Alcuin Reid, *The Organic Development of the Liturgy*, 2nd ed. (San Francisco: Ignatius Press, 2005) 22–27.

6   "Quaecumque in diocesi ad Dei cultum spectant, ab ordinario diligenter curari atque iis, ubi oportet, provideri aequum est." Council of Trent, Session XXI, *Decree concerning Reform* (16 July 1562), canon 8: *Decrees of the Ecumenical Councils*, ed. Norman Tanner, vol. II (London–Washington, DC: Sheed & Ward–Georgetown University Press, 1990) 731.

session (March 3, 1547), the council had already asserted liturgical discipline quite strongly:

> If anyone says that the received and approved rites of the Catholic Church in customary use in the solemn administration of the sacraments may, without sin, be neglected or omitted at choice by the ministers, or can be changed to other new ones by any pastor whatever: let him be anathema.[7]

In 1563 the council, in its final session, left the work of reforming the texts of the Missal and the Breviary to the pope personally.[8]

It is difficult to maintain that in taking this decision the council envisaged the liturgical centralism it would later bring about. Certainly, when Pope St. Pius V promulgated the subsequent *Breviarium Romanum* (1568) and the *Missale Romanum* (1570) he posited them as the norm for the Roman Rite. However, he also mandated respect for breviaries and missals of ancient use, where that use was of greater than two hundred years' standing.[9] As late as 1614, the "last" of the books of the liturgical reform of the Council of Trent to appear, the *Rituale Romanum*, was presented by Pope Paul V as a ritual, the use of which he exhorted, but did not impose.[10]

---

7   Council of Trent, Session VII, *Decree on the Sacraments* (3 March 1547), canon 13: "Si quis dixerit, receptos et approbatos ecclesiae catholicae ritus in solemni sacramentorum administatione adhiberi consuetos aut contemni, aut sine peccato a ministris pro libito omitti, aut in novos alios per quemcumque ecclesiarum pastorem mutari posse: anathema sit." Tanner, *Decrees*, 685. Compare article 22,3 of the Second Vatican Council's *Constitution on the Sacred Liturgy* (cited below).

8   See Council of Trent, Session XXV, *Concerning the Index of Books and the Catechism, Breviary and Missal* (4 December 1563): Tanner, *Decrees*, 797. For more on the work of this reform, see Reid, *The Organic Development*, 39–43.

9   *Breviarium Romanum Editio Princeps (1568)*, Monumenta Liturgica Concilii Tridentini 3, ed. Manlio Sodi and Achille M. Triacca (Vatican City: Libreria Editrice Vaticana, 1999), and *Missale Romanum Editio Princeps (1570)*, Monumenta Liturgica Concilii Tridentini 2, ed. Manlio Sodi and Achille M. Triacca (Vatican City: Libreria Editrice Vaticana, 1998).

10   *Rituale Romanum Editio Princeps 1614*, Monumenta Liturgica Concilii Tridentini 5, ed. Manlio Sodi and Juan Javier Flores Arcas (Vatican City: Libreria Editrice Vaticana, 2004).

Nevertheless, facilitated by the advance of printing technology, zealous new Counter-Reformation religious orders, as well as mendicants (also, later, zealous nineteenth-century ultramontane enthusiasts),[11] the Roman liturgical books in their Tridentine redaction came to dominate the Western Church in a way they had never previously.

Crucial to this new liturgical centralism was the establishment of the Sacred Congregation of Rites as part of the general reform of the Roman Curia carried out by Pope Sixtus V in 1588. Apart from competence in matters pertaining to the canonization of saints and ceremonial concerning visitors to the Papal court, the Congregation was charged with responsibility for "vigilance for the observance of sacred rites, restoration and reformation of ceremonies, reform and correction of liturgical books . . . the celebration of feast days . . . [and] solution of controversies over precedence and other liturgical matters."[12]

This heralded what the German liturgical scholar Theodore Klauser (1894–1984) loudly decried as the "epoch of rubricism."[13] There is no doubt that liturgical law and rubrics became a "growth industry" in the following centuries, hand in hand with an increase in centralism in papal governance in other areas. As the English polymath Adrian Fortescue (1878–1923) observed: "the Protestant revolt of the sixteenth century had its natural

---

11   In particular, Prosper Guéranger, OSB, in his understandable, though excessive, reaction to liturgical Gallicanism; see Reid, *The Organic Development*, 56–60.

12   McManus, *The Congregation of Sacred Rites*, 27.

13   Theodore Klauser, *A Short History of the Western Liturgy: An Account and Some Reflections*, trans. John Halliburton, 2nd ed. (Oxford: Oxford University Press, 1979) 119. Klauser claims that the Council of Trent's 1563 decision to place the reform of the Breviary and Missal in the hands of the pope (and therefore of his Curia) gave the Curia the sought-after prize of "exclusive right of jurisdiction in liturgical matters" (ibid., 118). While this in fact came with the establishment of the Sacred Congregation for Rites in 1588, it is difficult to recognize the seemingly political motivation Klauser attributes to this. It is possible that, in line with Counter-Reformation practice in other areas (catechesis, the formation of priests), this was a natural and appropriate step taken for the good of the Church at the time.

result in increased centralization among those who remained faithful."[14]

Rubricism—an excessive and exclusive concern for the *minutiae* of valid and legal celebration of the rites—is most certainly capable of reducing the sacred liturgy to a matter of the anxious or scrupulous public observance of positive law. Yet *rubrics* formed an integral part of the sacred rites and could not simply be set aside. Those learned in rubrics, whom we call "rubricists," were by no means intrinsically guilty of "rubricism." The rubrics and other liturgical rulings were complex and considerable skill was necessary to provide clergy with straightforward advice and useful manuals.

The famous Anglophone rubricist, Canon J. B. O'Connell († 1977), gives a clear explanation of the nature of rubrics:

> The rubrics are rules (laws, directions, suggestions) which are contained in the liturgical books for the right ordering of liturgical functions.[15] For the most part, if not entirely, the rubrics are positive ecclesiastical laws, and so (a) they bind under pain of mortal or venial sin, according to the gravity of the matter with which they are concerned; (b) apart from such considerations as the giving of scandal, contempt for the law, and the like, a sufficient and proportionately grave cause excuses from the observance of an (accidental) rubric.[16]

Accidental rubrics, he explains, are distinct from "substantial rubrics" and "do not concern the validity of a liturgical act, but regulate the rite in which it is enshrined." He continues: "Substantial rubrics are based on the divine law and, for the sacraments and Mass are immutable; the accidental rubrics are purely eccle-

14   Adrian Fortescue, *The Early Papacy to the Synod of Chalcedon in 451*, 4th ed. by Alcuin Reid (San Francisco: Ignatius Press, 2008) 36.

15   O'Connell adds in a footnote that "the rules which are found elsewhere (e.g., in the Code or in Papal Constitutions) are not termed 'rubrics' but 'decrees' or 'liturgical laws.'"

16   John Berthram O'Connell, *The Celebration of Mass: A Study of the Rubrics of the Roman Missal*, 4th ed. (Milwaukee: Bruce Publishing Co., 1964) 19.

siastical laws, and may be changed or dispensed from, but only by the Holy See."[17]

Certainly, by the twentieth century, the study of rubrics had largely eclipsed other areas of liturgical research: most seminaries taught liturgical law, not liturgical history or theology, and this is certainly one foundation for a certain disdain for the legislation of the Congregation of Sacred Rites. In 1920 Fortescue, more an historian than a rubricist (but who had nonetheless compiled what became the principal Anglophone rubrical manual),[18] complained bitterly of the need to revise his manual for a further edition:

> You cannot conceive how I loathe the idea of going into all that horrid business of the *minutiae* of tomfool modern ceremonies once again. I do not think there is any possible subject that seems to me more utterly devoid of interest or of any scientific attraction. It is always, of course, merely a matter of seeing what some footling Congregation of incompetent idiots at Rome has said we are to do. Not one halfpenny-worth of principle or of historic research is affected by the question whether the thurifer should stand on the left or on the right at any given moment. I would just as soon spend hours verifying the hours at which trains start on some railway line that I shall never use.[19]

Indeed, in his introduction to his 1931 work *Liturgical Law: A Handbook of the Roman Liturgy*, Charles Augustine, OSB (1872–1944), a monk of the Swiss-American Congregation, observed of the current state of liturgical law:

> The *Decreta Authentica* [of the Sacred Congregation of Rites] in its six volumes contains 4,284 numbers. If we multiply this num-

---

17   Ibid., 20.

18   Adrian Fortescue, *The Ceremonies of the Roman Rite Described* (London: Burns & Oates, 1918). To date a total of fifteen editions have been published, the third to the twelfth (1930–1962) under the editorship of J. B. O'Connell, the thirteenth to the fifteenth (1996, 2003, 2009) under the editorship of the present author.

19   Typewritten letter dated 20 May 1920: Cambridge University Library, Morison Papers, I, 16–18; quoted by kind permission of the Syndics of Cambridge University Library.

ber by five we have 21,420 *dubia* solved. And the multiplication is not too highly set. For more than one of the decisions solves twenty, thirty or even fifty *dubia*, each of them really constituting a decision or rule for itself. Then take all the changes made since 1913 in the Breviary and the Missal.[20]

He goes on to appeal: "Is it too much to say that a *rubrical disarmament parley* might produce some useful simplification?"[21]

From Fortescue and Augustine we can certainly see a reaction to the overgrowth of liturgical legislation, and indeed from the very subtitle of Augustine's book (*Liturgical Law: A Handbook of the Roman Liturgy*), we can appreciate the at least partial eclipse of liturgical history and theology by liturgical law at the time. Nevertheless, McManus and O'Connell rightly teach us that liturgical law is rooted in divine law, and also that because it is posited by due ecclesiastical authority it cannot simply be set aside without risk of at least the sin of disobedience. To put it more positively, love of Christ and his Church, and of the mysteries enshrined and celebrated by the sacred liturgy, above all love of the Holy Sacrifice of the Mass, led her ministers to strive always to obey her directives, even in the smallest details. Such obedience was a virtue, rightly cultivated and desired.

It is true that before the Second Vatican Council liturgical law was regarded more as a matter of jurisprudence within ecclesiology rather than as an integral part of liturgical theology. It is certainly true that many who readily accepted the rightful place of rubrics and liturgical law in the sacred liturgy before the council were eager for their simplification.[22] What remains to be seen is the juridical and theological place of liturgical law at the council and in its aftermath.

---

20   Charles Augustine, *Liturgical Law: A Handbook of the Roman Liturgy* (St. Louis–London: Herder, 1931) vi–vii.

21   Ibid., vii. Augustine concludes his introduction with a "request to our readers to refrain from sending us questions concerning the Sacred Liturgy: the S. Congregation of Rites is established for this purpose" (viii).

22   For some of the rubrical simplification desired and enacted before the council see Reid, *The Organic Development*, 145–301.

THE SECOND VATICAN COUNCIL

The Second Vatican Council's Constitution on the Sacred Liturgy, *Sacrosanctum Concilium* (December 4, 1963), has a clear theological foundation, articulated in Chapter I, Section I (articles 5–13) and two fundamental principles of reform—actual participation and liturgical formation—articulated in Chapter I, Section II (articles 14–20). These principles provide the "Why?" of the liturgical reform desired by the council. We read *Sacrosanctum Concilium* correctly only if we give *participatio actuosa* and liturgical formation a literally fundamental primacy.

There can be no question that the council wished the abolition of rubrics or of liturgical law. The constitution clearly envisages that rubrics remain part of the liturgy, explicitly referring to them six times: (articles 31, 35,2, 38, 63b, 97, 118). Furthermore, article 17 insists that:

> In seminaries and houses of religious, clerics shall be given a liturgical formation in their spiritual life. . . . In addition they must learn how to observe the liturgical laws, so that life in seminaries and houses of religious may be thoroughly influenced by the spirit of the liturgy.[23]

The constitution's view that learning how to observe liturgical law was a precondition *so that* these houses of formation may imbibe the spirit of the liturgy is noteworthy. It is also important to note that no opposition between liturgical law and the spirit of the liturgy can be found here;[24] indeed, the Italian scholar Cipriano

---

23   "Clerici, in seminariis domibusque religiosis, formationem vitae spiritualis liturgicam adquirant . . . pariter observantiam legum liturgicarum addiscant, ita ut vita in seminariis et religiosorum institutis liturgico spiritu penitus informetur."

24   See Francisco Gil Hellín, *Concilii Vaticani II Synopsis: Constitutio de Sacra Liturgia Sacrosanctum Concilium* (Vatican City: Libreria Editrice Vaticana, 2003) 62–63; Frederick McManus, "The Constitution on the Liturgy Commentary: Part I," in *Worship* 38 (1964) 314–374, at 329; Josef A. Jungmann, "Constitution on the Sacred Liturgy," in *Commentary on the Documents of Vatican II*, ed. Herbert Vorgrimler, vol. I (London–New York: Herder and Herder, 1967) 1–87, at 18; Herman Schmidt, *La Constitution de la Sainte Liturgie* (Brussels: Editions Lumen Vitae, 1966) 100.

Vagaggini, OSB (1909–1999), comments that in such formation, "nor is the juridical aspect to be neglected, since the external elements of worship belong to Liturgy and must be regulated by laws and rubrics."[25]

In article 22 the Second Vatican Council underlines the centralized liturgical authority of the Holy See, while foreseeing some devolution of this authority to bishops, individually or collectively:

1. Regulation of the Sacred Liturgy depends solely on the authority of the Church, that is, on the Apostolic See and, as laws may determine, on the bishop.

2. In virtue of power conceded by the law, the regulation of the liturgy within certain defined limits belongs also to various kinds of competent territorial bodies of bishops legitimately established.[26]

In the final number of article 22, the Second Vatican Council loudly echoes canon 13 of the seventh session of the Council of Trent (cited above), when it insists that, apart from the Apostolic See and bishops acting in accordance with the powers given them "no other person, even if he be a priest, may add, remove, or change anything in the liturgy on his own authority."[27] Liturgical law is by no means abolished by the Second Vatican Council.

I have spoken of the primacy of the principles of *participatio actuosa* and of liturgical formation for the whole of the constitution. Given that reality, it should come as no surprise that the council states in article 11 (which is one of the "general principles" of the constitution) that:

---

25   Cipriano Vagaggini, "General Norms for the Reform and Fostering of the Liturgy," in *The Commentary on the Constitution and on the Instruction on the Sacred Liturgy*, ed. Annibale Bugnini and Carlo Braga (New York: Benziger Brothers, 1965) 62–134, at 81.

26   "1. Sacrae Liturgiae moderatio ab Ecclesiae auctoritate unice pendet: quae quidem est apud Apostolicam Sedem et, ad normam iuris, apud Episcopum. 2. Ex potestate a iure concessa, rei liturgicae moderatio inter limites statutos pertinet quoque ad competentes varii generis territoriales Episcoporum coetus legitime constitutos."

27   "3. Quapropter nemo omnino alius, etiamsi sit sacerdos, quidquam proprio marte in Liturgia addat, demat, aut mutet."

In order that the liturgy may be able to produce its full effects, it is necessary that the faithful come to it with proper dispositions, that their minds should be attuned to their voices, and that they should cooperate with divine grace lest they receive it in vain [cf. 2 Cor 6:1]. Pastors of souls must therefore realize that, when the liturgy is celebrated, *something more is required than the mere observation of the laws governing valid and licit celebration*; it is their duty also to ensure that the faithful take part fully aware of what they are doing, actively engaged in the rite, and enriched by its effects.[28]

The council is insisting that *participatio actuosa* on the part of the faithful will come about only when the clergy *in addition to* the valid celebration of the sacred liturgy according to liturgical law also undertake the work of liturgical formation. Far from removing the duty of ensuring the valid and licit celebration of the liturgical rites, the council laid upon the clergy the additional and grave duty of the liturgical formation of their people. It is worth noting that this text caused no controversy and underwent no significant redaction at the council itself,[29] and that reputable and informed contemporary commentators of the likes of McManus, the German Josef Andreas Jungmann, SJ (1889–1975), Vagaggini, and the Dutch Herman Schmidt, SJ, saw here no denigration of liturgical law or license for going beyond the provisions of the liturgical books in order to facilitate actual participation,[30] but

---

28   "Ut haec tamen plena efficacitas habeatur, necessarium est ut fideles cum recti animi dispositionibus ad sacram Liturgiam accedant, mentem suam voci accommodent, et supernae gratiae cooperentur, ne eam in vacuum recipient [cf. 2 Cor 6:1]. Ideo sacris pastoribus advigilandum est ut in actione liturgica non solum observentur leges ad validam et licitam celebrationem, sed ut fideles scienter, actuose et fructuose eandem participent." Emphasis added.

29   See Gil Hellín, *Constitutio de Sacra Liturgia*, 48–49.

30   John J. McEneaney, in his review of Robert W. Hovda's *Manual of Celebration* (Washington, DC: The Liturgical Conference, 1970), reports that Hovda interprets this article as supporting "the position that rubrics must sometimes be consciously transcended;" John J. McEneaney, "Manual of Celebration," in *Worship* 44 (1970) 220–225, at 222.

rather the council's deliberate accentuation of the importance of liturgical formation as a precondition for *participatio actuosa*.[31]

This insistence on *participatio actuosa* by the council fathers is a pastoral policy of significant value which, when rightly understood,[32] is capable of bringing about that necessary and fruitful immersion in the Church's liturgical life and tradition so desired by the Liturgical Movement and indeed by council fathers themselves. That they assumed the integral place of liturgical law and discipline as self-evident in any future liturgical reform is another indicator that their intention was not rupture but continuity with what came before.

IN THE WAKE OF *SACROSANCTUM CONCILIUM*

The council's moderate and balanced position was not, however, held by a significant number of scholars, enthusiasts and activists.

In 1961, the Roman professor Adrien Nocent, OSB, published *L'avenir de la liturgie*,[33] in which he describes something of a mentality that was abroad and which came to flourish in the period following the promulgation of *Sacrosanctum Concilium*:

> There is [an] attitude, too impatient, sometimes inadequately informed, which rejoices beforehand at all "iconoclasm" and all burning of old idols. It confuses idle routine with true and legitimate tradition and is fond of change for its own sake, as a supreme manifestation of vitality.

Father Nocent continues, in part justifying this position:

---

31   McManus, "The Constitution on the Liturgy Commentary: Part I," 321; Jungmann, "Constitution on the Sacred Liturgy," 16; Vagaggini, "General Norms," 74–75; Schmidt, *La Constitution de la Sainte Liturgie*, 99–100.

32   See Alcuin Reid, "Active Participation and Pastoral Adaptation," in *Liturgy, Participation and Sacred Music: The Proceedings of the Ninth International Colloquium of Historical, Canonical and Theological Studies on the Roman Catholic Liturgy, Paris 2003* (Rochester: CIEL UK, 2006) 35–50, at 36–40.

33   Adrien Nocent, *L'avenir de la liturgie* (Paris: Éditions universitaires, 1961).

Still, we must sometimes excuse its vehemence and explain it by a wracking pastoral anxiety. What can be done, when we are faced with a whole people who cannot be reached by a liturgy encrusted with successive accumulations, inherited from past centuries where the religious culture and psychology have no connection with our own?[34]

The council fathers cannot have been ignorant of this phenomenon, and perhaps in part it explains their clear assertion of liturgical discipline in the constitution. We ought to note Nocent's underlining of the importance of the factors he describes as "pastoral," namely the liturgy's ability to "reach" people—a remarkably subjective quality—and its need to have a "connection" with the religious culture and psychology of contemporary man—something utterly subjective also, as well as intrinsically transitory. Nocent is writing before the constitution, of course, but these are recurring themes after it, and stand in contrast to *Sacrosanctum Concilium*'s fundamental principles of *participatio actuosa* and liturgical formation.

I submit that this post-conciliar phenomenon has three principle facets. The first is articulated in the January 1965 issue of *Paroisse et Liturgie*, a respected liturgical periodical published by the Abbey of Saint-André in Bruges. In an editorial entitled "On obedience in liturgical matters," Thierry Maertens, OSB (1921–2011), declared: "It is too obvious that there is a malaise. It is useless to behave like an ostrich and vain to appeal only to the virtue of priests: the problem is not primarily a moral issue."[35]

The issue was, in the opinion of the journal, therefore, not one of obedience to authority, but primarily pastoral: one of how priests could reach the people of "today" through the liturgy. The

---

34   Adrien Nocent, *The Future of the Liturgy,* trans. Irene Uribe (New York: Herder and Herder, 1963) 15–16.

35   "Il est trop évident qu'un malaise existe. Il est inutile de jouer à la politique de l'autruche et vain d'en appeler seulement à la vertu des prêtres: le problème n'est pas essentiellement un problème d'ordre moral." Thierry Maertens, "De l'obéissance en matière liturgique," in *Paroisse et Liturgie* 47 (1965) 1–2, at 1 (author's translation).

editorial team proposed the following criteria as essential for pastoral liturgy. A priest, they said, has:

a) To be in line with the Church—a Church that advances; to advance in the ways to which the Church has opened herself; to seek to open, in his place and according to his jurisdiction and his responsibilities, ways that become meaningful to others.

b) To be linked to his bishop and to inform him. To clearly accept that "he is one who forms, one who informs, but he is not one who conforms."

c) To inform himself from good sources; to follow the theological and liturgical research, etc.; to try to understand.

d) To consult, in his research to be linked to others (his team, deanery, etc.); to be a proponent of dialogue, listening to the experiences of others, despite all the risks of trial and error.

e) Finally, not to shock, to be a teacher of faith in everything one does, which not only means not to scandalize those of traditionalist spirit by novelties—but above all, not to impose the same requirements on one and all the communities; to respect the timelines and the pathways; to respect the freedom of the Spirit.[36]

---

36   "a) Etre dans le sens de l'Eglise—d'une Eglise qui marche; avancer dans les voies que l'Eglise a elle-même ouvertes; chercher à ouvrir, à sa place et conformément a son obédience et a ses responsabilités, des voies qui deviendront valables pour d'autres. b) Etre lié à son Evêque et l'informer. Accepter clairement « qu'il forme, qu'il informe, mais non qu'il conforme », a-t-on pu dire. c) S'informer aux bonnes sources ; suivre les recherches théologiques, liturgiques, etc.; chercher à comprendre. d) Se concerter, être dans sa recherche lié à d'autres (équipe, doyenné, etc.); être ardemment partisan du dialogue, attentif aux expériences des autres, malgré tous les risques de tâtonnements. e) Enfin ne pas scandaliser, être dans tout ce qu'on fait un éducateur de la foi; ce qui ne signifie pas seulement: ne pas scandaliser les esprits traditionalistes par des nouveautés—mais surtout ne pas imposer a tous et a toutes Communautés les mêmes exigences; respecter les délais et les cheminements; respecter la liberté de l'Esprit;" André Turck, "Le problème de la loi: Réflexions pastorales," in *Paroisse et Liturgie* 47 (1965), 3–13, at 10–11 (author's translation).

Another contributor wrote on the difficulty of reconciling the duty of being a pastor with the duty of obedience. He concluded that it is impossible for a pastor who is truly present to "where his people are at" to observe fixed liturgical law, calling rather for a dialogue that would lead to "open law" or frameworks, a "collective pastoral conscience of the *presbyterium* gathered around the bishop."[37] He observes that without collegial action to develop such frameworks there is the risk of falling into the dichotomy of either putting in place a coherent form of pastoral care, including an adapted liturgy, *or* of obeying the rubrics, and that the reality is that often priests are left to solve pastoral-liturgical questions in their individual consciences.[38]

The bishops of Belgium rebuked these opinions sharply, insisting that "we cannot accept anything that is likely to lead our priests to evade the rules and engage in personal or collective free improvisation" in the liturgy,[39] reminding the journal that "the

---

37   ". . . une conscience pastorale collective du *presbyterium* autour de l'évêque;" Emile Marcus, "Réconcilier le devoir d'être pasteur avec celui d'obéir," in *Paroisse et Liturgie* 47 (1965) 36–49, at 48 (author's translation).

38   See ibid., 49: "Le sacerdoce ministériel qui est investi de la tâche pastorale assume également la présidence de l'assemblée liturgique. Mais les deux responsabilités sont à ce point liées qu'il est impossible de s'accommoder pour la seconde d'une réglementation totalement fixe, alors que la première consiste a rejoindre les hommes là où ils en sont dans leur cheminement vers Dieu. Le peuple doit être initié au mystère du salut à partir des pierres d'attente déposées en chaque individu. Et il est rassemblé de tous milieux et de toutes races. Mais rien ne se fera tant que la diversification de la pastorale en même temps que la fidélité à des normes liturgiques 'ouvertes' (loi-cadre) ne seront pas effectivement prises en charge par le *presbyterium* de l'évêque. Car faute de ce *presbyterium*, le jugement pastoral ne peut s'exercer valablement, l'individu prêtre se retrouvant seul avec sa conscience pour résoudre un problème qui relève de la compétence de l'ensemble. De plus il risque toujours de retomber dans ce faux dilemme: mettre en place une pastorale cohérente, et donc adapter la liturgie, ou obéir aux rubriques. Cet exercice collégial du sacerdoce suppose la mise en place de structures de dialogue. Elle suppose aussi un véritable apprentissage et sans doute beaucoup de vertu! La longue habitude de l'*idem facere* et du *sub uno esse* ne nous a pas préparés a l'*agere ut pars*."

39   ". . . nous ne pouvons accepter tout ce qui est de nature à conduire nos prêtres à se soustraire aux règles établies et à se livrer à la libre improvisation personnelle

Holy See intends to maintain a strict discipline in all aspects of the liturgy, and that this discipline is the very condition for a happy progressive adaptation [of the liturgy]."[40] The journal's editors published an unequivocal acceptance of the bishops' position.[41]

However, the stance of *Paroisse et Liturgie* was not an isolated one. In the February 1966 edition of *Concilium,* Theodore Vismans, OP, in an article "Liturgy or Rubrics?" (the very juxtaposition in the title indicates something of the crisis of the time), insists that the questions raised in Belgium "are real questions, should not be stifled in silence and must be given a satisfactory answer some day if the renewal of the liturgy is not to remain suspended in mid-air."[42] Vismans also notes the "live contemporary issue" of pleas "for a liturgy which is really close to life and not alien to it."[43]

This, then, is the first face of a particularly powerful post-conciliar liturgical demon: an obsession with the supposed pastoral relevance of liturgical celebrations, judged according to the tastes, expectations or subjective desires of individuals or groups. I venture to call this "liturgical *pastoralism*"—the phenomenon by which the sacred liturgy as handed on in the tradition of the Church is treated at best as a resource, and at worst as a quaint historical memory, and is left behind in the quest of transient pastoral relevance.[44]

The second face of this demon manifests itself in the article of Patrick Regan, OSB (1938–2017), in the January 1966 edition of the American journal, *Worship*:

---

ou collective;" "Une lettre de l'épiscopat Belge a la rédaction de la revue," in *Paroisse et Liturgie* 47 (1965), before 241 (author's translation).

40   "Faut-il rappeler que le Saint-Siège entend maintenir une stricte discipline en tout ce qui touche la liturgie et que cette discipline est la condition même d'une heureuse adaptation progressive?" Ibid. (author's translation).

41   See ibid.

42   Theodore Vismans, "Liturgy or Rubrics," in *Concilium* 2 (1966) 45–49, at 48.

43   Ibid. Vismans is referring to the article by Gotthold Hasenhüttl, "Die Konstitution über die heilige Liturgie: Eine theologische Besinnung," in *Bibel und Liturgie* 38 (1964/5) 187–192.

44   Prescinding from the significant questions one can raise about the place of the post-conciliar reform in the Church's liturgical tradition, one can also apply this definition to how the modern liturgical books have been received.

When public worship abounds in signs, gestures, and language which, however beautiful or rubrically correct, are nonetheless considerably devoid of real significance, a kind of identity crisis arises in the church.

Liturgy reveals and creates the church body. But when the church consistently expresses herself in faulty signs, a false front or mask is built up and she begins to think of herself in strange ways which only vaguely correspond to her real nature. There is no accidental relationship between triumphalism in the church and triumphalism in liturgy; between centralization in the church and centralization in liturgy. As liturgy becomes more humble, poor, and sensitive to local needs, there is every reason to believe that the Christian people will become so too. And in so doing, the church will become what she truly is.

The liturgical renewal, then, has as its principal goal the restoration of authenticity in liturgical signs. The rigid demands of past legislation are being relaxed in order that liturgical expression may be grounded in the life-experiences of the worshipers.[45]

Regan articulates a position that

. . . lays stress on the relativity of liturgical rites. It understands liturgy as the function of the assembled people of God and refuses to view it as the implementation of an unconditioned system of formulae. The starting point for planning the kind of worship described here is regard for the specific needs and abilities of the community. It is motivated by the necessity of bringing the people of God into fresh existence in every time and place, through active participation in worship, leading to active participation in one another's lives, and active participation in the world. The norms by which this is done arise out of the very nature of liturgical celebration and not merely from external directives.[46]

---

45   Patrick Regan, "The Change behind the Changes," in *Worship* 40 (1966) 36–45, at 38.
46   Ibid., 45.

Regan's arguments evacuate the objective theological content of the sacred liturgy and reduce it to a human function ("the function of the assembled people of God"). The end of the liturgy, as Regan articulates it here, is "active participation in the world." Whilst the theology of *Sacrosanctum Concilium* admits that the liturgy is "the outstanding means whereby the faithful may express in their lives, and manifest to others, the mystery of Christ and the real nature of the true Church,"[47] it does not view this as its ultimate or overriding purpose. The council teaches that the sacred liturgy is:

> ... an exercise of the priestly office of Jesus Christ. In the liturgy the sanctification of man is signified by signs perceptible to the senses, and is effected in a way which corresponds with each of these signs; in the liturgy the whole public worship is performed by the Mystical Body of Jesus Christ, that is, by the head and his members.[48]

There is, then a theological objectivity to the Church's liturgy. It is primarily the work of Christ, not of man. It is perhaps true that this objectivity was stressed to the exclusion of other (primarily pastoral) considerations before the work of the twentieth-century Liturgical Movement, but that does not justify its relativization, dissipation or denial. However this phenomenon, which I call the "theological evacuation of the sacred liturgy," that emerged in some places following the council was capable of reducing it to a subjective human gathering. In such a gathering the Church's liturgical law has little or no place or relevance.

---

47   *Sacrosanctum Concilium*, no. 2: "Liturgia enim, per quam, maxime in divino Eucharistiae Sacrificio, 'opus nostrae Redemptionis exercetur,' summe eo confert ut fideles vivendo exprimant et aliis manifestent mysterium Christi et genuinam verae Ecclesiae naturam. ..."

48   Ibid., no. 7: "Merito igitur Liturgia habetur veluti Iesu Christi sacerdotalis muneris exercitatio, in qua per signa sensibilia significatur et modo singulis proprio efficitur sanctificatio hominis, et a mystico Iesu Christi Corpore, Capite nempe eiusque membris, integer cultus publicus exercetur."

This subjectivity spread rapidly,[49] leaving liturgical law in, at best, a tenuous position. In a 1968 article in *The Jurist* entitled "The Authority of Liturgical Law," the American Walter J. Kelly (†2009), spoke of "an ever-widening gulf" between unauthorized liturgical celebrations and those holding to a strict interpretation of liturgical law.[50] Kelly maintained that "a resolution cannot be expected to be achieved in the context of traditional ground-rules of liturgical discipline."[51] "Until the dichotomy between the pastoral and legal aspects of the liturgy can be removed, what is the priest to do," Kelly asks, "who is provided with a liturgy foreign to the genius of the place, time, and people he serves?"[52] Kelly offers a canonical solution:

> There must be a broader use of certain basic principles of law—epikeia, presumptive revocation, presumptive cessation, and above all . . . that no-one is held to obey a merely ecclesiastical law if grave harm would result from its observance . . .
>
> When, to be specific, many liturgical laws occasion the rejection of the liturgy by large numbers of people, then it seems that great objective harm is being done to the liturgy, and it can be

---

49   At the 1967 North American Liturgical Week, one of its Board of Directors would argue: "I am personally convinced that we must ultimately arrive at a variety of liturgies, in order to express adequately in worship the varied levels of Christian awareness which are operative at any given time or place within the People of God;" Thomas E. Ambrogi, "A Mass of the Future," in *Experiments in Community: Twenty-eighth North American Liturgical Week: Kansas City, Missouri, August 12–24, 1967* (Washington, DC: The Liturgical Conference, 1967) 42–59, at 43. Crispian McNaspy, *Our Changing Liturgy* (London: Frederick Muller, 1967) 24–25, explains something of the influence of contemporary culture when he asserts: "Another reason why change is particularly urgent today, in liturgy as in other human elements of the Church's work, is the unprecedented acceleration of change in the world as a whole. . . . If the Church is reluctant to change in those areas in which she is permitted to change, the lag between civilization and the Church's work on earth will continue to increase at a stupefying pace. And this would make her *role* ever more irrelevant."

50   Walter J. Kelly, "The Authority of Liturgical Laws," in *The Jurist* 28 (1968) 397–424, at 398.

51   Ibid., 399.

52   Ibid., 418.

said that either the law may be disregarded or may be considered
to have been presumptively revoked.[53]

Kelly consummates this relativization of liturgical law by specu-
lating that:

> If the law, however new, was not formulated with real consid-
> eration for pastoral needs nor in the light of pastoral experience
> primarily, it might well be said to be obsolete almost immedi-
> ately and subject to presumptive revocation or cessation in the
> judgement of those most closely engaged in pastoral activity.[54]

Here we find the third face of this liturgical demon: a juridical
relativism whereby *any* liturgical law is viewed as *legally* devoid
of obligation in the light of pastoral considerations in the judgment of the individual alone. Frederick McManus would even
argue this possibility in respect of the liturgical law of the new
rites in 1974.[55]

Obsessive pastoralism, the theological evacuation of the sacred
liturgy, and juridical relativism were significant realities in the

---

53   Ibid.
54   Ibid., 418–419. Somewhat more calmly Kelly adds: "Only in the presence
of a clear need and after mature judgment would such a course of action [contraven-
ing article 22,3 of *Sacrosanctum Concilium*] seem to be warranted. For each celebrant
to begin to decide what the liturgy should be would be the genesis of chaos. In general, then, it would seem to be at least undesirable for priests to invoke the principles
spoken of, perhaps simply wrong. Still, in the face of growing disregard for the liturgy
and indeed for the Church itself, some accommodation to the needs of pastoral work
must be made; some norms for pastoral obedience to liturgical legislation have to be
developed." Ibid., 420–421.
55   "When there are grave inhibitions in the present rite, no one should hesitate
to consider the several possibilities of relief for the good of the praying and worshipping people." Frederick R. McManus, "Liturgical Law and Difficult Cases," in *Worship*
48 (1974) 347–366, at 366. McManus appears torn in his article, and goes on to con-
clude the above sentence: "more often the solution is in trying to celebrate effectively
the received rite." John M. Huels notes that neither Kelly or McManus "was totally
satisfied" with the approach advocated in their writings: see John M. Huels, *One Table,
Many Laws: Essays on Catholic Eucharistic Practice* (Collegeville, MN: Liturgical Press,
1986) 17–18.

immediate post-conciliar years and beyond, and gave rise to wide-spread abuses of the sacred liturgy, which sprang up throughout the Western Church. In retrospect, Archbishop Bugnini himself admits that "it cannot be denied that real abuses occurred and that they did harm to the faithful and to the reform generally."[56]

Bugnini, and the *Consilium* for the Implementation of the Constitution on the Sacred Liturgy itself, cannot be accused of encouraging these abuses,[57] and he rightly draws attention to the protests made by the Holy See against liturgical abuse.[58] But it remains an historical reality that, while Bugnini was orchestrating the (not uncontroversial) work of the *Consilium*,[59] the conditions in which the council and the Holy See had assumed that the official reform would be received—formation in a sound and integrated liturgical and pastoral theology, in which respect for liturgical discipline played its proper part—simply did not exist in many places.

This resulted in the fact that the new liturgical books in both their *editiones typicae* and in the various (and, at times, questionable) vernacular translations often came to rest not on the stable soil of a liturgically well-disciplined Church, enriched by sound liturgical formation towards the pastoral goal of *actuosa participatio* as envisaged by the council fathers. Rather, the debilitating effects of the ideologies and abuses abroad in the intervening years saw them arrive—in many places—on the quicksand of liturgical subjectivity and relativism which quickly swallowed much, if not most, of the liturgical renewal intended.[60]

---

56   Annibale Bugnini, *The Reform of the Liturgy: 1948–1975*, trans. Matthew J. O'Connell (Collegeville, MN: Liturgical Press, 1990) 259.

57   Though a case could be made that the pace (for some too slow, for some too fast), and at times seemingly contradictory elements of the official reform contributed to a destabilization of liturgical discipline.

58   See Bugnini, *The Reform of the Liturgy*, 257–262.

59   The evaluation of which is beyond the scope of this paper.

60   For example: In the year 1969 in which the new *Ordo Missae* was introduced, the President of the Dutch National Liturgical Commission would argue: "The Church's worship, as the expression of communion of living men with the living God, must respect the conditions of liberty, truth, and dynamic development, for these are basic traits of life itself. If respect for these conditions were to lead a Christian com-

There is no need to survey in detail the further literature that perpetuated these ideologies, or to recount *ad nauseam* yet more accounts of the liturgical abuses experienced throughout the Church in the 1970s and 1980s: we know them well enough. Perhaps this was in part fueled by the many legitimate options permitted in the new liturgical books, perhaps by enthusiastic talk about liturgical creativity and inculturation?[61] My own opinion is that the potent liturgical demon, the three principal "faces" of which I have described above, once unleashed, proved very difficult to exorcise.

ATTEMPTING TO REASSERT LITURGICAL DISCIPLINE

On the feast of Saints Peter and Paul, 1972, Blessed Paul VI made the astonishing assertion that "from some fissure the smoke of Satan has entered the Temple of God."[62] At the time this state-

---

munity to seek its forms of liturgical expression beyond the law, would we have to regard such a community as a sect tending to detach itself from communion with the universal church? Would it not be better in such cases to question the law itself, to challenge its validity? After all, law is made for men, not men for the law. If we take seriously what the documents of Vatican II have to say concerning the importance of local communities, are we not led to require for these communities a larger measure of autonomy and initiative?" "Chronicle," in *Worship* 44 (1970) 49–53, at 49–50. In November 1970 the Editor of *Worship*, Aelred Tegels, OSB (1922–2003), responded to the promulgation of the new *Missale Romanum* with the observation that "the book contains relatively few new texts, and most of these are not very 'new' in the sense of being expressive of contemporary Christian understanding and experience of worship." He regarded it as "a very valuable, indeed indispensable, phase of liturgical reform," and hoped that in forthcoming articles by "evaluating in terms of tradition and contemporary experience" the texts of the new Missal, "to promote the work of renewal and make a modest contribution to the next *non-definitive* edition of the Roman Missal." "Chronicle," in *Worship* 44 (1970) 561–568, at 561 and 566, emphasis added.

61   See Anscar J. Chupungco, *Liturgies of the Future: The Process and Methods of Inculturation* (New York: Paulist Press, 1989).

62   ". . . da qualche fessura sia entrato il fumo di Satana nel tempio di Dio." Pope Paul VI, "Per il nono anniversario dell'Incoronazione di Sua Santità: 'Resistite fortes in fide'" (29 June 1972), in *Insegnamenti di Paolo VI*, vol. 10 (Vatican City: Tipografia Poliglotta Vaticana, 1973) 707.

ment was seen as a general reference to the widespread crisis in the Church. However, in May 2008 Virgilio Cardinal Noè (1922–2011), a trusted collaborator in the modern liturgical reforms and Master of Pontifical Ceremonies from 1970–1982, revealed in an interview that Paul VI

> . . . spoke of the smoke of Satan because he maintained that those priests who turned Holy Mass into straw in the name of creativity, in reality were possessed of the vainglory and the pride of the Evil One. So, the smoke of Satan was nothing other than the mentality that wanted to distort the traditional and liturgical canons of the Eucharistic ceremony.[63]

Given this, Paul VI's lament is a terrible indictment coming from the very mouth of him under whose personal authority the postconciliar reform was carried through and promulgated, and perhaps also an early indication of what Archbishop Piero Marini has described as "a tendency to return to a preconciliar mindset" in the respect of the liturgy, which Marini regards as one of the "limitations" of the pontificate of Paul VI.[64] It does, however, also indicate that the supreme authority in the Church understood clearly that all was not well with liturgical discipline and practice.

In part, this may well be due to the almost impossible demands that the "spirit" of the new liturgy was perceived to have placed on individual priests, subjectivizing even the relatively loose norms of the new liturgical books. This was based on a not uncommon misinterpretation of *Sacrosanctum Concilium*, no. 11 as calling for

---

63   "Parlò di fumo di Satana perché sosteneva che quei preti che della Santa Messa facevano paglia in nome della creatività, in realtà erano posseduti dalla vanagloria e dalla superbia del Maligno. Dunque, il fumo di Satana altro non era che la mentalità che voleva stravolgere i canoni tradizionali e liturgici della cerimonia Eucaristica." Interview with Bruno Volpe in the magazine *Petrus*, now available at http://difenderelafede.freeforumzone.com/discussione.aspx?idd=8664389 (author's translation).

64   Piero Marini, *A Challenging Reform: Realizing the Vision of the Liturgical Renewal,* ed. Mark R. Francis, John R. Page, Keith F. Pecklers (Collegeville, MN: Liturgical Press, 2007) 157.

liturgical creativity as the *means* to bring about *participatio actuosa* (the article was calling for the work of formation of people to bring about participation in the sacred liturgy, not the re-formation of the liturgy to "enthrall" people). A monk of Collegeville, Minnesota, R. Kevin Seasoltz, proposed this misinterpretation in 1979:

> No longer may ministers feel that they have done their duty if they have carried out the norms in the liturgical books; they must go beyond the norms, in the sense that they must bring the liturgy to life for people. Consequently they must develop a sensitive ministerial style that enables them to be aware of the pastoral needs of the people and to structure and execute celebrations in such a way that they truly respond to people's needs. This presupposes an understanding of both the theological and aesthetic dimensions of the liturgy.[65]

The effect of this misinterpretation of the council was to allow, if not indeed to insist upon, the subjugation of liturgical law—and indeed the liturgical rites themselves—to subjective pastoral ends. The Constitution on the Sacred Liturgy did not intend this, but many liturgists and canonists interpreted it in this way.[66] In such a climate, many faithful pastoral clergy felt bullied by vociferous liturgists, innumerable chancery directives and even informed and committed parishioners into implementing "creative" liturgical practices that went well beyond liturgical law. One student of post-conciliar liturgical law asked:

> Does the degree of responsibility on the part of the priest required by the new legislation place unreasonable demands on

---

65   R. Kevin Seasoltz, *New Liturgy, New Laws* (Collegeville, MN: Liturgical Press, 1979) 207.

66   Huels, *One Table, Many Laws*, 32–33, sees article 11 of *Sacrosanctum Concilium* as mitigating the "uncompromising impact" of article 22,3 and states "As strict and unyielding as the *text* of this law reads, it cannot be understood apart from its *context,* namely, that liturgical law seeks to promote the pastoral aims of the liturgy. This is the substance behind all liturgical law, and no single norm can supersede it."

him? Can each pastor be a poet, public relations director, administrator, musician, public speaker, theologian and mystagogue?[67]

The answer, I submit, in the decades following the council is that these were indeed unreasonable and unrealistic demands. As the American canonist John M. Huels, OSM, observes of liturgical law, "If the laws are good and its implementers have a solid formation, problems and tensions in the interpretation and observance of liturgical law will be greatly diminished."[68] The problem is that the laws were no longer all that clear—options, recommendations and directives all appeared in the new liturgical books—and the liturgical formation of those who had to implement them varied starkly. The result was a liturgical *praxis* in the Western Church very different from that envisaged by the council fathers.

So much so that Saint John Paul II, in his first encyclical letter, *Redemptor Hominis*, found it necessary to teach a liturgical theology that reasserted liturgical discipline. Having explained that the Blessed Eucharist is "the most perfect sacrament" of our union with Christ, he insists:

> It is not permissible for us, in thought, life or action, to take away from this truly most holy Sacrament its full magnitude and its essential meaning. It is at one and the same time a Sacrifice-Sacrament, a Communion-Sacrament, and a Presence-Sacrament. And, although it is true that the Eucharist always was and must continue to be the most profound revelation of the human brotherhood of Christ's disciples and confessors, it cannot be treated merely as an "occasion" for manifesting this brotherhood. When celebrating the Sacrament of the Body and Blood of the Lord, the full magnitude of the divine mystery must be respected, as must the full meaning of this sacramental sign in which Christ is really present and is received, the soul is filled with grace and the pledge of future glory is given (cf. *Sacrosanctum Concilium*, 47).

---

67   Thomas Richstatter, *Liturgical Law Today: New Style, New Spirit* (Chicago: Franciscan Herald Press, 1977) 177.

68   Huels, *One Table, Many Laws*, 36.

This is the source of the duty to carry out rigorously the liturgical rules and everything that is a manifestation of community
worship offered to God himself, all the more so because in this
sacramental sign he entrusts himself to us with limitless trust, as
if not taking into consideration our human weakness, our
unworthiness, the force of habit, routine, or even the possibility
of insult.[69]

His pontificate would see repeated efforts on the part of the Holy
See to reassert liturgical discipline, from the 1980 Instruction *Inaestimabile Donum* to the Instruction *Redemptionis Sacramentum* of
2004.[70] Towards the end of his pontificate his final encyclical,
Ecclesia de Eucharistia (2003), would lament the "shadows" cast by
the implementation of the liturgical reform. His lament was more
explicit than that of Paul VI:

In various parts of the Church abuses have occurred, leading to
confusion with regard to sound faith and Catholic doctrine concerning this wonderful sacrament. At times one encounters an
extremely reductive understanding of the Eucharistic mystery.
Stripped of its sacrificial meaning, it is celebrated as if it were
simply a fraternal banquet. Furthermore, the necessity of the
ministerial priesthood, grounded in apostolic succession, is at
times obscured and the sacramental nature of the Eucharist is
reduced to its mere effectiveness as a form of proclamation. This
has led here and there to ecumenical initiatives which, albeit
well-intentioned, indulge in Eucharistic practices contrary to
the discipline by which the Church expresses her faith. How can
we not express profound grief at all this? The Eucharist is too
great a gift to tolerate ambiguity and depreciation.

69   John Paul II, Encyclical Letter at the Beginning of his Papal Ministry
Redemptor Hominis (4 March 1979) no. 20.
70   See Sacred Congregation for the Sacraments and Divine Worship, Instruction Concerning Worship of the Eucharistic Mystery *Inaestimabile Donum* (3 April
1980); Congregation for Divine Worship and Discipline of the Sacraments, Instruction on Certain Matters to be Observed or to be Avoided Regarding the Most Holy
Eucharist *Redemptionis Sacramentum* (25 March 2004).

It is my hope that the present Encyclical Letter will effectively help to banish the dark clouds of unacceptable doctrine and practice.[71]

John Paul II clearly locates liturgical law within Eucharistic theology and asserts its validity and importance in the twenty-first century and beyond. However, that the Sovereign Pontiff judged it necessary to address this lament to the whole Church in 2003 is another indictment of the reality of the post-conciliar liturgical reform, and of the efforts to restore discipline in the preceding decades, which, in addition to the instructions mentioned above, saw new editions of the General Instruction of the Roman Missal in 1975 and 2000, the new Code of Canon Law in 1983, and various new editions of other ritual books, not to mention the ongoing clarification of and insistence upon liturgical discipline by the Congregation for Divine Worship.[72]

These efforts were not without some success. In 2006 Huels published a volume *Liturgy and Law*, which is a serious delineation of the relationship between modern canon and liturgical law. His introduction articulates an important precept, which had often been obscured in the liturgical practices of previous decades: "Fidelity to the liturgical laws in keeping with sound principles of liturgical celebration serves to ensure the liturgy's authenticity and upholds the right of the faithful to the prayer which is truly that of the Church."[73] This is not a bad principle from which to start.

---

71   John Paul II, Encyclical Letter on the Eucharist and Its Relationship to the Church *Ecclesia de Eucharistia* (17 April 2003) no. 10. It must be added that while Archbishop Piero Marini served as the Master of Pontifical Ceremonies, many questioned elements introduced into papal liturgical celebrations by him. He offers his defense in Piero Marini and Bruno Cescon, *Io sono un Papa amabile: Giovanni Paolo II* (Milan: Edizioni San Paolo, 2011).

72   A helpful database of the responses to questions of liturgical discipline published by the Congregation for Divine Worship in their journal *Notitiae* may be found at http://notitiae.ipsissima-verba.org/. It is perhaps not without irony that a collection of the official responses of the Congregation to questions of liturgical discipline should now be made almost fifty years after the Second Vatican Council.

73   John M. Huels, *Liturgy and Law: Liturgical Law in the System of Roman Catholic Canon* Law (Montreal: Wilson & Lafleur, 2006) 25–26. Denis C. Smolarski,

But very few indeed will have the inclination, patience or skill to make a detailed study of modern liturgical law, and Huels' work, while a valuable reference, remains academic.

The widespread misinterpretation of *Sacrosanctum Concilium*, no. 11, to which I have referred, and its reading through an *a posteriori* hermeneutic of rupture that finds in it, not the call for liturgical formation *so that* the faithful may actually participate in rubrically correct celebrations of the sacred liturgy, but a justification for departure from the rites as given in the liturgical books in pursuit of liturgical creativity and adaptation according to perceived pastoral needs in a given place and time, remains. And there are other examples of reading the council's liturgical constitution with a hermeneutic of rupture.[74]

Others still have "moved on," as it were, and devote their attention to "post-modern liturgy"[75] or to liturgical inculturation and "the organic progression of the liturgy."[76] For such as these, modern liturgical law, even according to Huels, belongs to a past age.

A "HIGHER WAY"—*ARS CELEBRANDI*?

Perhaps there is a "higher way" (see 1 Cor 12:31) to consider liturgical law and rubrics in the twenty-first century; one which places this sound principle expounded by Huels into a larger, more meaningful context?

SJ, articulated this stance in a more popular publication two decades earlier: "… law tries to enflesh more important underlying principles and less important cultural options for the purpose of preserving the heritage within a given tradition and in a cultural manner which most people would feel comfortable with." *How Not to Say Mass: A Guidebook for all Concerned about Authentic Worship* (New York: Paulist Press, 1986) 10.

74   See Alcuin Reid, "*Sacrosanctum Concilium* and the Organic Development of the Liturgy," in *The Genius of the Roman Rite: Historical, Theological, and Pastoral Perspectives on Catholic Liturgy. Proceedings of the 2006 Oxford CIEL Colloquium*, ed. Uwe Michael Lang (Chicago: Hillenbrand Books, 2010) 198–215.

75   See *Liturgy in a Postmodern World*, ed. Keith Pecklers (London and New York: Continuum, 2003).

76   See Anscar Chupungco, "Inculturation and the Organic Progression of the Liturgy," in *Ecclesia Orans* 7 (1990) 7–21.

In his 2007 Apostolic Exhortation *Sacramentum Caritatis*, Pope Benedict XVI asserted that the liturgical "changes which the Council called for need to be understood within the overall unity of the historical development of the rite itself, without the intro- duction of artificial discontinuities."[77] He goes on to note, "I am referring here to the need for a hermeneutic of continuity also with regard to the correct interpretation of the liturgical develop- ment which followed the Second Vatican Council."[78] Already, in this call for continuity of outlook, of attitude—which was surely that of the council fathers, even if it may not have been that of the officials of the *Consilium* charged to implement its reform—we can begin to see the correct approach to liturgical law and rubrics: it must be one of continuity, not rupture.

However, Benedict XVI goes on to report that at the 2005 Synod, of which *Sacramentum Caritatis* is the subsequent magiste- rial act, there was "insistence on the need to avoid any antithesis between the *ars celebrandi*, the art of proper celebration, and the full, active and fruitful participation of all the faithful." He then teaches:

> The primary way to foster the participation of the People of God in the sacred rite is the proper celebration of the rite itself. The *ars celebrandi* is the best way to ensure their *actuosa participatio*. The *ars celebrandi* is the fruit of faithful adherence to the liturgical norms in all their richness; indeed, for two thousand years this way of celebrating has sustained the faith life of all believers, called to take part in the celebration as the People of God, a royal priesthood, a holy nation (cf. 1 Pet 2:4-5, 9).[79]

---

77   Benedict XVI, Post-Synodal Apostolic Exhortation on the Eucharist as the Source and Summit of the Church's Life and Mission *Sacramentum Caritatis* (22 Feb- ruary 2007) no. 3.

78   Ibid., fn. 6. I have occasionally been criticised for using this "mere" footnote as indicative of Benedict XVI's thought. The use of the first person singular and its consonance with his other writings on the topic give me confidence that its use is apposite. Its appearance as a note may be due to a personal intervention by Benedict XVI late in the drafting of the text.

79   Ibid., no. 38.

I should like to underline the phrase: "the fruit of faithful adherence to the liturgical norms in all their richness." Adherence to the liturgical norms is not here an imposition, an undue restriction, an impeding of what should be. Nor is it pastoral sloth on the part of the clergy. No, it is the precondition of liturgical fecundity. The "richness" of the liturgical norms is sufficient, as it always has been. The liturgical books are not resource books or mere points of departure, but books that provide all that is needed for fruitful and truly pastoral liturgical celebrations. We do not need to look for canonical "get-out" clauses or for other excuses to do something different to be pastoral: the liturgical rites when celebrated as the Church intends them to be celebrated are true pastoral liturgy.

Also, the norms of the liturgical books are more than simply "stage directions," as Msgr. Guido Marini has explained:

> The liturgical norms . . . serve as the closest guardian of the mystery being celebrated. The rubrics affirm and equally guarantee ritual unity and, consequently, are capable of giving expression to the Catholicity of the Church's liturgy. At the same time norms serve as a vehicle for liturgical and doctrinal content that a centuries-old tradition and proven experience have transmitted to us and which it is wrong to treat with superficiality and to pollute with our poor subjectivity.[80]

Malcolm Cardinal Ranjith, Archbishop of Colombo, has explained *ars celebrandi* as

> . . . not so much a matter of a series of actions put together in a harmonious way as much as a deeply interior communion with Christ—the art of conforming to Christ the High Priest and his sacrificial and salvific action. It does not so much connote the freedom to do as one pleases as much as the freedom to be united to Christ's priestly mission.[81]

---

80   Guido Marini, *Liturgical Reflections of a Papal Master of Ceremonies,* trans. Nicholas L. Gregoris (Pine Beach, NJ: Newman House Press, 2011) 20–21.

81   Malcolm Ranjith, "Towards an *Ars Celebrandi* in the Liturgy," in *Antiphon* 13 (2009) 7–17, at 10.

Cardinal Ranjith distinguishes three elements of this communion: interiority, obedience to norms, and devoutness.[82] We can see here that *ars celebrandi* is not about liturgical law or rubrics. It is about fidelity to Christ and communion with the one Church he founded. Within this *relationship* of faithful communion, its liturgical celebrations are justly governed by laws and the ritual books rightly give directions called rubrics. They are but one expression of our fidelity to Christ and our love for and communion with his Church.[83] Were it not for the fact that they surround and protect the greatest mysteries of our faith, the sacraments and indeed Christ himself, they might even be able to be called a small part of that relationship. But even were that to be the case, as Saint Augustine said, "What is small is indeed small, but whoever would be faithful in small things is great."[84]

This larger perspective—of fidelity to Christ and to his Church in small things as well as in great—gives a meaning and a place, indeed a theological importance, to liturgical law and to rubrics in the twenty-first century.

It is this spirit of love, and of the fidelity that is its fruit, that has motivated authors such as Bishop Peter Elliott as well as Father André Philippe Mutuel with Peter Freeman to publish ceremonial manuals for the modern rites in English and in French, manuals grounded in the *ars celebrandi* of which *Sacramentum Caritatis* speaks.[85] Would that more shall appear.

---

82   See ibid., 10–15.

83   James P. Moroney asserts that "the secret of the *ars celebrandi*" is that "obedience, authenticity, humility, and love for the sacred rites and texts are by-products of a life lived in close communion with Christ;" "In Pursuit of an *Ars Celebrandi*: Presuppositions and Possibilities," in *Sacrosanctum Concilium and the Reform of the Liturgy*, ed. Kenneth D. Whitehead (Chicago: University of Scranton Press, 2009) 27–35, at 29–30.

84   "Quod ergo minimum est, minimum est; sed in minimo fidelem esse, magnum est." Augustine of Hippo, *De doctrina christiana,* IV, XVIII, 35: ed. R. P. H. Green, Oxford Early Christian Texts (Oxford: Clarendon Press, 1995) 240.

85   See Peter J. Elliott, *Ceremonies of the Modern Roman Rite*, 2nd ed. (San Francisco: Ignatius Press, 2005), and *Ceremonies of the Liturgical Year* (San Francisco: Ignatius Press, 2002); André Philippe M. Mutuel and Peter Freeman, *Cérémonial de la*

CONCLUSION

I have not discussed here the place of liturgical law in the *usus antiquior* of the Roman Rite. One of its joys is that the place of liturgical law and of rubrics in its celebration has never seriously been in doubt, and has indeed been reaffirmed by the instruction *Universae Ecclesiae*[86] (in spite of, or perhaps in answer to, attempts to undermine its integrity).[87] Nor have I addressed the crucial and urgent question of the deficiencies and possible discontinuities of the modern liturgical rites themselves: that is for another work. Rather I have sought to demonstrate the place within the modern rites promulgated after the council of that traditional respect for rubrics and obedience to the Church's liturgical law that was once a matter of honor for clergy and laity alike.

Recent decades, beginning even before the Second Vatican Council, regarded rubrics and liturgical law as dry, and even in opposition to true worship, and often too readily set them aside. Perhaps the reason for this crisis lies in the fact that when love grows cold through routine, is seduced by other "apparent" goods, is poisoned by ideology, or becomes diseased through infidelity, love's little rules—those small, seemingly insignificant conventions that spring from and in fact protect and guard love itself—when this happens, those little rules loom unusually large and seem themselves to be the cause of oppression. They appear out of all context and proportion.

In respect of this crisis I submit that what we need first is to recapture, to revive, perhaps even to reconcile the fundamental relationship into which we are immersed at our baptism: the rela-

---

sainte messe à l'usage ordinaire des paroisses: suivant le missel romain de 2002 et la pratique léguée du rit romain (Perpignan: Éditions Artège, 2010).

86   See *Universae Ecclesiae*, no. 28.

87   See John M. Huels, "Reconciling the old with the new: Canonical questions on *Summorum Pontificum*," in *The Jurist* 68 (2008) 92–113. My response to this article (which seems to be consonant with that outlined in *Universae Ecclesiae*) can be found in *The Ceremonies of the Roman Rite Described*, ed. Adrian Fortescue, J. B. O'Connell and Alcuin Reid (London: Burns & Oates/Continuum, 2009) 18–19.

tionship of being sons and daughters of the Father, in Christ, through the power of the Holy Spirit working in the one true Church founded by Christ. When we live in and live from this ecclesial communion, a communion sustained in love by Love Himself, rubrics and laws take their proper place in our life of worship, and fidelity to them is nothing other than our act of love and of fidelity to God Himself.

René Girard and the Holy Sacrifice of the Mass: Re-Assessing the Twentieth-Century Liturgical Reform

RYAN J. MARR

After being exposed to the writings of René Girard, it came as no surprise to me to learn that he supported the movement to provide for a wider use of the "Tridentine Mass."[1] Given the centrality of Christ's sacrificial self-offering to Girard's later work, it makes sense that he would have been sympathetic to a ritual form that, perhaps more than any other Christian liturgy, involves a re-presentation of Christ's Passion.[2] Unfortunately, nowhere in his published writings did Girard directly comment on the theological significance of the older form of the Roman Rite. In fact, for the most part, Girard kept his distance from discussions of liturgical matters. Thus, while his work has made significant waves in the fields of anthropology and systematic theology, the

---

1   See "Italian Intellectuals Sign 'Tridentine Manifesto,'" at http://rorate-caeli.blogspot.com/2006/12/italian-intellectuals-sign-tridentine.html.

2   Early in his career, Girard rejected a sacrificial interpretation of Christ's Passion, arguing that such an approach perpetuated the scapegoat mechanism that was operative in archaic notions of sacrifice. Correspondingly, he was critical of the Letter to the Hebrews, which he blamed for planting the seed of this line of interpretation. Girard subsequently modified his position, after coming to recognize the great distance between the sacrifice of Christ (as that which undid the law of scapegoats) and archaic sacrifice. Girard discussed this development in his thinking in *The One by Whom Scandal Comes*, trans. Malcolm B. DeBevoise (East Lansing, MI: Michigan State University Press, 2014) 33–45. See also Avery Dulles, "The Death of Jesus as Sacrifice," in *Josephinum Journal of Theology* 3 (1996) 4–17, at 6.

field of liturgical studies remains ripe for a deeper engagement with Girard's work. The underlying contention of the following study is that Girard's scholarship can provide a fuller understanding of the mystery of the Eucharist in relation to Christ's sacrificial work on the cross, thereby providing a fuller appreciation of the particular strengths of what is now known as the Extraordinary Form of the Roman Rite.[3] The first section of the article will examine how Girard's thoughts concerning sacrifice provide a helpful grammar for talking about atonement, while the second section will bring his work into conversation with Catholic Eucharistic theology, specifically, with the notion of the Eucharist as an unbloody sacrifice. The third section of the paper will be more polemical in nature, arguing that certain aspects of the liturgical reform following the Second Vatican Council, in particular the *Novus Ordo Missae*, obscure the sacrificial character of the Mass, thereby blunting the force of the rite to communicate the way in which Christ's sacrifice frees us from the cycle of violence that has plagued human culture from its very beginnings. My comments in this section of the paper will focus on the *Ordo Missae* strictly speaking. A broader analysis of the reform of the Missal could examine its different aspects—e.g., the structure of the liturgical year, the various prayers, lectionary readings, etc.—but this article will limit itself to an assessment of the Order of Mass. Finally, the conclusion will set forth a constructive proposal for concretizing Benedict XVI's hope that the two forms of the Roman Rite might be mutually enriching.

VIOLENCE AND THE SACRED: SACRIFICE IN THE THOUGHT OF RENÉ GIRARD

Before getting to the heart of my argument, some brief comments on Girard's theory of mimesis and its application to a Chris-

---

3   Admittedly, my article advances an application of Girard's thought beyond anything specific that he wrote regarding the celebration of the liturgy. Nevertheless, I hope to show how Girard's insights can fruitfully inform questions about the prudential nature of certain alterations that were made to the Mass. Hopefully, the reader will judge this exercise to be a judicious extension of Girard's project.

tian understanding of atonement are in order. In Girard's view, human beings do not possess "natural" desires; rather, we learn what to desire by observing what others desire. While on the surface this mimetic desire seems harmless enough, it has a darker side in that shared desire inevitably leads to violence.[4] Mimetic conflict represents a crisis not only in the relationships between individuals, but also at a societal level, due to the contagious nature of violence.[5] Because of the human propensity to seek revenge, acts of violence tend to escalate into heightened levels of conflict, until the very structures of social order reach the brink of destruction. As a means of resolving this crisis, primitive societies often fell back upon the scapegoat mechanism, in which the anger and hostility of the community were directed against a randomly chosen victim. Just as two rivals can find solidarity through a shared enemy, so also this dynamic appears to work at the societal level. In a very real sense, social cohesiveness is constructed around the lynched body of a sacrificial victim.[6] Throughout most of human history, it seems, societies have operated according to the principle of Caiaphas, that it is better for one man to die for the people than that the whole nation should perish (see Jn 11:50).[7]

Building on this idea of the scapegoat mechanism, Girard showed how religion plays a central role in the process of culture formation. Over time, a community (without realizing precisely what it is doing) will cover up the originating violence upon which it was founded with an elaborate system of ritual and myth.[8]

---

4   René Girard, Jean-Michel Oughourlian, and Guy Lefort, *Things Hidden Since the Foundation of the World*, trans. Stephen Bann and Michael Metteer (Stanford, CA: Stanford University Press, 1987) 90–93. See also René Girard, João Cezar de Castro Rocha, and Pierpaolo Antonello, *Evolution and Conversion: Dialogues on the Origins of Culture* (New York: Continuum, 2007) 56–57.

5   René Girard, *Violence and the Sacred*, trans. Patrick Gregory (Baltimore, MD: Johns Hopkins University Press, 1977) 30–31.

6   Girard, *Evolution and Conversion*, 64.

7   Girard discusses this passage in *The Scapegoat*, trans. Yvonne Freccero (Baltimore, MD: Johns Hopkins University Press, 1986) 112–115.

8   Ibid., 95.

Ritual, Girard pointed out, serves as a way for the community to re-enact the collective murder that made social order possible in the first place—but in an organized manner, thus ensuring that the expression of violence remains within "acceptable" boundaries. As Girard put it, "Ritual is nothing more than the regular exercise of 'good' violence."⁹ From this perspective, "Religion . . . is far from 'useless.'" In Girard's words, religion "humanizes violence; it protects man from his own violence by taking it out of his hands, transforming it into a transcendent and ever-present danger to be kept in check by the appropriate rites appropriately observed and by a modest and prudent demeanor."¹⁰

Within this framework, myth represents an organic development of ritual sacrifice.¹¹ Through the formulation of myth, human societies construct a cultural memory that explains the community's existence while at the same time fostering the unitive forces that make the community possible. Just as in the case of ritual, myth turns the community's vision back to the founding murder, but does so in such a way that the community's complicity in the violence is effectively obscured—in some cases, even transforming the original victim into a deity who at some point in the distant past saved the community from certain catastrophe.¹² From Girard's perspective, then, myth is always "*against* the victim."¹³ Within the orbit of the mythical worldview, the victim is assumed to be guilty of some primeval crime, even if he remains unaware of the violation he has committed. Alongside this dynamic, myth offers further justification of the originating violence by obscuring that violence.

---

9   Girard, *Violence and the Sacred*, 37.
10   Ibid., 134. See also Girard, *Things Hidden*, 28–32.
11   Simply stated, myth is a way of "narrating the sacred." This phrase comes from Chris Fleming's study of Girard's project, *René Girard: Violence and Mimesis* (Malden, MA: Polity Press, 2004) 77.
12   As James Alison explains, "Because the expelled victim has brought about . . . peace, after its expulsion it becomes sacralized: it becomes the god whose visitation has first chaos, then order, a being to be worshiped with gratitude and to be feared." *The Joy of Being Wrong: Original Sin Through Easter Eyes* (New York: Crossroad, 1998) 19.
13   Girard, *Evolution and Conversion*, 196.

In short, myth is always written from the perspective of the persecutors, and, as a result, the cry of the victim goes unheard. Juxtaposed against standard mythology, Hebraic religion stands out as a monumental cultural achievement. In contrast to the myths of other cultures, the Hebrew Scriptures tell Israel's history in such a way that the voice of the victim is heard for the first time. From the very beginning of Scripture, but even more so as the narrative unfolds, history is told from the perspective of the victim. An especially important point in this process is the exodus, in which God's people realize that their election is intrinsically connected to their status as victims—or, to put it another way, that God remains on the side of the oppressed, not the persecutors.[14] Apart from any questions about the historicity of the biblical accounts, the Bible, according to Girard, constitutes authentic revelation, in that it demystifies narratives that implicitly present "scapegoating" as necessary for maintaining social harmony.[15]

The paradoxical character of the Hebrew Scriptures has to do with the way in which the biblical authors weave together texts that foster "the intelligence of the victim" with those that seem to perpetuate mimetic violence, or at the very least to gloss it over.[16] Within the Old Testament, we hear a plurality of voices—some clearly on the side of the victim,[17] but others standing in tension with this perspective. The significance of Christ emerges when

14   On God's people coming to understand his preferential option for the oppressed and on the freedom this realization brings, see James Alison's discussion of "the intelligence of the victim" in *Knowing Jesus* (Springfield, IL: Templegate Publishers, 1994) 31–58.

15   See Girard, *Evolution and Conversion*, 200: "I think there is a fundamental opposition between biblical texts and myths. The truth of the biblical text isn't a question of referentiality/non-referentiality. It doesn't have to be referential to be true. It is true in so far as it is *the denial of myths*, which are the source of the lie, since they always confirm the scapegoat mechanism, and in so doing cover it up."

16   One thinks especially of the conquest narratives and also of what biblical scholars refer to as "texts of terror." For a feminist treatment of the latter topic, see Phyllis Trible, *Texts of Terror: Literary-Feminist Readings of Biblical Narratives* (Philadelphia: Fortress Press, 1984).

17   E.g., Exodus, Job, the psalms of lament, etc.

his life is viewed against this backdrop. With the coming of Christ, the scapegoat mechanism is definitively exposed, because in this unique historical instance God not merely sides with the victim but, in fact, freely chooses to be the victim of human violence, thus bringing an end to any need for further sacrifice.[18]

As we know from the Gospels, the disciples did not comprehend the full significance of Christ's paschal self-offering until they encountered him as risen Lord. On the surface, the resurrection of Christ seems to follow the pattern of scapegoating myths, in that the victim is brought back to life, deified, and then depicted as the one who can ensure future communal harmony. But, as James Alison points out, the key difference resides in the fact that in his post-resurrection body Christ continues to bear the marks of his crucifixion:

> [W]hen Jesus rose it was not a simple continuation of his life. . . , but rather that he was given back to the disciples as simultaneously dead and alive. . . . [T]he resurrection life has emptied death of its power by showing the *form* of death (the marks of crucifixion) without its content. . . . So the risen presence is of the dead-and-risen one as gratuitous forgiveness revealing love beyond death.[19]

Following the resurrection, this risen presence is mediated through the ritual of the Eucharist: Christ remains present to his followers through the sharing of bread and wine (e.g., Lk 24:13–35), which make present in their midst his body and blood (1 Cor 11:23–26). In this way, the primary ritual of Christian worship transforms and perfects the sacrificial offerings of human history.[20] At the center of

---

18   Girard, *Evolution and Conversion*, 203. In light of this insight, we can better understand why Christ framed his mission not as the abolition of the law, but as its fulfillment (Mt 5:17), as well as the New Testament's insistence that Christ is the Lamb of God who takes away sins (Jn 1:29), the one slain from the foundation of the world (Rev 13:8).

19   Alison, *The Joy of Being Wrong*, 76.

20   The Roman Canon majestically expresses this reality, when the priest prays to God, "Be pleased to look upon these offerings with a serene and kindly countenance, and to accept them, as once you were pleased to accept the gifts of your servant

Christian ritual stands the crucified body of an innocent victim, but in this case the victim is the incarnate Son of God, who has freely offered himself in loving obedience to the Father, and thereby made possible the realization of authentic community, founded as it is upon a process of reconciliation rather than coercion.[21]

SACRIFICE AND COMMUNITY: CHRISTIAN EUCHARIST AND UNION WITH GOD

As numerous commentators have pointed out, Girard's thought presents a helpful framework for understanding the Christian doctrine of atonement. Specifically, Girard's approach provides a way of thinking through the difficult issue of violence being so central to Christ's atonement for human sin. Within certain strands of the Christian tradition, the violence that Christ underwent in the Passion almost came to be seen as *necessary*, in the sense that the punishment inflicted upon Christ appeased the wrath of God the Father.[22] According to this sort of atonement

---

Abel the just, the sacrifice of Abraham, our father in faith, and the offering of your high priest Melchizedek, a holy sacrifice, a spotless victim." *The Roman Missal: Renewed by Decree of the Most Holy Second Ecumenical Council of the Vatican, Promulgated by Authority of Pope Paul VI and Revised at the Direction of Pope John Paul II*, English translation according to the third typical edition (Totowa, NJ: Catholic Book Publishing, 2011) The Order of Mass, Eucharistic Prayer I (The Roman Canon), no. 93.

21   The New Testament writings describe this reality simultaneously as the in-breaking of the Kingdom of God and the disarming of the principalities and powers of this world. The principalities and powers rely upon the threat of further violence to maintain order, but Christ, in freely assuming the role of scapegoat, has disarmed these powers by making a public spectacle of them (Col 2:15; see Girard, *The Scapegoat*, 189). As Christ's followers share in the Eucharist, they begin to experience the Kingdom of God firsthand. In the partaking of Christ's body and blood, they themselves are built up into the Body of Christ and are made to be a "sacrament of saving unity" to the world; Second Vatican Council, Dogmatic Constitution on the Church *Lumen Gentium* (21 November 1964) no. 9.

22   For a critical analysis of the classic penal substitutionary theology of atonement, see S. Mark Heim, *Saved From Sacrifice: A Theology of the Cross* (Grand Rapids, MI: Eerdmans, 2006) 297–302. See also James Alison, *Undergoing God: Dispatches from the Scene of a Break-In* (New York: Continuum, 2006) 55.

theory, the suffering of Jesus on the cross pays the penalty for
human sinfulness, thus providing satisfaction for humanity's violation of God's justice. If interpreted in a simplistic manner, this
theology can give the impression that the dynamic at work in the
Passion is one of inter-Trinitarian violence, in which God the
Father directs the full force of his righteous anger against his innocent Son, who stands in the place of sinful human beings.[23] In
contradistinction to this vision of the cross, Girard's writings dramatically highlight the way in which Christ's execution is fundamentally the product of human violence, not divine violence.[24]
From a Girardian perspective, the atoning work of Christ does not
provide salvation by balancing the cosmic scales of justice; rather,
it does so by exposing the scapegoating violence that resides at the
root of human culture, thus revealing the inadequacy of any
human effort to achieve peace by means of sacrificial violence. In
this way, Girard's approach effectively restores a proper balance
to the Trinitarian dynamics at work in the Gospel. In the Passion
the Father's and the Son's wills were perfectly united, dispelling
any notion that God the Father "required" the death of Christ to
appease his wrath.[25]

---

23   Without totally dismissing the artistic merit of Mel Gibson's *The Passion*,
one can see why his film, which draws upon a penal substitutionary understanding
of the atonement, telescopically focuses in on the violent nature of Jesus' death in an
almost "pornographic" way. If the suffering of Christ appeases God's wrath within a
broader matrix of justice, then it makes sense that Christians would dwell upon the
intensity of Christ's suffering. In contrast, the Gospels provide only brief descriptions
of this facet of the Passion, instead focusing upon the larger movements at work in
the dramatic events of Jesus' final hours.
24   In conversation with the work of Girard, James Alison develops a great
deal of his theological reflection from the foundational insight that "there is no violence in God." See, e.g., Alison, *Raising Abel: The Recovery of the Eschatological Imag-
ination* (New York: Crossroad, 1996) 41–48.
25   Heim, *Saved from Sacrifice*, 309. In his meditations on the seven last words,
Stanley Hauerwas follows a trajectory similar to Heim's. As Hauerwas sees the matter,
"[A]ny account of the cross that suggests God must somehow satisfy an abstract theory
of justice by sacrificing his Son on our behalf is clearly wrong. Indeed such accounts
are dangerously wrong. The Father's sacrifice of the Son and the Son's willing sacrifice

This approach to the atonement lays the groundwork for understanding the sacrificial character of the Eucharist. On the evening of his betrayal, Christ celebrated the Last Supper with his disciples, and in the context of this meal communicated to them that the suffering he was about to undergo was not something imposed upon him, but something he freely accepted for the sake of reconciling humanity. After the resurrection, this Eucharistic meal became the primary means by which Christ's followers remembered his death and experienced his living presence. From earliest times, Christian communities understood the Eucharist as possessing a clearly sacrificial character. A crucial witness to this conviction was the Fourth Gospel, which set Jesus' death against the backdrop of the paschal lambs being sacrificed in the Temple.[26] Along similar lines, the book of Hebrews portrayed Christ as both priest and victim, arguing that his sacrifice brought about the sanctification that the Levitical sacrifices only foreshadowed (Heb 10:11–14). Thus, when the author of Hebrews talked about how "we have an altar from which those who officiate in the tent have no right to eat" (Heb 13:10 NRSV),[27] Christians could not help but read this statement in light of their Eucharistic practice.

As is well known, at the time of the Protestant Reformation the longstanding tradition of viewing the Eucharist in a sacrificial

---

is God's justice. Just as there is no God who is not the Father, Son, and Holy Spirit, so there is no god who must be satisfied that we might be spared. We are the spared because God refuses to have us lost." Stanley Hauerwas, *Cross-Shattered Christ: Meditations on the Seven Last Words* (Grand Rapids, MI: Brazos Press, 2004) 65–66.

26   See Raymond E. Brown, *The Death of the Messiah: From Gethsemane to the Grave*, vol. 1 (Garden City, NY: Doubleday, 1994) 846–848. Besides the fact that Jesus' death occurs at the time of the paschal sacrifices, the Gospel of John draws attention to this connection through a number of devices, as for example, by narrating that Jesus' bones remained unbroken (see Ex 12:46, Jn 19:33–34). Debate rages among scholars about whether the background to the Eucharist is the *tōda* or Passover meal. For an instructive article on these matters, see Jack Custer's analysis of Ratzinger's theology of the Eucharist, "The Eucharist as Thanksgiving Sacrifice," in *Antiphon* 12 (2008) 46–65.

27   *The Holy Bible: New Revised Standard Version* (New York: Harper Collins, 1993).

light became a point of contention between Protestant and Roman Catholic theologians.[28] For Luther, the idea of the Mass as a sacrifice offered to God was a threat to the gratuity of salvation that was the heart of the Gospel.[29] Calvin, meanwhile, protested principally against the idea that the Mass could obtain the remission of sins.[30] In spite of the impassioned critiques leveled by the Protestant Reformers, the Catholic Church continued to defend the notion of the Mass as a sacrifice, and at the Council of Trent, this doctrine achieved dogmatic form. Drawing in large part upon the theology of Thomas Aquinas,[31] the council fathers taught unambiguously that the Mass was an unbloody sacrifice, a re-presentation of Christ's atoning work, and efficacious for the remission of sins.[32]

---

28   Matthew Levering traces out these debates in *Sacrifice and Community: Jewish Offering and Christian Eucharist*, Illuminations: Theory and Religion (Malden, MA: Blackwell, 2005) 12–17.

29   See Martin Luther, "The Babylonian Captivity of the Church," trans. Bertram Lee Woolf, in *Martin Luther: Selections from His Writings*, ed. John Dillenberger (New York: Doubleday, 1962) 286.

30   John Calvin, *Institutes of the Christian Religion*, trans. Henry Beveridge (Grand Rapids, MI: Eerdmans, 1989) IV.18. Quoted in Levering, *Sacrifice and Community*, 14.

31   For a helpful introduction to the Eucharistic theology of Aquinas, see Damian C. Fandal, *The Essence of the Eucharistic Sacrifice* (River Forest, IL: The Aquinas Library, 1960) 16–82. See also Matthew Levering, "Aquinas on the Liturgy of the Eucharist," in *Aquinas on Doctrine: A Critical Introduction*, ed. Thomas Weinandy, Daniel A. Keating, and John Yocum (New York: Continuum, 2004) 183–197.

32   For instance, Council of Trent, Session XXII, *Doctrine on the Sacrifice of the Mass*, Chapter II (17 September 1562): "In this divine sacrifice that is celebrated in the Mass, the same Christ who offered himself once in a bloody manner [*cf. Heb 9:14, 27f.*] on the altar of the Cross is contained and is offered in an unbloody manner. Therefore, the holy council teaches that this sacrifice is truly propitiatory [*can. 3*], so that, if we draw near to God with an upright heart and true faith, with fear and reverence, with sorrow and repentance, through it 'we may receive mercy and find grace to help in time of need' [*Heb 4:16*]. For the Lord, appeased by this oblation, grants peace and the gift of repentance, and he pardons wrongdoings and sins, even great ones. For, the victim is one and the same: the same now offers himself through the ministry of priests who then offered himself on the Cross; only the manner of offerings is different. The fruits of this oblation (the bloody one, that is) are received in abundance through this unbloody (oblation). By no means, then, does the latter detract

The dogmatic articulation of Trent represents a necessary supplement to Girard's perspective. On the one hand, Girard's approach guards against an understanding of the Passion as an occasion of divine violence intended to rectify humanity's violation of an abstract notion of justice. In this respect, Girard's position undercuts the misguided idea that in the Eucharist Christ is sacrificed again, as if there was still some continuing need for sacrifice to effect reconciliation and peace.[33] On the other hand, if Girard's thought is isolated from a fully Catholic perspective, there is a sense in which he can be misunderstood as promoting a soteriology with Gnostic and Pelagian elements.[34] According to this line of misinterpretation, Christ's life, death, and resurrection had to do with conveying knowledge (*gnosis*) to humanity. If this were true, human beings would be saved simply by appropriating the anthropological insight that Christ revealed, that is to say, by seeing the scapegoat mechanism for what it is and then by willfully refusing to participate in it.[35]

However, the dogmatic articulation of Trent closes off the possibility of reducing the salvific work of Christ to a matter of conveying knowledge, by demonstrating the way in which Christian worship stands in continuity with the sacrifices instituted

---

from the former [*can. 4*]. Therefore, it is rightly offered according to apostolic tradition, not only for the sins, punishments, satisfaction, and other necessities of the faithful who are alive, but also for those who have died in Christ but are not wholly purified [*can. 3*]." *Enchiridion symbolorum definitionum et declarationum de rebus fidei et morum*, ed. Heinrich Denzinger and Peter Hünermann, 43rd ed. (San Francisco: Ignatius Press, 2012) no. 1743.

33   The *locus classicus* for grounding the "once and for all" nature of Christ's sacrifice is Heb 10:11–18.

34   At an earlier point in his career, Girard himself seemed to come perilously close to falling into this error—for instance, as in *Things Hidden*, 205–215, when he argued in favor of a completely non-sacrificial understanding of the Passion. Girard has since repudiated that viewpoint, acknowledging that he came to a more nuanced approach to this issue, in part, through a closer reading of Hebrews. See Girard, *Evolution and Conversion*, 40 and 214–215.

35   Heim warns against this kind of reductive approach to Girard's theory. See Heim, *Saved from Sacrifice*, 196–197.

under the Law. Certainly, Christ's sacrifice differed from the Levitical in that he offered a single sacrifice for all time, thus doing away with any need for further sacrifices (Heb 10:11–18). Nevertheless, his sacrifice must be viewed as the fulfillment of the sacrifices under the Law, and not as their abolishment. In both cases, the purpose of the sacrifice is to effect reconciliation among the people of God, so as to enable true communion with God.[36] In this light, salvation has to do with much more than grasping an anthropological insight. Salvation could not be achieved through the transmission of knowledge, but required sacrifice—not just any sacrifice, but a perfect sacrifice, the sacrifice to end all sacrifice (Heb 9:23–28). In making a perfect offering for the forgiveness of sins, Christ also left his followers the memorial of his death and resurrection—the Eucharist—by which we continue to experience the forgiveness of our sins and are brought into loving communion with the Triune God through our incorporation into the Mystical Body of Christ.[37]

Only with all of the above in view can I hope to defend my contention that Girard's support for wider availability of the traditional form of the Roman Mass was not accidental, but made sense in light of his developed understanding of sacrifice, particularly in relation to the Passion. If Christ's self-offering signals "the

---

36   Levering, *Sacrifice and Community*, 113.

37   See, for instance, Pope Pius XII, Encyclical on the Mystical Body of Christ *Mystici Corporis Christi* (29 June 1943) no. 82: "By means of the Eucharistic Sacrifice Christ our Lord willed to give the faithful a striking manifestation of our union among ourselves and with our divine Head, wonderful as it is and beyond all praise. For in this Sacrifice the sacred minister acts as the vice-regent not only of our Savior but of the whole Mystical Body and of each one of the faithful. In this act of Sacrifice through the hands of the priest, by whose word alone the Immaculate Lamb is present on the altar, the faithful themselves, united with him in prayer and desire, offer to the Eternal Father a most acceptable victim of praise and propitiation for the needs of the whole Church. And as the Divine Redeemer, when dying on the Cross, offered Himself to the Eternal Father as Head of the whole human race, so 'in this clean oblation' [Mal 1:11] He offers to the heavenly Father not only Himself as Head of the Church, but in Himself His mystical members also, since He holds them all, even those who are weak and ailing, in His most loving Heart."

end of Satan's mechanism" and the in-breaking of God's Kingdom, as Girard contended, then it is not only natural, but necessary, for true worship to have as its central focus the perfect sacrifice of Christ. The mystery and solemnity of Catholic worship
have to do with the Church's conviction that the Mass does not
simply memorialize Christ's Passion, but in fact re-presents it, such
that the faithful assisting at the celebration are brought into real
contact with the sacred mysteries of salvation.[38] The final section
of this paper will argue that the Extraordinary Form of the Roman
Rite,[39] more clearly conveys the sacrificial character of the
Eucharist than does its Ordinary Form, which resulted from the
post-conciliar reform of the liturgy. In short, it will contend that
by diminishing the sacrificial character of the Mass the *Novus Ordo
Missae* runs the risk of obscuring a central affirmation of the
Catholic faith.

THE HOLY SACRIFICE OF THE MASS:
A CURSORY ANALYSIS OF THE LITURGICAL REFORM

The *Novus Ordo Missae* differs from its historical predecessor
in a number of significant ways, and a substantive treatment of
the reform could easily occupy a thesis in its own right. For the
purposes of the present study, however, a brief look at just a few
of the changes made will suffice to demonstrate the way in which
the reformed liturgy downplays the sacrificial character of the
Mass.[40] One of the most noticeable alterations to the liturgical cel-

---

38   See the *Catechism of the Catholic Church*, 2nd ed. (Washington, DC: United
States Catholic Conference, 2000) no. 1366: "The Eucharist is thus a sacrifice because
it *re-presents* (makes present) the sacrifice of the cross, because it is its *memorial* and
because it *applies* its fruit" (emphasis original).

39   See the relevant remarks in Pope Benedict XVI, Letter to the Bishops
Accompanying the Motu Proprio *Summorum Pontificum* (7 July 2007).

40   The analysis that follows draws somewhat from a 2001 document published
by the Society of Saint Pius X, *The Problem of the Liturgical Reform: A Theological and
Liturgical Study* (Kansas City, MO: Angelus Press, 2001). Even though I glean a number of insights from this work, I do think there are some methodological shortcomings
in it. For example, the authors of this critique are harshly critical of the *Novus Ordo's*

ebration can be found at the very beginning of the rite.[41] In the Extraordinary Form, the priest and servers begin the Mass with a series of prayers at the foot of the altar, including a recitation of Psalm 42 (*Iudica me*), which pleads for deliverance from enemies and mentions "going unto the altar of God." Following these prayers, there is a double recitation (priest and servers) of the *Confiteor*, or public confession, followed by additional pleas for God's mercy. Finally, upon ascending to the altar, the priest offers a moving prayer for purification, asking God to take away the sins of those present, as within this sacred ceremony we will be entering into the Holy of Holies.[42]

In contrast to this elaborate opening ritual, the new Order of Mass suppresses the prayers at the foot of the altar, leaving only a greeting and a truncated penitential rite.[43] Alongside the omission

---

orientation to the Paschal Mystery (see pp. 39–51)—a theological term meant to encompass the entire mystery of Christ's atoning work, from Holy Thursday to the resurrection and ultimately his ascension. While I agree with the SSPX's contention that the crucifixion constitutes a kind of fulcrum for the liturgy, I also have a deep appreciation for the renewed sense in the post-conciliar era that the liturgy draws the faithful into an encounter with the full drama of salvation, not simply Christ's death. In making this point, I do not mean to imply a shortcoming in the Extraordinary Form, but merely to signal my puzzlement at the SSPX's adamant resistance to the concept of the Paschal Mystery. For further elaboration on the theology of the Paschal Mystery as it applies to the liturgy, see Rita Ferrone, *Liturgy: Sacrosanctum Concilium* (New York: Paulist Press, 2007) 23–25 and 91–94.

41   The English translation of the Order of Mass in the Extraordinary Form is taken from http://sanctamissa.org/en/tutorial/ordo-missae-1.html. The original Latin can be found in *Missale Romanum ex decreto SS. Concilii Tridentini restitutum Summorum Pontificum cura recognitum*, Editio typica (Vatican City: Typis Polyglottis Vaticanis, 1962). For the Ordinary Form, see *Missale Romanum ex decreto Sacrosancti Oecumenici Concilii Vaticani II instauratum auctoritate Pauli PP. VI promulgatum Ioannis Pauli PP. cura recognitum*, Editio typica tertia reimpressio emendata (Vatican City: Typis Vaticanis, 2008) and *The Roman Missal*.

42   "Take away from us our iniquities, we beseech Thee, O Lord, that we may be worthy to enter with pure minds into the Holy of Holies. Through Christ our Lord. Amen. We beseech Thee, O Lord, by the merits of Thy Saints whose relics are here and of all the Saints, that Thou wouldst vouchsafe to forgive me all my sins. Amen."

43   The *Novus Ordo Missae* retains the Confiteor as an option for the penitential rite (to be recited by the priest and assembly together), though this feature has

of preparatory prayers at the foot of the altar, the fact that many churches built or renovated after the council lack architectural features—such as altar rails—that section off the sanctuary from the nave further obscures the reality that in the Mass the Church intends to offer through her priests a holy and perfect sacrifice, not merely to celebrate a thanksgiving meal. The older form of the rite, through a logical progression of rubrics and prayers, undeniably displays the sacrificial nature of what is taking place in the liturgy. Spatially, the distinct architectural features of historic Catholic churches heighten this signification. In the Extraordinary Form, before approaching the altar, the priest confesses his unworthiness and asks for God's mercy. Moreover, when the priest recites the Canon of the Mass, he does so silently, indicating that at the point of the Eucharistic prayer he is entering into the greater and more perfect Holy of Holies (see Heb 9:11–14 and 10:19–22), just as the Levitical priests drew near to the Holy Place to purify the people from their sins.

The dramatic difference between the two forms of the Roman Rite can also be seen through a comparison of the traditional offertory with the new "presentation of the gifts." As a preface to the Eucharistic prayer, the reformers of the liturgy replaced the supplicatory prayers of the traditional offertory "with the ritual *berakoth* of the Jewish meal,"[44] which reads: "Blessed are you, Lord God of all creation, for through your goodness we have received the bread we offer you: fruit of the earth and work of human hands, it will become for us the bread of life"—with similar words of thanksgiving offered over the wine.[45] Besides this change, the revised offertory also omits the *Suscipe* prayer—asking God to receive the spotless host that the priest offers on behalf of his and the congregation's

---

been edited through an excising of invocations to blessed Michael the Archangel, blessed John the Baptist, and the Holy Apostles Peter and Paul. At the conclusion of the penitential rite, the liturgy transitions immediately into the *Kyrie*—or, into the *Gloria* if the *Kyrie* has already been used in one of the forms of the act of penance.

44   Louis Bouyer, *Eucharistie: Théologie et spiritualité de la prière eucharistique* (Paris: Desclée, 1990) 109, my translation.

45   *The Roman Missal*, The Order of Mass, nos. 23 and 25.

sins—as well as the offering of the chalice of salvation ("*Offerimus tibi...*") and a moving prayer to the Most Holy Trinity. Perhaps more than any other revision, the changes made to the offertory conspicuously display the shift in theological orientation in the transition that took place in the post-conciliar liturgical reform. In the reformed *Ordo Missae*, immediately prior to offering up the gifts on the altar, the priest communicates that the act to follow primarily entails a thanksgiving meal. In the process, the sacrificial character of the celebration recedes into the background.[46] One of the members (J. M. Martin Patino) of the *Consilium* that oversaw the reform confirmed this shift, noting that, "We have gone from an offertory in the strict sense of the word to a simple presentation of gifts which will become 'the bread of life and the cup of salvation.'"[47]

A third alteration to the Roman liturgy worth drawing attention to is a change that was not explicitly called for by the reform and that remains optional within the celebration of the Mass— namely, the widespread move away from celebrating *ad orientem*— or, towards the "liturgical east"—to celebrating *versus populum*, with the priest facing the people.[48] While this particular shift was not mandated by the official documents promulgated by the *Consilium*, the practice of the priest facing the congregation as he celebrates the Eucharist has become nearly ubiquitous since the time of the reform. As Joseph Ratzinger points out, the "turning of the priest toward the people has turned the community into a self-enclosed people," thereby collapsing the eschatological orientation of the liturgical celebration.[49] He writes,

46   Without disappearing altogether, of course, as the revised offertory retains the *In spiritu humilitatis* and *Orate, fratres*.

47   José María Martin Patino, Andrés Pardo, Alberto Iniesta and Pere Farnes, *Nuevas normas de la missa* (Madrid: Biblioteca de Autores Cristianos, 1969) 125, my translation.

48   For a thorough overview of this topic, see Uwe Michael Lang, *Turning Towards the Lord: Orientation in Liturgical Prayer*, 2nd ed. (San Francisco: Ignatius Press, 2009).

49   Joseph Cardinal Ratzinger, *The Spirit of the Liturgy*, trans. John Saward (San Francisco: Ignatius Press, 2000) 80. Most of Joseph Ratzinger's writings on the liturgy

[A] common turning to the east during the Eucharistic Prayer remains essential. This is not a case of something accidental, but of what is essential. Looking at the priest has no importance. What matters is looking together at the Lord. It is not now a question of dialogue but of common worship, of setting off toward the One who is to come. What corresponds with the reality of what is happening is not the closed circle but the common movement forward, expressed in a common direction for prayer.[50]

The move away from *ad orientem* worship has minimized not only the eschatological orientation to the Eucharistic, but also its sacrificial character—especially in light of the fact that in the Catholic liturgical scheme turning towards the east involves at the same time a turning towards the crucifix.

The theological import of the *ad orientem* posture is a hotly debated issue, and doing the topic justice would require a longer study. For the purposes of this article, a few brief remarks will have to suffice. The above quotation from Cardinal Ratzinger, while primarily highlighting the eschatological symbolism of facing east, also moves us toward a better understanding of how the *ad orientem* form of celebrating Mass properly expresses the sacrificial nature of what is taking place. In Ratzinger's concise phrasing, "Looking at the priest has no importance. What matters is looking together at the Lord." When one keeps in view the historic Catholic confession that the Mass is an unbloody sacrifice, Ratzinger's conclusion makes complete sense. The priest, standing *in persona Christi*, sacramentally offers up the body and blood of Christ to God the Father. In fulfilling this liturgical role, it is only proper that the priest would turn towards the one to whom he is making this sacrificial offering.

---

are conveniently assembled in the volume: *Theology of the Liturgy: The Sacramental Foundation of Christian Existence,* Joseph Ratzinger Collected Works 11, ed. Michael J. Miller (San Francisco: Ignatius Press, 2014). From Ratzinger's perspective, a renewal of the liturgy will necessarily involve a recovery of the ancient practice; see *Spirit of the Liturgy,* 81.

50   Ibid., 81.

This point was thoughtfully addressed in a letter from 25 September 2000, in which Cardinal Jorge Arturo Medina Estévez, the then-Prefect of the Congregation for Divine Worship and the Discipline of the Sacraments, offered a response to the question of whether article 299 of the General Instruction of the Roman Missal excludes the possibility of celebrating *versus orientem*. The Prefect responded in the negative, highlighting the fact that the Eucharist as a sacrifice is fundamentally an offering made to the triune God:

> [W]hatever may be the position of the celebrating priest, it is clear that the Eucharistic Sacrifice is offered to the one and triune God, and that the principal, eternal, and high priest is Jesus Christ, who acts through the ministry of the priest who visibly presides as His instrument. . . . It would be a grave error to imagine that the principal orientation of the sacrificial action is [toward] the community. If the priest celebrates *versus populum*, which is legitimate and often advisable, his spiritual attitude ought always to be *versus Deum per Iesum Christum* (towards God through Jesus Christ), as representative of the entire Church. The Church as well, which takes concrete form in the assembly which participates, is entirely turned *versus Deum* (towards God) as its first spiritual movement.[51]

In this response, the Congregation for Divine Worship under the leadership of Cardinal Medina does not impose one posture as normative for the celebration of the Mass, but the letter does emphasize that the spiritual attitude of priest and people ought to be directed *versus Deum*.[52] Given the fact that the *ad orientem* posture

---

51   Congregatio de Cultu Divino et Disciplina Sacramentorum, "Responsa ad quaestiones de nova *Institutione Generali Missalis Romani*," in *Communicationes* 32 (2000) 171–172. English translation: *Adoremus Bulletin Online Edition*, vol. 6, no. 9 (December 2000–January 2001), at https://adoremus.org/2007/12/31/Letter-on-the-Position-of-the-Priest-during-the-Eucharistic-Liturgy/.

52   Notably, during his time on the Chair of Peter, Ratzinger made it a regular practice at papal liturgies to offer the Mass with a crucifix at the center of the altar, thus orienting the celebration towards the sacrifice of Calvary and as a way of modeling a kind of compromise between the traditional liturgical orientation and the *versus populum* orientation which is most common today.

all but disappeared in the decades following the reform of the liturgy, wider use of this way of celebrating could help to reorient the collective mindset of the Catholic faithful, helping them to recognize more clearly the sacrificial character of the Mass.

In a nuanced and in-depth study of orientation in liturgical prayer, Uwe Michael Lang helpfully unpacks the symbolic resonance of the priest facing the "liturgical east." Working from the Council of Trent's affirmation that Christ left his Church a "visible sacrifice," Lang maintains that "the question needs to be asked how the sacrificial character of the Eucharist is to be expressed in the liturgical celebration."[53] While "the notion of the eucharistic sacrifice is clearly present in the prayers of the *Missale Romanum* of 1970," it is worth asking, what are the proper means for expressing its "ritual actualisation?"[54] In formulating an answer to this question, Lang quotes Thomas Witt, who succinctly captures the way in which the *ad orientem* posture accentuates the sacrificial character of the Mass:

> When the Lord's sacrifice is made present, the direction of this sacrifice is maintained. The Lord's sacrifice is directed to the Father—for the salvation of men. The basic direction of the sacrifice is indicated in his words on the Cross: "Father, into thy hands I commit my spirit" (Lk 23:46). . . . Christ returns to the Father and takes those who hope in him with him on this journey. In this respect, the final movement at which Christ's sacrifice aims is not downward, but upward. If, therefore, Christ's sacrifice is made present as his self-offering to the will of the Father, the direction of prayer "facing east" makes sense. For Christ's sacrifice has a direction of its own, qua being a sacrifice, and that is upward, to the Father.[55]

---

53   Lang, *Turning Towards the Lord,* 124.
54   Ibid., 125.
55   Thomas Witt, *Repraesentatio Sacrificii: Das eucharistische Opfer und seine Darstellung in den Gebeten und Riten des Missale Romanum 1970. Untersuchungen zur darstellenden Funktion der Liturgie,* Paderborner theologische Studien, 31 (Paderborn: Ferdinand Schöningh, 2002) 328. Translation provided by Lang, *Turning Towards the Lord,* 126.

To reiterate, this particular liturgical question is not an issue of prioritizing one form of the Roman Rite over another: the *ad orientem* posture is a legitimate option in the celebration of the Ordinary Form, and the current Prefect of the Congregation for Divine Worship has encouraged priests to celebrate in this manner more regularly.[56] That being said, for various reasons of historical accident, the *versus populum* manner of celebrating Mass has become virtually associated with the Ordinary Form and *ad orientem* with the Extraordinary Form, such that working towards a broader use of the *ad orientem* posture within parishes could be viewed as one way to promote mutual enrichment between the two forms of the Roman Rite. As Lang notes, "Pastoral experience of the last four decades shows that the understanding of the Mass as the sacrifice of Christ and the sacrifice of the Church has diminished considerably, if not faded away among the faithful."[57] If Witt's point, noted above, holds true, then bringing about more regular use of the *ad orientem* posture might serve as one way of reasserting the theological affirmation of the Mass as a sacramental re-presentation of Christ's sacrifice at Calvary. The following section of this article will propose one other key recommendation for advancing this effort.

UNBLOODY SACRIFICE AND SACRED MEAL

The above section has detailed some of the ways in which the alterations to the liturgy following the Second Vatican Council diminished the sacrificial character of the Mass. In seeking to establish a case for this argument, I would not want to overstate the matter, as the *Novus Ordo Missae* undoubtedly has retained certain markers that indicate a sacrifice is being offered.[58] In recent

---

56   See Robert Cardinal Sarah, "Towards an Authentic Implementation of *Sacrosanctum Concilium*," in *Authentic Liturgical Renewal in Contemporary Perspective: Proceedings of the Sacra Liturgia Conference Held in London, 5–8 July 2016*, ed. Uwe Michael Lang (London: Bloomsbury, 2017) 3–19, at 16–17.

57   Lang, *Turning Towards the Lord*, 127.

58   Most explicitly, perhaps, when the priest uses Eucharistic Prayer I, commonly known as the Roman Canon. As an indication of the commitments of the

years, Church officials (particularly during the pontificate of Pope Benedict XVI) have sought to emphasize the continuity in the reforms, in part, by reemphasizing the sacrificial character of the Mass.[59] While such efforts are commendable, one concrete way of fostering continuity could be to reintroduce into the Ordinary Form some of the prayers and rubrics from the older form that undeniably express that the Mass involves a sacrificial action.

Undoubtedly, the Mass does have the element of a Eucharistic meal, and the emphasis on communion with God through the partaking of Christ's body and blood should never be downplayed or forgotten. Still, given the evidence that we have examined above, the greater danger in our day seems to be that the balance might shift so determinatively towards the meal aspect of the Eucharist that we completely lose sight of the sacrificial aspect.[60] While some liturgical experts have justified a prioritization of the community meal over the sacrificial element by appealing to the

---

architects of the reform, however, it is telling that the Roman Canon in its traditional form was preserved only through an intervention by Paul VI late in the process of the reform. See Cassian Folsom, "From One Eucharistic Prayer to Many: How It Happened and Why," in *Adoremus Bulletin Online Edition* vol. 2, nos. 4–6 (September–November 1996), at https://adoremus.org/2011/09/15/from-one-eucharistic-prayer-to-many-how-it-happened-and-why/.

59   Already by the mid-eighties, Joseph Ratzinger realized that certain changes to the liturgy had caused an imbalance in liturgical understanding. Commenting on notable trends within Catholic theology, he remarked: "Some apparently see liturgy narrowly in terms of the Eucharist alone, and only under the aspect of the 'brotherly meal.' But the Mass is not only a meal among friends who have come together to remember the Lord's Last Supper through the common breaking of bread. The Mass is the common sacrifice of the Church, in which the Lord prays with us and for us and communicates himself to us. It is the sacramental renewal of Christ's sacrifice: consequently its redeeming power extends to all men, those present and those far away, the living and the dead." Joseph Cardinal Ratzinger, with Vittorio Messori, *The Ratzinger Report: An Exclusive Interview on the State of the Church,* trans. Salvator Attanasio and Graham Harrison (San Francisco: Ignatius Press, 1985) 132. See also Pope John Paul II, Encyclical on the Eucharist and its Relationship to the Church *Ecclesia de Eucharistia* (17 April 2003) no. 10.

60   For Ratzinger's explanation of the sacrificial character of the Eucharist, see *God Is Near Us: The Eucharist, the Heart of Life,* trans. Henry Taylor (San Francisco: Ignatius Press, 2003) 44–51.

Eucharist's relation to the tradition of the Passover, Ratzinger argues that this move operates according to a false dichotomy, since "even in the earliest period, when the Passover was still a family feast, the slaughtering of the lambs already had a sacrificial character."[61] In his 1981 work on the liturgy, *The Feast of Faith*, Ratzinger brings together the eschatological and sacrificial dimensions of the Mass to demonstrate the error of placing an inordinate emphasis on the meal element to the detriment of the notion of sacrifice:

> To speak of the Eucharist as the community meal is to cheapen it, for its price was the death of Christ. And as for the joy it heralds, it presupposes that we have entered into this mystery of death. Eucharist is ordered to eschatology, and hence it is at the heart of the theology of the Cross. This is why the church holds fast to the sacrificial character of the Mass; she does so lest we fail to realize the magnitude of what is involved and thus miss both the real depth of what it means to be human and the real depth of God's liberating power.[62]

At any rate, it is difficult to see how the meal aspect of the Eucharist could be lost altogether, given the fact that the Mass always involves the offering of bread and wine, and normally concludes with the communal partaking of these elements. In our

---

61   Joseph Cardinal Ratzinger, "Theology of the Liturgy," in *Looking Again at the Question of the Liturgy with Cardinal Ratzinger: Proceedings of the July 2001 Fontgombault Liturgical Conference*, ed. Alcuin Reid (Farnborough: Saint Michael's Abbey Press, 2003) 18–31, at 23. Ratzinger adds: "[P]recisely through the tradition of the Passover, the idea of sacrifice is carried right up to the words and gestures of the Last Supper, where it is present also on the basis of a second Old Testament passage, Exodus 24, which relates the conclusion of the Covenant at Sinai. . . . The new Christian Passover is thus expressly interpreted in the accounts of the Last Supper as a sacrificial event, and on the basis of the words of the Last Supper would be an empty gesture without the reality of the Cross and of the Resurrection, which is anticipated in it and made accessible for all time in its interior content" (ibid.).

62   Joseph Cardinal Ratzinger, *The Feast of Faith: Approaches to a Theology of the Liturgy*, trans. Graham Harrison (San Francisco: Ignatius Press, 1986) 65.

own day, the sacrificial dimension to the liturgy seems to face a much greater risk of being neglected.[63]

CONCLUSION

Admittedly, my study has followed a circuitous path—beginning with Girard's theory of sacrifice, then moving to an investigation of the Catholic teaching that the Eucharist possesses a sacrificial character, before concluding with a critique of the twentieth-century liturgical reform, arguing that this reform obscures in significant ways the sacrificial character of the Mass. As a way of unifying this diverse material, I would point again to Girard's public support of Benedict XVI's decision to widen the availability of the older form of the Roman Rite. If Girard is correct that Christ's free offering of himself on the cross constitutes the sacrifice to end all sacrifices, then it not only makes sense, but is imperative that the worship of God by the community that Jesus Christ founded would be oriented towards the Passion—in other words, that the center of Christian worship would be the holy and perfect sacrifice of Calvary. As suggested briefly at the start of this paper, the traditional Latin Mass focuses worshippers' attention on Christ's sacrifice in a particularly memorable and potent manner, and Catholic Christians who have been formed within the liturgical context of the post-conciliar reforms would likely derive great benefit through exposure to the originating stream from which they flowed.

In the letter that Benedict XVI sent to bishops regarding the promulgation of *Summorum Pontificum*, he highlighted the potential benefit of this kind of "cross-pollination" by expressing his hope that "the two Forms of the usage of the Roman Rite [could] be mutually enriching."[64] One way this might be done, I would suggest, is by inserting certain prayers and liturgical actions from

---

63   In contrast to the time around the Reformation, in which communion by the laity (in the West) was quite rare.

64   Benedict XVI, Letter to the Bishops Accompanying the Motu Proprio *Summorum Pontificum*.

the Extraordinary Form—such as the prayers at the foot of the altar and the traditional offertory—into the regular celebration of the Ordinary Form. This minor reform would underline the essential continuity between the two forms of the Roman Rite, and at the same time help to reinvigorate a sense of the sacrificial character of the Mass among the Catholic faithful. Furthermore, it would signal that the Extraordinary Form is not a museum piece, but has an important place in the ongoing life of the Church.

Augustine's Conception of Sacrifice in *City of God*, Book X, and the Eucharistic Sacrifice

Uwe Michael Lang

INTRODUCTION

In the tenth book of his monumental work on the *City of God*, Saint Augustine of Hippo (354–430) develops a conception of sacrifice that has received considerable attention among theologians, not least in a number of recent scholarly contributions, including an essay by then-Cardinal Joseph Ratzinger.[1] This lively

---

1   Among the literature, see especially Joseph Lécuyer, "Le sacrifice selon saint Augustin," in *Augustinus Magister (Congrès International Augustinien, Paris, 21–24 septembre 1954)*, vol. 2 (Paris: Études Augustiniennes, 1954) 905–914; Ghislain Lafont, "Le sacrifice de la Cité de Dieu: Commentaire au *de ciu. Dei*, l. X, ch. I–VII," in *Recherches de science religieuse* 53 (1965) 177–219; John F. O'Grady, "Priesthood and Sacrifice in 'City of God,'" in *Augustiniana* 21 (1971) 27–44; Basil Studer, "Das Opfer Christi nach Augustins 'De Civitate Dei' X, 5–6," in *Lex orandi, lex credendi: Miscellanea in onore di P. Cipriano Vagaggini*, Studia Anselmiana 79, ed. Gerard J. Békés and Giustino Farnedi (Rome: Editrice Anselmiana, 1980) 93–107; Gerald Bonner, "The Doctrine of Sacrifice: Augustine and the Latin Patristic Tradition," in *Sacrifice and Redemption: Durham Essays in Theology*, ed. Stephen W. Sykes (Cambridge: Cambridge University Press, 1991) 101–117 (reprinted in Gerald Bonner, *Church and Faith in the Patristic Tradition: Augustine, Pelagianism and Early Christian Northumbria* [Aldershot: Variorum, 1996] no. II); Roland J. Teske, "The Definition of Sacrifice in the *De Civitate Dei*," in *Nova Doctrina Vetusque: Essays in Early Christianity in Honor of Fredric W. Schlatter, S.J.*, American Universities Studies, Series VII: Theology and Religion, vol. 207, ed. Douglas Kries and Catherine Brown Tkacz (New York: Peter Lang, 1999) 153–187; Stéphane Toulouse, "Que le vrai sacrifice est celui d'un cœur pur," in

conversation centers on the question of how to interpret Augustine's dense exposition, which, at first sight, would seem to propose an understanding of sacrifice that is entirely interiorized and detached from ritual expression. An initial reading of the text may well recall the third verse of the "Morning Hymn" (*Morgenlied*) by the Lutheran divine Paul Gerhard (1606–1676), written in 1666:

> Come ye with singing,
> To God be bringing
> Goods and each blessing—
> All we're possessing—
> All be to God as an offering brought.
> Hearts with love glowing,
> With praises o'erflowing,
> Thanksgiving voices,
> In these God rejoices,
> All other off'rings without them are nought.[2]

Recherches Augustiniennes 32 (2001) 169–223; Goulven Madec, "Le livre X du *De civitate Dei*: le sacrifice des chrétiens," in *Lettura del De Civitate Dei Libri I–X. Lectio Augustini XV–XVI–XVII. Settimana Agostiniana Pavese (1999–2001)*, Studia Ephemeridis Augustinianum 96 (Rome: Institutum Patristicum Augustinianum, 2003) 235–246; John Joy, "Love and Self-Gift: Sacrifice in St Augustine's City of God," in *Antiphon* 11 (2007) 78–85; Daniel Jones, "The *verum sacrificium* of Christ and of Christians in De Civitate Dei 10: Eucharist, Christology, and Christian Identity," in *Celebrating the Eucharist: Sacrifice and Communion. Proceedings of the Fifth Fota International Liturgical Conference, 2012*, Fota Liturgy Series 5, ed. Gerard Deighan (Wells: Smenos Publications, 2014) 135–172; Joseph Ratzinger, "Theology of the Liturgy: A Lecture Delivered during the Journées Liturgiques de Fontgombault, 22–24 July 2001," in *Theology of the Liturgy: The Sacramental Foundation of Christian Existence*, Joseph Ratzinger Collected Works 11, ed. Michael J. Miller (San Francisco: Ignatius Press, 2014) 541–557.

2   *Paul Gerhardt's Spiritual Songs*, trans. John Kelly (London: Alexander Strahan, 1867) 271. The German original is available at http://gutenberg.spiegel.de/buch/-7513/53:

> Lasset uns singen,
> Dem Schöpfer bringen
> Güter und Gaben,
> Was wir nur haben,
> Alles sei Gotte zum Opfer gesetzt!

Lovely as it is, this hymn entails a firm rejection of the sacrificial character of the Mass, especially when Gerhard insists, in literal translation, that "songs of thanksgiving are incense and ram (Dankbare Lieder/ Sind Weihrauch und Widder)," and hence the only offering that is holy and pleasing to God.

Gerhard's poetical assertion stands for an interpretation of Augustine that had some currency in the religious upheavals of the sixteenth century. For the Lutheran theologian Martin Chemnitz in his 1566 *Examination of the Council of Trent*, Augustine provided the justification for rejecting the council's teaching about the sacrificial character of the Mass and for setting against it "the true interior, invisible and spiritual sacrifices of the faithful."[3] Sacrifice is thus disconnected from ritual or symbolic expression and re-conceived as an interior attitude of religious devotion and moral conduct of life.[4] On the Catholic side, we find among the propositions of the Louvain theologian Michael Baius that were condemned by Pope Pius V in 1567 the following statement: "The sacrifice of the Mass is a sacrifice for no other reason than for that general one by which 'every work is performed that man may cling to God in holy fellowship' [*City of God*, X, 5]."[5]

Die besten Güter
Sind unsre Gemüter,
Dankbare Lieder
Sind Weihrauch und Widder,
An welchen Er sich am meisten ergötzt.

3   Martin Chemnitz, *Examen Concilii Tridentini*, locus VI: De Missa, c. II, art. 1, ed. Eduard Preuss (Berlin: Gustav Schlawitz, 1861) 383.

4   See Johannes Zachhuber, "Modern Discourse on Sacrifice and its Theological Background," in *Sacrifice and Modern Thought*, ed. Julia Meszaros and Johannes Zachhuber (Oxford: Oxford University Press, 2013) 12–28.

5   Pius V, Bull *Ex Omnibus Afflictionibus* (1 October 1567), *Errors of Michael Baius on the Nature of Man and Grace*, no. 45: *Enchiridion Symbolorum: Compendium of Creeds, Definitions, and Declarations of the Catholic Church*, ed. Heinrich Denzinger and Peter Hünermann, 43rd ed. (San Francisco: Ignatius Press, 2012) no. 1945. Baius had in fact retracted this thesis even before the papal condemnation. See Marius Lepin, *L'idée du sacrifice de la Messe d'après les théologiens depuis l'origine jusqu'à nos jours* (Paris: Beauchesne, 1926) 357–360. Considerable attention to the interpretation of *City of*

On the other hand, the vast corpus of Augustine's works is full of sacrificial language with precise and specific references not only to the cross, but also to the Eucharist, both of which he calls "the most true sacrifice" (*uerissimum sacrificium*).[6] How can these passages be squared with those sections in the *City of God* that would seem to advocate an entirely spiritual concept of sacrifice consisting in any work of mercy done to our fellow human beings for the sake of attaining God, our supreme good? In this article I argue that the hermeneutical key to reading the much-discussed exposition in the *City of God* is the apologetic context of the work. Augustine intends above all to contrast Christian sacrifice with pagan sacrifice and hence to reject the latter. In doing so, he presents a theology of sacrifice that has considerable spiritual depth; far from contradicting the by-then traditional understanding of the Eucharist as a sacrifice, Augustine enriches it by exploring its Christological and ecclesiological dimensions.

God, X is given by Robert Bellarmine, *De Sacramento Eucharistiae*, lib. V, cap. 2, in *Disputationes de controversiis christianae fidei adversus huius temporis haereticos*, vol. 3 (Venice: J. Malachinus, 1721) 373–377. The interpretation of Augustine was also disputed in Anglicanism, as shown in *An Epistolary Dissertation Addressed to the Clergy of Middlesex, wherein the Doctrine of St. Austin, concerning the Christian Sacrifice, is set in a true Light: By Way of Reply to Dr Waterland's late Charge to them. By a Divine of the University of Cambridge*. The treatise, which is contained in William Cunningham, *S. Austin and His Place in the History of Christian Thought* (London–Cambridge: C. J. Clay and Sons–Cambridge University Press, 1886) 199–276, may have been written by the nonjuror George Smith (1693–1756). The question resurfaced in the interpretation of Augustine proposed by Yves de Montcheuil, "L'unité du sacrifice et du sacrement dans l'Eucharistie," in id., *Mélanges théologiques* (Paris: Aubier-Montaigne, 1946) 49–70, which prompted the refutation of Guy de Broglie, "La notion augustinienne du sacrifice 'invisible' et 'vrai'," in *Recherches de science religieuse* 48 (1960) 135–165.

6   To list just a few of them: *Confessiones* IX,XII,32 (ed. Martin Skutella, rev. Heiko Jürgens and Wiebke Schaub [Leipzig: Teubner, 1996] 203): "sacrificium pretii nostri" (about Monica's burial); *De Trinitate* IV,XIII,17 (CCSL 50:183): "Morte sua quippe uno uerissimo sacrificio pro nobis oblato. . .;" *De spiritu et littera* 11,18 (CSEL 60:170): "In ipso uerissimo et singulari sacrificio, Domino Deo nostro agere gratias admonemur;" see also *Sermo* 228B (ed. Germain Morin, in *Sancti Augustini Sermones post Maurinos reperti*, Miscellanea Agostiniana, vol. 1 [Rome: Typis Polyglottis Vaticanis, 1930] 18–20).

As so often in this prolific and supple thinker, we need to hold various strands in his writings together in order to avoid one-sided interpretations that can easily lead to a fractured vision of the Christian faith, as happened in history with the readings of Augustine on grace, free will and predestination.

THE APOLOGETIC CONTEXT OF THE
CITY OF GOD

Any analysis of the tenth book of the *City of God* needs to be clear about what Augustine wants to achieve with it. This book belongs to the first part of a large-scale apology against paganism. As the more recent study of late antiquity has shown, the Christianization of the Empire was a long process that only gradually transformed established customs and practices in society, including religion. The *City of God* is Augustine's response to a particular charge laid on the Christians. The sack of Rome by the troops of Alaric the Goth in AD 410 had a devastating effect on the identity and self-confidence of Roman civilization. Although the occupation of the city lasted only three days and the physical damage remained limited, the event exposed the fragile and vulnerable state of the Empire. This anguish over the fall of the "eternal city" is reflected in Augustine's own preaching at the time.[7] Some of the aristocratic elite who retained an allegiance to pagan religion, such as the circle of senator Volusianus, saw the disaster of 410 as a consequence of the neglect of the gods, especially by means of the traditional sacrifices that were their due. Ritual sacrifice was an essential element of the contractual relationship between the gods and humankind. Practicing such ritual dutifully and correctly would result in the *pax deorum*, the "peace of the gods" that would ensure divine protection for the welfare and prosperity of Rome.

7   For instance, *Sermo* 81, 105, 296 and 397; see Jean-Claude Fredouille, "Les sermons sur la chute de Rome," in *Augustin predicateur (395–411): Actes du Colloque International de Chantilly (5–7 septembre 1996)*, Collection des Etudes Augustiniennes: Série Antiquité 159, ed. Goulven Madec (Paris: Institut d'Etudes Augustiniennes, 1998) 439–448.

The religious context of late antiquity provides the background for Augustine's exposition: while the offering of animals
and of the land's produce to the gods had been outlawed by the
legislation of Christian emperors and was on the wane, it still had
a lingering presence in the Mediterranean world. This is fundamentally different from Western societies today, where the success
of Christianization over centuries led to the total abandoning of
such ritual sacrifice.[8] Moreover, the memory of the Jewish sacrificial system, the abolition of which was contingent upon the
destruction of the Jerusalem Temple in AD 70, was sustained by
its presence in the Sacred Scriptures. The thrust of Augustine's
argument is apologetic, in continuity with the work of a Justin,
Tertullian, or Origen. In the *City of God*, the bishop of Hippo
seeks to unmask pagan sacrifices as a perversion of right worship,
because what is owed to God alone is offered to lesser beings. By
contrast, he states a limited but real appreciation of the sacrifices
of the Old Covenant (against its Manichean detractors).

According to Augustine's own instructions to Firmus on how
to have the manuscript of the *City of God* bound, the work can be
divided into two parts: the first ten books are primarily dedicated
to refuting "the vanity of the impious" and the other twelve to
describing and defending the Christian religion, though the two
major intentions of the work are present in each part of it. The
first part of the *City of God* can be further divided into two sections: books one to five argue "against those who contend that the
worship not of gods, but of demons profits the happiness of this
life;" books six to ten contend with "those who hold that either

---

8   The Emperor Julian (reigned 361–363), called the "apostate," because he was
brought up in the Christian faith, which he knew well and consciously rejected, wrote
in his *Contra Galilaeos*: "Why do you not sacrifice. . . . The Jews agree with the Gentiles, except that they believe in only one god. That is indeed peculiar to them and
strange to us; since all the rest we have in a manner in common with them—temples,
sanctuaries, altars, purifications, and certain precepts. For as to these we differ from
one another either not at all or in trivial matters." Cited after *The Works of the Emperor
Julian*, vol. 3, trans. Wilmer C. Wright, Loeb Classical Library (Cambridge, MA: Harvard University Press, 1923) 306.

such gods or many gods of any kind ought to be worshipped by ceremonies and sacrifices for the sake of the life that is to come after death." Augustine's treatise on sacrifice in book ten thus forms the climax of his apology against classical Roman religion.[9]

Book ten opens with a generally agreed premise: the universal human desire for happiness;[10] how to attain it, however, has been disputed among the philosophers. Augustine singles out the Platonists for their insight that a happy life can only be reached by "clinging with pure and holy love to the one supreme good, which is the unchangeable God."[11] Clinging to God in pure and holy love is not simply an interior disposition, but also a matter of right worship, designated by the Greek term *latreia*. Augustine spends some time on the question how to translate *latreia* into Latin and finds no single expression that would convey its full meaning; whether it is rendered *cultus, seruitus, religio,* or *pietas*, what is intended is the worship due "to that God who is the true God, and who makes his worshippers gods"[12]—a remarkable phrase that resonates with the Greek Christian doctrine of deification.

The pagans, Augustine argues, fell into the error of offering worship—and this means offering sacrifice—to lesser beings and so committed idolatry. Such sacrifices are to be abhorred because what is owed to the one true God is usurped by demons. False worship fails to reach its end, Augustine explains, for

> . . . whoever the immortal and blessed beings in their heavenly habitations may be, if they do not love us and do not wish us to

---

9   Augustine, *Ep.* 1*A,1 (CSEL 88:7–8).

10   "Omnium certa sententia est, qui ratione quoquo modo uti possunt, beatos esse omnes homines uelle;" *De civitate Dei* X,1,1–2 (CCSL 47:271). In this article, the English translation of William Babcock, *The City of God (De Civitate Dei), Books 1–10,* The Works of Saint Augustine: A Translation for the 21st Century, I/6 (Hyde Park, NY: New City Press, 2012) is used, with some modifications. See also *De beata vita* II,10 (CCSL 29:70–71) and *De Trinitate* XIII,iv,7 (CCSL 50A:387–389).

11   ". . . illi uni optimo, quod est incommutabilis Deus, puritate casti amoris adhaeserit;" *De civitate Dei* X,1,20–21 (CCSL 47:271–272).

12   ". . . qui uerus est Deus facitque suos cultores deos;" *De civitate Dei* X,1,95–96 (CCSL 47:271).

be blessed, they are certainly not to be worshipped. If, however, they do love us and want us to be blessed, they clearly want us to attain our blessedness from the same source from which they attain theirs. For how could there be one source of blessedness for them and another for us?[13]

TRUE WORSHIP—TRUE SACRIFICE

Latreia is thus owed to God alone, "whether we render it in certain sacred actions (*in quibusque sacramentis*) or in ourselves (*in nobis ipsis*)."[14] Augustine introduces here a distinction between outward and inward worship, external acts and interior dispositions. For visible, external worship he uses the expression *sacramenta*, which should not be translated as "sacraments" in the scholastic meaning the term acquired in the course of the Middle Ages. In patristic use, *sacramenta* would rather indicate a wider reality of sacred signs that communicate divine grace, and these would include the sacraments in the later theological sense. The reason for the twofold nature of worship lies in the inhabitation of God in each individual and in the community:

> . . . for we are his temple, at the same time all of us together and each one of us, because he deigns to dwell in the concord of all (*omnium concordiam*) and in each individual, being no greater in all than in each, since he is neither expanded nor divided.[15]

This passage is crucial for Augustine's argument, because it lays the ground for his essentially ecclesial understanding of Christian sacrifice and hence would seem to preclude the individualistic interpretation that emerged in the Reformation period. This is borne out in the following section, despite its almost pietistic or revivalist tone:

---

13   "Quicumque igitur sunt in caelestibus habitationibus inmortales et beati, si nos non amant nec beatos esse nos uolunt, colendi utique non sunt. Si autem amant et beatos uolunt, profecto inde uolunt, unde et ipsi sunt; an aliunde ipsi beati, aliunde nos?" *De civitate Dei* X,1,96–100 (CCSL 47:273–274).

14   *De civitate Dei* X,3,19–20 (CCSL 47:275).

15   *De civitate Dei* X,3,10–14 (CCSL 47:275).

Our heart, when lifted up to him, is his altar; it is with his Only-Begotten One as our priest that we propitiate him; to him we sacrifice bleeding victims when we fight for his truth even unto [shedding our] blood; we honour him with the sweetest incense when, in his sight, we burn with pious and holy love; to him we devote and surrender his gifts in us and ourselves; to him, by solemn feasts and on appointed days, we dedicate and consecrate the memory of his benefits, lest ungrateful forgetfulness creep in through the lapse; to him we offer, on the altar of our heart, the sacrifice of humility and praise, kindled by the fire of love.[16]

A closer look at this passage reveals the presence of characteristically liturgical language. The heart (*cor*) rising to God (*ad illum sursum*) would seem to echo the introductory dialogue to the Eucharistic prayer, which in Augustine's North African use had the distinct invitation "*sursum cor*" (rather than "*corda*"). I would even go so far as to suggest that highly rhetorical expressions like "*dona eius . . . uouemus et reddimus*," "*beneficiorum . . . dicamus sacramusque memoriam*," "*sacrificamus hostiam humilitatis et laudis*," exhibiting typical features of contemporary Latin euchological style,[17] may refer to the Eucharistic prayer used by Augustine, of which we do not know from primary sources but from which we can only gather snippets in his preaching and writing.

It would be anachronistic to read into Augustine a disparity between external liturgical worship, interior religious devotion and moral conduct of life. His concept of *religio* is indebted to the Roman classical tradition and its transformation in the earlier Latin Fathers. The classical understanding of *religio*, as exemplified in Cicero, sees at its center the public and sacrificial worship of the gods, though without ignoring its connection with the moral life.[18] In the eighth book of the *City of God* Augustine speaks of

---

16   *De civitate Dei* X,3,14–23 (CCSL 47:275).

17   See Uwe Michael Lang, *The Voice of the Church at Prayer: Reflections on Liturgy and Language* (San Francisco: Ignatius Press, 2012) 73–115.

18   See, e.g., Cicero, *De natura deorum* II,xxviii,71 (trans. Harris Rackham, Loeb Classical Library [Cambridge, MA: Harvard University Press, 1956] 193): "But the best and also the purest, holiest and most pious way of worshipping the gods (*cultus*

the "true religion, which our faith (*fides nostra*) takes up and defends."[19] *Religio* is thus understood as the form or shape, in which the Christian faith finds its visible expression. The German liturgical scholar Walter Dürig has shown that in biblical, patristic, and early liturgical texts the use of the terms *pietas* and *pius* for expressing man's relation to God cannot be reduced to an interior attitude or disposition; the outer form, or rite, is not to be neglected. *Pietas* towards God always includes carrying out cultic acts as demanded by divine precepts, and hence can be equated with *religio, cultus Dei*, or *cultura Dei*. While man's inner dispositions or convictions are meant to be in harmony with these external acts of worship, early Christian *pietas* is liturgical piety, or, to use Dürig's word, "*Kultfrömmigkeit.*" Moreover, by being liturgical, *pietas* is never merely the action of the isolated subject; rather, the individual acts as a part of the community, that is, as a member of the Church.[20] Only the later Middle Ages, especially the Gothic period, saw an internalization of man's relationship to God to such an extent that private forms of religious devotion came to be regarded as more important than external acts of worship. This change was not only a characteristic

---

deorum) is ever to venerate them with purity, sincerity and innocence both of thought and of speech." Also *De domo sua* XLI,107 (trans. Nevile H. Watts, Loeb Classical Library [Cambridge, MA: Harvard University Press, 1955] 261): ". . . and a right fulfillment of duty to the gods (*erga deos pietas*) is impossible without a disinterested conviction as to their designs and purposes, combined with a belief that they grant no petitions which are unjust or unseemly."

19   *De civitate Dei*, VIII,4,46–47 (CCSL 47:220): ". . . religioni uerae, quam fides nostra suscepit ac defendit." See Ernst Feil, *Religio: Die Geschichte eines neuzeitlichen Grundbegriffs vom Frühchristentum bis zur Reformation* (Göttingen: Vandenhoeck & Ruprecht, 1986) 72. Also Bernard Botte, "Pietas," in *L'ordinaire de la messe: Texte critique, traduction et études*, ed. Bernard Botte and Christine Mohrmann, Études liturgique, 2 (Paris–Louvain: Cerf–Abbaye du Mont César, 1953) 243.

20   Walter Dürig, *Pietas liturgica: Studien zum Frömmigkeitsbegriff und zur Gottesvorstellung der abendländischen Liturgie* (Regensburg: Pustet, 1958) 220: "Sie ist Kultfrömmigkeit, bei der die innere Gesinnung und der äußere kultische Akt in gleicher Weise wesentlich sind." See also ibid., 38, 90, 92, and 94.

of the Protestant movements but affected early modern Catholicism as well.[21]

Augustine insists that sacrifice is not limited to its cultic forms (as was a tendency in Roman religion), but embraces every aspect and dimension of life. Through right worship we are cleansed from our sins and evil desires and consecrated to God's name. This in turn enables us to cling to God, who is the "fountain of our happiness" and "the end of all desire."[22] Such clinging to God is shown very concretely in the observance of

> . . . those two commandments on which hang all the law and the prophets: "You shall love the Lord your God with all your heart, and with all your soul, and with all your mind;" and "You shall love your neighbor as yourself."[23]

Love of self comes naturally to us (for good or ill), and if it is an informed or intelligent love, then it is governed by that supreme good, which is none other than God. Love of neighbor is enjoined upon us as a commandment, and for Augustine, it consists in doing what we can to commend to our neighbor the love of God. When Augustine adds that "this is the worship of God (*Dei cultus*), this is true religion (*uera religio*), this is right piety (*recta pietas*), this is the service due to God only (*tantum Deo debita seruitus*),"[24] he does not mean to exclude the external cult. This is clear from his

---

21   See Christopher Dawson, *The Dividing of Christendom* (San Francisco: Ignatius Press, 2009; originally published in 1965) 33: ". . . the Post-Reformation period is characterized by the interiorization of religion and the intensive cultivation of the spiritual life." Dawson singles out the flowering of mysticism in Spain and Italy, and the ascetic spirituality as represented in the Ignatian *Spiritual Exercises*, with their roots in the *devotio moderna*. On the other hand, regarding the late Middle Ages, historians have noticed the sheer materiality of popular religiosity, with its focus on relics, the miraculous and pilgrimages. See Caroline Walker Bynum, *Christian Materiality: An Essay on Religion in Late Medieval Europe* (New York: Zone Books, 2011).

22   "Ipse enim fons nostrae beatitudinis, ipse omnis appetitonis est finis;" *De civitate Dei* X,3,26–27 (CCSL 47:275).

23   *De civitate Dei* X,3,37–41 (CCSL 47:275), quoting Mt 22:37 and 39.

24   *De civitate Dei*, X,3,47–48 (CCSL 47:276).

train of thought, which right at this point resumes the apologetic against pagan sacrifices. The perversion of the pagans lies not in their observance of external rituals per se but in the fact that their rituals are ordered to lesser creatures rather than the true God. In typical fashion, Augustine pinpoints his argument with a biblical quotation: "Whoever sacrifices to any god, save to the Lord only, shall be utterly destroyed" (Ex 22:20).[25] In the following chapter, he adds:

> And how ancient a part of God's worship sacrifice is, those two brothers, Cain and Abel, sufficiently show, of whom God rejected the elder's sacrifice, and looked favourably on the younger's.[26]

To sum up, far from rejecting sacrifice as such, Augustine is concerned with true sacrifice, which is, first, owed to the one true God alone and, secondly, not limited to the cultic sphere, but extends to the whole of Christian living.[27]

RESUMING THE PROPHETIC CRITIQUE OF SACRIFICE

As a next step, Augustine reinforces his case against pagan worship by applying the Old Testament prophets' critique of sacrifice to the notion underlying classical Roman religion; that the gods are somehow in need of sacrificial offerings to sustain them. Evidently, the one true God is not in need of any material good offered to him. The argument is taken further when Augustine asserts that God has no need even of man's righteousness; the right worship we offer God benefits not him, but us. The images used

---

25   *De civitate Dei*, X,3,54–55 (CCSL 47:276); also *Enarrationes in Psalmos* 135,3 (CCSL 40:1959).

26   *De civitate Dei* X,4,9–13 (CCSL 47:276).

27   This section is indebted to the profound discussion of Johannes Nebel, "Von der *actio* zur *celebratio*: Ein neues Paradigma nach dem Zweiten Vatikanischen Konzil," in *Operation am lebenden Objekt: Roms Liturgiereformen von Trient bis zum Vaticanum II*, ed. Stefan Heid (Berlin: be.bra wissenschaft, 2014) 53–90, esp. 65–67.

to illustrate this point are striking: one does not benefit a fountain by drinking from it, nor benefit light by the act of seeing.

The total absence of need in the true God provides Augustine with a hermeneutic to interpret the animal sacrifices of the Old Testament, which were of course no longer continued in his day, but had an enduring presence in the Scriptures: "... their role was to signify what is now done among us, for the purpose of clinging to God and helping our neighbor to the same end."[28] In other words, the blood sacrifices of the Old Covenant were genuine expressions of those interior dispositions, which, when translated into the practice of love of God and love of neighbor, enable us to attain union with God. The meaning and purpose of sacrifice does not lie in the actual slaughtering of the animal or the destruction of the victim, but in the right intention of those who offered it. Hence comes Augustine's widely received definition: "Sacrifice, therefore, is the visible sacrament of an invisible sacrifice; that is, it is a sacred sign."[29]

Augustine finds a warrant for his reading of the sacrifices under the Law in the Old Testament itself, that is, in the prophetic critique of sacrifice, above all Psalm 50(51), from which he quotes extensively: the sacrifice acceptable to God is a contrite and humble heart. Early Christianity (and rabbinical Judaism, though from a different perspective)[30] had an ambiguous relationship towards the sacrificial worship practised until the destruction of the Temple, and this ambiguity is brought into sharp relief by Augustine's

---

28   "Nec ... aliud intellegendum est, nisi rebus illis eas res fuisse significatas, quae aguntur in nobis, ad hoc ut inhaereamus Deo et ad eundem finem proximo consulamus." *De civitate* X,5,10–14 (CCSL 47:276–277). Augustine's positive understanding of sacrifice under the Law is also attested in a short treatise of c. 420 against detractors of the Old Testament, who may have followed the Marcionite tradition. See Roland J. Teske, "Sacrifice in Augustine' *Contra Aduersarium Legis et Prophetarum*," in *Studia Patristica* 33 (1997) 254–259.

29   "Sacrificium ergo uisibile inuisibilis sacrificii Sacramentum, id est sacrum signum est." *De civitate Dei* X,5,15–16 (CCSL 47:277).

30   See Guy G. Stroumsa, *The End of Sacrifice: Religious Transformations in Late Antiquity,* trans. Susan Emanuel (Chicago: University of Chicago Press, 2009).

discussion. He notes that the psalmist, "in the very place where he said that God does not desire sacrifice, he showed that God does desire sacrifice."[31] The sacrifice God wants is not the slaughtering of an animal, but humility and contrition for sins. And yet, the sacrifice that, according to the psalm, God does not want *signifies* the sacrifice that he wants. The sacrifices of the Old Law cannot therefore be simply dismissed as idolatrous, as the Manichees would have it, because they were commanded by God and fulfilled a purpose in his economy of salvation. Their real significance lay not in the external act but in the interior disposition with which this act was performed. Augustine continues:

> And the reason why those sacrifices had to be changed, at the opportune and pre-established moment, was precisely to keep people from believing that such sacrifices in themselves, rather than the things they signified, were desirable to God or at least acceptable in us.[32]

A series of biblical quotations follows, which includes Micah 6:6-8 and culminates in Christ's saying, "I desire mercy rather than sacrifice" (Mt 9:13; 12:7), understood "simply to mean that one kind of sacrifice is preferred to another. For the kind of sacrifice that everyone calls sacrifice is a sign of the true sacrifice."[33] The sacrifices of the Tent of Meeting or the Temple can therefore be read as signs of the true sacrifice, which is love of God and love of neighbor.

THE SACRIFICE OF CHRISTIANS

Augustine proceeds to give a definition of "true sacrifice," which is

---

31   *De civitate Dei* X,5,19–22 (CCSL 47:277).

32   *De civitate Dei* X,5,30–33 (CCSL 47:277). See also *Contra Faustum* 6,5 and 18,6 (CSEL 25:290–292 and 494–495), where Augustine defends the sacrifices of the Old Covenant as prefiguring the one sacrifice of Christ, which is now commemorated in the Eucharist.

33   *De civitate Dei* X,5,55–57 (CCSL 47:278).

. . . every work done in order that we might cling to God in holy fellowship, that is, every work which is referred to the final good in which we can be truly blessed.[34]

The first thing to note here is the theocentric conception of sacrifice: not every act of mercy towards a fellow human being is a sacrifice but only such that is done for God's sake. A sacrifice, Augustine explains, though being prepared or offered by a human agent, is a "divine matter (*res diuina*)." This is implied in the Latin expression *res diuinam facere*, "to make a thing sacred," which is often simply shortened to *facere* in the sense of "to sacrifice" and puts an emphasis on consecration, which is an act of handing over to God. The consecrated reality is no longer under human control but in the ownership of God.[35] This can refer not only to objects, but also to persons; hence a consecrated person who dies to the world in order to live for God alone, can be himself or herself a sacrifice.[36]

Not every good work or work of mercy or act of renunciation is a sacrifice; rather, it is its purpose of finality that makes it a sacrifice. That finality is to cling to God, our supreme good and fountain of happiness, "*in sancta societate.*" This last phrase is often rendered as "in holy fellowship," but this would seem too broad to convey the ecclesial implications of *societas* in the context of the *City of God*. The "holy society" can be identified with that commonwealth, whose citizens are totally formed by love of God.

Augustine goes on to quote extensively from Romans 12, where the Apostle urges his readers "by the mercy of God, to present your bodies as a living sacrifice, holy and pleasing to God, which is your reasonable service" (v. 1). Augustine reads "body"

---

34   *De civitate Dei* X,6,1–3 (CCSL 47:278).

35   See "Sacrifice, Roman," in *Oxford Classical Dictionary,* ed. Simon Hornblower and Antony Spawforth (3rd ed., Oxford: Oxford University Press, 1999) 1345–1346, at 1345. While sacrifice thus clearly implies setting a thing apart and making it "sacred," the expression *sacrum facere*, from which *sacrificare* and *sacrificium* are derived, is better translated generically as "to perform a religious ceremony."

36   Teske, "The Definition of Sacrifice in the *De Civitate Dei*," 158, observes that for Augustine "consecrated by God's name" can connote baptism, in *Ep.* 23,4 (CSEL 34/1:67) and *Sermo* 352 (PL 39:1551).

here not only in the literal sense that would suggest an exhortation to the ascetic life, but also in an ecclesiological sense. The sacrifice holy and pleasing to God is that of the whole body of Christ, which is the communion of saints, and it is offered through Christ the head, Christ the high priest:

> . . . the whole redeemed city (*ciuitas*), that is, the congregation and society of the saints (*congregatio societasque sanctorum*), is offered to God as a universal sacrifice through the great priest, who, in his passion, offered himself for us in the form of a servant, to the end that we might be the body of such a great head. For it was this servant form that he offered, and it was in this form that he was offered, because it is according to this form that he is the mediator, in this form that he is the priest, and in this form that he is the sacrifice.[37]

One thing would seem very clear now: for Augustine the sacrifice to which Christians are called can never be reduced to the individual believer's interior religious devotion and personal moral conduct. Rather, as the bishop of Hippo comments with reference to Romans 12: "This is the sacrifice of Christians: we, being many, are one body in Christ."[38] And this offering is made possible only in and through of the supreme act of mercy, which is the sacrifice that Christ, the mediator and high priest, offered "in the form of a servant" (Phil 2), that is, in his humanity, on the cross. Finally, Augustine makes the link with the sacrifice of the Mass, when he concludes:

---

37   *De civitate Dei*, X,6,33–39 (CCSL 47:279).
38   *De civitate Dei*, X,6,52–53 (CCSL 47:279). Here Augustine would seem to be indebted to Cyprian of Carthage, *De dominica oratione*, 23–24 (CSEL 3,284–285). Cyprian comments on the petition of the Lord's Prayer, "forgive us our trespasses, as we forgive those who trespass against us" and emphasizes the need for peace and reconciliation in the unity of God's people: "Sic nec sacrificium Deus recipit dissidentis et ab altari revertentem prius fratri reconciliari iubet [see Mt 5:23], ut pacificis precibus et Deus possit esse placatus. Sacrificum Deo maius est pax nostra et fraterna concordia et de unitate Patris et Filii et Spiritus Sancti plebs adunata."

This is also the sacrifice that the Church continually celebrates in the sacrament of the altar (which is well known to the faithful), where it is made plain to her that, in the offering she makes, she herself is offered.[39]

This Eucharistic turn concludes what the noted Augustinian scholar Gerald Bonner has acclaimed as "an astonishing piece of theological exposition." His appraisal renders justice to the subtlety of this discussion and is worth being quoted in full:

> The complexity of construction of the argument of this passage is remarkable, even by Augustine's standards. Starting from his premise that a sacrament is every act which is designed to unite us to God in holy fellowship, he argues that acts of compassion are sacrifices, and immediately applies this conception to the Eucharist, in which Christ, the priest, offers his Body, which is at one and the same time the human body which suffered on Calvary; the bread and wine on the altar, which are offered by the Faithful; and the Faithful themselves.[40]

Bonner argues that Augustine's theological conception of the Eucharistic sacrifice is traditional and rooted in the Latin Fathers, above all Cyprian's widely received *Letter 63*. There are in fact plenty of passages in Augustine's work where he affirms the sacrificial and propitiatory character of the Eucharist, and he does so at a later stage in book ten of the *City of God*. This passage comes after a long hiatus, when Augustine returns to the main apologetic thrust of the book, which is his argument against false worship that is exemplified in sacrifices offered to lesser beings and not to the one true God.

After this lengthy treatment Augustine resumes his earlier definition of sacrifice and introduces an analogy between acts of sacrifice and words of prayer and praise:

---

39   *De civitate Dei* X,6,53–55 (CCSL 47:279).
40   Bonner, "The Doctrine of Sacrifice," 109–110. Lafont, "Le sacrifice de la Cité de Dieu," speaks of the "sacrifice triforme," a notion that is explored at length by Jones, "The *verum sacrificium* of Christ and of Christians in *De Civitate Dei* 10."

> . . . these visible sacrifices are signs of invisible sacrifices in the
> same way that spoken words are signs of things. Therefore, just
> as in the case of prayer and praise we direct to God words that
> signify and offer to him the things in our hearts that are signified
> by our words, so also we should understand that, in the case of
> sacrifice, visible sacrifice is to be offered only to God and that,
> in our hearts, we should present our very selves as an invisible
> sacrifice to him.[41]

The passage is reminiscent of the theory of signs, which Augustine
develops in *De doctrina christiana*.[42] Just as the spoken words of
prayer and praise reveal the invisible thoughts and sentiments of
our hearts, so the external actions of sacrifice are meant to express
the interior act of offering ourselves to God. This theory provides
a hermeneutic for understanding the daily sacrifice[43] offered by
the Church as a sacrament of Christ's supreme and true sacrifice.
What follows is hailed by Bonner as "the finest short statement of
Augustine's thought in the whole of his writings:"[44]

> In the form of God, then, the true mediator—since, by taking
> the form of a servant, he became the mediator between God
> and man, the man Jesus Christ—receives sacrifice together with
> the Father, with whom he is one God. In the form of a servant,
> however, he chose to be a sacrifice rather than to receive sacri-
> fice, and he did so in order to keep anyone from thinking that
> sacrifice should be offered even in this case to any creature at
> all. At the same time, he is also the priest, himself making the
> offering as well as himself being the offering. And he wanted

---

41   *De civitate Dei* X,19,4–10 (CCSL 47:293).

42   See Robert A. Markus, "St. Augustine on Signs," and B. Darrell Jackson,
"The Theory of Signs in St. Augustine's *De doctrina christiana*," in *Augustine: A Collection of Critical Essays*, ed. Robert A. Markus (Garden City, NY: Anchor Books,
1972) 61–91 and 92–147.

43   While the following passage would imply a daily offering of the Eucharistic
sacrifice, Augustine is aware that this was not generally observed; see *Ep.* 54,2 (CCSL
31:227). It is not entirely clear from his writings whether there was a daily celebration
of Mass in Hippo.

44   Bonner, "The Doctrine of Sacrifice," 107.

the sacrifices offered by the Church to be a daily sacrament of his sacrifice, in which the Church, since she is the body of which he is the head, learns to offer her very self through him. The sacrifices of the saints of old were the manifold and varied signs of this true sacrifice, for this one sacrifice was prefigured by many, just as one thing may be expressed by a variety of words, in order to recommend it highly but not monotonously. To this supreme and true sacrifice all false sacrifices have now given way.[45]

CHRIST THE HIGH PRIEST AND SACRIFICE

The apologetic perspective of the *City of God* may obscure the Christocentrism in Augustine's theology of sacrifice[46]: the acts of mercy, through which we cling to God, our supreme good, in a holy society, are made possible only through Christ, the true mediator, who offered himself on the cross in his humanity (in the form of a servant) and also received this sacrifice as the Second Person of the Blessed Trinity (in the form of God). Hence the self-offering of Christ, accomplished once for all on Calvary, is an eternal reality and is made present in the Holy Eucharist, as Augustine elucidates in one of his sermons:

So Christ our Lord, who offered by suffering for us what by being born he had received from us, has become our high priest for ever, and has given us the order of sacrifice which you can

---

45   *De civitate Dei* X,20 (CCSL 47:294); see also X,31,33–38 (CCSL 47:309): "They [the angels] do not command us to offer sacrifice except to him alone, whose sacrifice—as I have often said, and as must be said again and again—we ought to be, with them, in our very selves. This sacrifice is to be offered through the priest who, in the humanity he assumed and in accord with which he also willed to be a priest, lowered himself to become a sacrifice for us, even to the point of death."

46   See Bonner, "The Doctrine of Sacrifice," 101, and Teske, "The Definition of Sacrifice in the *De Civitate Dei*," 158, who objects to the reading of O'Grady, "Priesthood and Sacrifice in 'City of God,'" that it misses precisely this Christocentric matrix of Augustine's thought, which in the *City of God* also has anti-Pelagian connotations. A lucid presentation of this topic is given by Jones, "The *verum sacrificium* of Christ and of Christians in *De Civitate Dei* 10."

see (*sacrificandi dedit ordinem quem uidetis*), of his body that is to say, and his blood. . . . Recognize in the bread what hung on the cross, and in the cup what flowed from his side.[47]

The doctrine of Christ the one and true eternal high priest after the order of Melchizedek, following the Letter to the Hebrews, was a particularly strong element in North African Christianity, as is evident from Tertullian and Cyprian of Carthage, but it is also found in Ambrose of Milan.[48] The diffusion of this teaching is attested in the Roman Canon of the Mass, as cited by Ambrose at the end of the fourth century,[49] and not least in the artistic representations of Melchizedek's offering of bread and wine as a type of the Eucharistic sacrifice in the central nave of the Roman Basilica of Saint Mary Major, dating from the pontificate of Sixtus III (432–440), and in the sixth-century churches of Ravenna.[50]

Augustine's emphasis on Christ the high priest also highlights that the true sacrifice is not simply constituted by the fact of Jesus being put to death (or, to use classical sacrificial language, by the immolation of the victim), but in his voluntary act of offering himself to the Father for the salvation of the world. Thomas Aquinas is acutely aware of this, when in the *Summa theologiae* he discusses the question whether the Passion of Christ operated by way of sacrifice. In the third objection to this proposition it is claimed that "whoever offers sacrifice performs some sacred rite, as the very word 'sacrifice' shows. But those men who slew Christ did not perform any sacred act, but rather wrought a great wrong. Therefore Christ's Passion was rather a malefice than a

---

47   Augustine, *Sermo* 228B (ed. Morin, 18–19), trans. Edmund Hill, *Sermons (184–299Z) on the Liturgical Seasons*, The Works of Saint Augustine: A Translation for the 21st Century, III/6 (Brooklyn, NY: New City Press, 1993) 261–262. The centrality of Hebrews in Augustine's understanding of sacrifice is shown by Lécuyer, "Le sacrifice selon saint Augustin."

48   See the lucid presentation of Bonner, "The Doctrine of Sacrifice," 105–108.

49   See Lang, *The Voice of the Church at Prayer*, 60–66.

50   Hugo Brandenburg, *Die frühchristlichen Kirchen in Rom* (2nd ed., Regensburg: Schnell und Steiner, 2005) 184.

sacrifice."[51] Aquinas's response departs from *Ephesians* 5:2 ("He gave himself up for us, an oblation and a sacrifice to God for an odour of sweetness") and quotes Augustine's definition of true sacrifice as "every work done in order that we might cling to God in a holy society, that is, every work which is referred to the final good in which we can be truly blessed." The sacrifice is offered in Christ's "voluntary enduring of the Passion," and this was "most acceptable to God, as coming from charity."[52] Likewise, Robert Bellarmine argues that the Passion of Christ is a sacrifice properly and strictly speaking, because Christ has the freedom and the power to offer his life. One of the scriptural passages Bellarmine cites to support this point is John 10:17–18, "I lay down my life. . . . No one takes it from me, but I lay it down of my own accord." This sovereign freedom distinguishes the death of Christ from that of the martyrs, who are entirely passive in their suffering; hence martyrdom can be called a "sacrifice" only in a loose sense according to Bellarmine.[53]

Early modern Catholic theology on the sacrificial character of the Eucharist in response to the Protestant challenge largely focussed on the *victima* and its immolation in the sacrificial act. From an Augustinian-Thomist perspective the essence of sacrifice lies not so much in the destruction of the victim as it does in the interior act of offering. Hence comes the definition, which has been so widely received in the Christian tradition and at the same time has spurred much controversy, that sacrifice properly understood is the visible sacrament of an invisible sacrifice.

By insisting that the interior act of offering is the true sacrifice, Augustine does not reject the sacrificial character of the visible sign by which this true sacrifice is signified. The faithful are joined to the sacrifice of Christ the high priest precisely in the ritual offer-

---

51   Thomas Aquinas, *Summa theologiae* III, q. 48, a.3, obj. 3; the English version is taken, with modifications, from the online edition of the translation by Fathers of the English Dominican Province, available on www.newadvent.org/summa/.

52   *Summa theologiae* III, q. 48, a. 3, co. See also the discussion of Zachhuber, "Modern Discourse on Sacrifice," 18–24, which includes a discussion of the early Protestant theory of Christ's "priestly office" (*munus sacerdotale*).

53   Bellarmine, *De Sacramento Eucharistiae*, lib. V, cap. 3 (p. 377).

ing of his sacrifice in the Eucharist. While Augustine provides a brilliant theological rationale for the interiority of sacrifice, which is a characteristic of early Christianity as such, he would not be content with the claim, often found in modern discussions of the subject, that the visible sacrifice (the sacred sign) is called a sacrifice only in a metaphorical sense.[54]

At this point, however, the question may be asked what makes the Eucharist a *visible* sacrifice, which according to the Council of Trent is demanded by human nature?[55] The most convincing answer is I believe found in the Thomist tradition, which holds that the essence of the Eucharistic sacrifice consists in the double consecration of bread and wine and hence in the mystical separation of Christ's body from his blood, which signifies his death on the cross. According to Aquinas, the sacrifice is offered to God in the consecration of the Eucharist.[56] I should like to argue that this is a legitimate development from Augustine's own position. In a remarkable sermon on Easter Sunday, dated between 412 and 417, the bishop of Hippo explains to neophytes the sacrament of the Eucharist:

> That bread which you can see on the altar, sanctified by the word of God, is the body of Christ. That chalice, or rather what the chalice contains, sanctified by the word of God, is the blood of Christ. It was by means of these things that the Lord Christ

---

54   See Teske, "The Definition of Sacrifice in the *De Civitate Dei*," 155–156: "When Augustine says that the true sacrifice is what is signified by the visible sacrifice, he is, then, not denying that the visible sacrifice is a sacrifice in the proper sense, but stressing that it is the interior act which in the pregnant sense realizes the proper meaning in a full or richer way and that in the typological sense the term 'sacrifice' which properly applies to the visible sign is transferred to the realities symbolized. Though Augustine does not, as De Broglie has shown, deny that the visible sacrifice—'what everyone calls sacrifice'—is properly a sacrifice, he clearly does place the emphasis upon the interior act of the one who offers sacrifice rather than upon the external and visible sign."

55   Council of Trent, Session XXII (17 September 1562), *Doctrine and Canons on the Sacrifice of the Mass*, ch. 1: Denzinger–Hünermann, *Enchiridion Symbolorum*, no. 1740.

56   Thomas Aquinas, *Summa theologiae* III, q. 82, a. 10, co. and ad 1; also III, q. 74, a. 1, co. and q. 76, a. 2, ad 1. See Reginald Garrigou-Lagrange, *Reality—A Synthesis of Thomistic Thought*, trans. Patrick Cummings (St. Louis: Herder, 1950) 254.

wished to present us with his body and blood, which he shed for our sake for the forgiveness of sins. If you receive them well, you are yourselves what you receive. You see, the apostle says, *We, being many, are one bread, one body* (1 Cor 10:17). That is who he explained the sacrament of the Lord's table: one bread, one body, is what we all are, many though we be.[57]

Later in the same sermon Augustine, having commented on the introductory dialogue of that part of the Eucharistic prayer we commonly call "Preface," he returns to the "sanctification of the sacrifice of God" (*sanctificatio sacrificii Dei*), which refers to the consecration of bread and wine by means of the word of God, that is, the Eucharistic words of institution. Characteristically, Augustine unites the sacrifice of Christ the Head with that of Christ the Mystical Body, when he elaborates:

> Then, after the sanctification of the sacrifice of God, because he wanted us to be ourselves his sacrifice, which is indicated by where that sacrifice was first put [*sc.* on the altar], that is the sign of the thing that we are . . .[58]

This passage is fraught with some difficulties and possibly corruptions in the received text, but it is clear enough in affirming Augustine's sacrificial understanding of the Eucharistic consecration. It is again characteristic of his thinking that he does not dwell on the presence of Christ in the Eucharistic species, but is rather interested in the grace signified and effected in the sacrament. In medieval terms, his exposition focuses not on the *res et sacramentum*, the reality signified by the sacramental sign, but on the *res tantum*, the grace ultimately conferred by the sacrament.

CONCLUSION

Any interpretation of the *City of God* needs to be guided, first, by an awareness of the religious-historical background and, sec-

---

57   Augustine, *Sermo* 227 (SC 116:234–236); trans. Hill, 254 (slightly modified).
58   *Sermo* 227 (SC 116:240); trans. Hill, 255 (slightly modified).

ondly, by the apologetic character of the work. In the first place, blood sacrifice constituted the essence of religious worship in the ancient world, both Jewish and pagan. One of the most momentous religious transformations of late antiquity was the interiorization and spiritualization of sacrifice, which was achieved in early Christianity through Christ's once-for-all sacrifice of the cross, and in rabbinical Judaism as a consequence of the destruction of the Jerusalem Temple in AD 70. Still, it was taken for granted that some kind of sacrifice had to be offered to God and that this sacrifice had to be carried out in an external, ritual form of worship.

In the second place, the *City of God* is a monumental apologetic treatise "against the pagans," and this context conditions Augustine's exposition in a significant way. As Roland Teske notes, the emphasis on the "interior and spiritual character of true sacrifice" is "part of his strategy to convert contemporary Platonists to Christianity and specifically to the worship of the Christian God in the Church." The aim is not to advance a complete doctrine of Christian sacrifice, but rather to present it in such terms that "[a] Platonist exploring the possibility of becoming a Christian would not necessarily find anything off-putting or incompatible with Platonic spiritualism at its best."[59] This is borne out, for instance, by the remarkable similarity, with obvious differences, between Augustine's account of the spiritual nature of sacrifice and that of Porphyry's *Letter to His Wife Marcella*.[60]

The apologetic framework is not a limitation, however, at least not when the contender in debate is the Platonic philosophical tradition, and it has generated what Gerald Bonner has praised as "one of the most profound discussions of the nature of sacrifice in Christian literature"[61]—a discussion that even after centuries of reflection continues to generate interest among contemporary theologians and liturgists.

---

59   Teske, "The Definition of Sacrifice in the *De Civitate Dei*," 158.
60   See Stroumsa, *The End of Sacrifice*, 59–60.
61   Bonner, "The Doctrine of Sacrifice," 105.

The Whence and Whither of the Kiss of Peace in the Roman Rite[1]

Michael P. Foley

One of the more conspicuous features of the renewed *Missale Romanum* of Pope Paul VI published in 1970[2] is the liberalization of the sign of peace in the Mass, a liberalization that has in many quarters been embraced with great enthusiasm. While the *pax* is something of a rarity in Masses celebrated according to the *Missale Romanum* of 1962,[3] reserved as it usually is to Solemn High Mass, it is commonplace in those according to the post-conciliar Missal, which allows the rite of peace to be used *pro opportunitate*.[4] For many, this alleged reintroduction of a ritual held with the utmost reverence by the early and medieval Church marks one of the greatest triumphs of the modern liturgical reforms. Indeed, on a popular level it has become, as one of my priest friends has been told by several of his parishioners, "the highpoint of the Mass."

---

1   An earlier version of this essay was given as a presentation at the 2007 Society for Catholic Liturgy conference, and a popularized and less developed version appeared as "A Crisis of Meaning in the Sign of Peace" in *The Latin Mass* 16 (Advent/Christmas 2007) 36–39. The author wishes to express his profound gratitude to Rev. Neil J. Roy for his sagacious recommendations.

2   *Missale Romanum ex decreto Sacrosancti Oecumenici Concilii Vaticani II instauratum auctoritate Pauli PP. VI promulgatum*, Editio typica (Vatican City: Typis Polyglottis Vaticani, 1970) no. 129 (p. 473). The second typical edition of the Pauline Missal was published in 1975; the third typical edition was approved by Pope John Paul II in 2000, published in 2002, and emended in 2008.

3   *Missale Romanum ex decreto SS. Concilii Tridentini restitutum Summorum Pontificum cura recognitum*, Editio typica (Vatican City: Typis Polyglottis Vaticanis, 1962).

4   *Missale Romanum* 1970, no. 129 (p. 473).

Such robust but theologically inaccurate testimonies may also account for the growing concern that all is not right with the way the peace is currently kept. The 2005 Synod on the Eucharist asserts that the greeting of peace has, "in certain cases," assumed "a dimension that could be problematic," as for example "when it is too prolonged or even when it causes confusion."[5] In his Post-Synodal Apostolic Exhortation *Sacramentum Caritatis*, Pope Benedict XVI elaborates on this confusion when he mentions the sign of peace becoming "exaggerated" by emotion and causing "a certain distraction in the assembly just before the reception of Communion;"[6] he therefore calls for "greater restraint" and "sobriety" in the gesture. Indeed, dissatisfaction with the rite of peace is as old as its reintroduction. In 1978, Bruce Harbert noted, "The sign of peace . . . is often either distant or chilly or trivialized to the level of a superficial chumminess."[7] Such criticism is also shared by the non-Catholic Christian communities which incorporated a similar peace ritual into their worship around the same time. A Lutheran theologian speaks of "real incoherence and inappropriateness" in his community's sharing of the peace, describing it as "mawkish, unbecoming, and pointless."[8] A Presbyterian minister writes: "The longer I am in ministry, the more convinced I become that the church simply does not know what to do with the tradition of 'passing the peace.'"[9] Some Anglicans bemoan a "touchy-feely element" that has crept into their kiss of peace, an element "which

5   Synod of Bishops, XI Ordinary General Assembly on "The Eucharist: Source and Summit of the Life And Mission of the Church" (2–23 October 2005) [henceforth: 2005 Synod], Proposition 23, available at http://www.pjp2ea.org/pjp2ea/eventswrk.asp?strArticle=Events/ZenitSynodOct2005.htm.

6   Benedict XVI, Post-Synodal Apostolic Exhortation on the Eucharist as the Source and Summit of the Church's Life and Mission *Sacramentum Caritatis* (22 February 2007) no. 49.

7   Bruce Harbert, "The Church, the Kingdom and the English Mass," *The Clergy Review* 63 (January 1978) 2–8, at 6.

8   David Yeago, "Unfashionable Thoughts on Sharing the Peace," in *Dialog – A Journal of Theology* 23 (August 1984) 292–294, at 292.

9   Shelley E. Cochran, "Passing the Peace, Restoring Relationships," in *The Christian Ministry* 24 (1993) 18–20, at 18.

assumes the right to intrude on another person's defensible space" and promotes "a whole pseudo-communitarian ideology" reinforced by a "cult of raw spontaneity."[10] The Anglican Church in Canada, combining wryness and formality, reminded its flock that the peace is a "sign of reconciliation," not "a foretaste of the coffee hour."[11] Suffering at the hands of sentimental, unseemly, and meaningless demonstrations of peace appears to be so common in different Christian circles that it may, ironically, be one of their stronger ecumenical sources of commiseration and solidarity.

It is little wonder, then, that scholars such as Graham Woolfenden have offered thoughtful arguments for moving the kiss of peace from its current position in the Roman Rite and that the 2005 synod moved to consider this possibility despite the fact that the Roman *pax* has remained where it is for the past 1,500 years.[12] In *Sacramentum Caritatis*, Benedict XVI obliged the synod and wrote:

> Taking into account ancient and venerable customs and the wishes expressed by the Synod Fathers, I have asked the competent curial offices to study the possibility of moving the sign of peace to another place, such as before the presentation of the gifts at the altar. To do so would also serve as a significant reminder of the Lord's insistence that we be reconciled with others before offering our gifts to God (cf. Mt 5:23 ff.); cf. *Propositio* 23.[13]

How could the restoration of an ancient practice lead so swiftly to thoughts of departing from ancient practice? To answer this question, we must first understand what the kiss of peace is in traditional Christian life and thought. From there, we will be in a

---

10   David Martin, "Personal Identity and a Changed Church," in *No Alternative: The Prayer Book Controversy*, ed. David Martin and Peter Mullen (Oxford: Blackwell, 1981) 12–22, at 20. Also Margaret Doody, "Our Fathers, Often Faithless Too," in ibid., 36–56, at 52.

11   *The Holy Eucharist: The Third Canadian Order* (Toronto: Anglican Book Center, 1981) 9.

12   Graham Woolfenden, "'Let us offer each other the sign of peace'—An Enquiry," in *Worship* 67 (1993) 239–252.

13   *Sacramentum Caritatis*, no. 49, n. 150.

position to ascertain if there are any distinctive features to the kiss of peace in the spirituality of the Roman liturgy and whether or how these features should continue to be fostered.

BIBLICAL WITNESS

The origins of what St. Paul calls the "holy kiss" (*philêma hagion*)[14] and St. Peter the "kiss of charity" (*philêma agapês*)[15] are not clear. The custom may have derived from Jewish Palestinian practices at the time. Jesus, for example, chides his host Simon the Pharisee for not kissing him as if he should have known better (Lk 7:45), and Judas acts as if publicly kissing his master would be a recognizable yet unremarkable sign by which to carry out his stratagem (Lk 22:47). On the other hand, early Judaism "does not appear to have had any practice closely related to the Christian ritual kiss"[16] either inside its liturgy or without, and so if kissing was common in Jesus' day, it was probably not common because of any religious significance attached to it. This is not to say, however, that kissing is absent from the Old Testament. To take two out of many examples: Jacob and Esau reconciled with a kiss (Gen 33:4), and Jonathan and David parted with a kiss (1 Sam 20:41). Related actions were also construed as instances of kissing. Elisha's mouth-to-mouth resuscitation of the woman of Sunam's dead son was seen as a kiss (2 Kgs 4:32-35), and the Jewish rabbinical tradition recognizes two "cosmic" kisses at the beginning and end of history: the breathing of the breath of life into man (Gen 2:7) and the breathing of God's spirit into his people at the resurrection of the dead (Ezek 37:14).[17] None of these biblical associations, as we shall see, would be overlooked by the early Church.

---

14   See Rom 16:16; 1 Cor 16:20; 2 Cor 13:12; 1 Thess 5:26.

15   1 Pet 5:14.

16   Michael Philip Penn, *Kissing Christians: Ritual and Community in the Late Ancient Church* (Philadelphia: University of Pennsylvania Press, 2005) 19.

17   *Shir Hashirim Zuta*, ch. 1, T. S. 21, 144; see Nicolas James Perella, *The Kiss Sacred and Profane: An Interpretive History of Kiss Symbolism and Related Religio-Erotic Themes* (Berkeley: University of California Press, 1969) 273, n. 12.

Less disputable is the salience of kissing in the Greek and Roman worlds, where kisses held a wide range of meaning: as tokens of friendship and family, as greetings and farewells, as gestures of veneration and submission, as expressions of mind and speech, and of course, as libidinous and even obscene acts. Grammarians contradistinguished the three Latin words *basium, suavium,* and *osculum* by defining the first two as different kinds of erotic kisses and the third as a non-erotic kiss, even though these distinctions were sometimes more honored in the breach than in the observance.[18] Interestingly enough, kissing played a small role in Greco-Roman religion, being generally limited to the occasional veneration of priests.[19] Christians, beginning with the apostles or their contemporaries, drew from these meanings and conventions, but they were careful to modify them as well. The Church fathers used only the words *osculum* and *pax* to designate the holy kiss, promoted chaste kissing over licentious osculation and, in extending the kiss to all baptized members of the flock, moved it from the margins of religious life to a much more central location.[20]

Whatever its origin, the Christian kiss was already well known by the time Paul was writing in the mid-first century: otherwise he would probably not have mentioned it four times without also explaining or introducing it.[21] Paul refers to the holy

---

18   E.g., Isidore of Seville, *Differentiae* 1,398 (PL 83:51): "Basia coniugibus, sed et oscula dantur amicis/ Suavia lascivis miscentur grata labellis;" also Servius, *Commentary on the Aeneid of Vergil* 1,256. See Penn, *Kissing Christians*, 11; Philippe Moreau, "*Osculum, basium, suavium,*" in *Revue de Philologie* 52 (1978) 87–97; Willem Frijhoff, "The Kiss Sacred and Profane: Reflections on a Cross-cultural Confrontation," in *A Cultural History of Gesture*, ed. Jan Bremmer and Herman Roodenburg (Ithaca, NY: Cornell University Press, 1992) 210–236, at 211.

19   Michael Penn finds that only two percent of all references to kissing in the pagan literature of Greece and Rome are to kisses in a religious setting (*Kissing Christians*, 16). While kissing people as a religious act was rather rare, kissing objects, however, was not: indeed, the word "adore," which comes from the Latin words "to the mouth," can refer to the kissing of statues.

20   Penn, *Kissing Christians*, 16.

21   Paul Bradshaw suggests that Paul instituted or at least encouraged the kiss; see *The Search for the Origins of Christian Worship*, 2nd ed. (New York: Oxford

kiss as a special salutation or greeting that is reserved for the "brethren," i.e., fellow Christians only, and he links it contextually to the God of peace and love (2 Cor 13:12), Christ's grace, and the fellowship of the Holy Spirit (2 Cor 13:12, 16:23; 1 Thess 5:28). Some passages in which the holy kiss is mentioned also bespeak a concern for unity in Christ free from doctrinal error (Rom 16:16-17, 1 Cor 16:20-22), and all passages are found in the concluding paragraph of the epistle, thus functioning as a "seal" for the entire work. Moreover, according to L. Edward Phillips, there is a pneumatological significance to the holy kiss. Phillips notes that the three epistles in which Paul does not enjoin his Christian audience to salute each other with a kiss contain the blessing "the grace of the Lord Jesus Christ be with your spirit," as if this benediction and the holy kiss were two different facets of the same practice. Thus, the kiss was seen by Paul as a communication of Christ's grace or spirit (that is, the Holy Spirit[22]) into the spirit of the believer.[23] Further supporting this thesis is Phillips's analysis of how the word "holy" in Paul's epistles has a pneumatological meaning.[24]

Finally, although St. Peter uses a different term for the holy kiss (an indication, perhaps, of a plurality of practices or at least of nomenclature), his single reference to the kiss of charity is also linked contextually to salutation, fellow Christians, seal, and peace or grace (1 Pet 5:14), and he too presupposes that his audience is already familiar with the custom.[25] At least one scholar, influenced by the increasingly discredited "myth of the Constantinian fall of

---

University, 2002) 17–19, 95–96; however, as Michael Penn points out, "the evidence points more strongly in the other direction" (*Kissing Christians*, 18).

22   For both Paul and John, the spirit of Christ is in some sense the Holy Spirit. See Rom 8:9, 2 Cor. 3:17, Jn 20:22.

23   L. Edward Phillips, *The Ritual Kiss in Early Christian Worship* (Cambridge: Grove, 1996) 812.

24   Ibid., 8.

25   The Vulgate translates 1 Pet 5:14b, "*Eirênê humin pasin tois Christô*," as "Gratia vobis omnibus qui estis in Christo Jesu." This too may be linked to "pneuma" if one views "charity" in terms of the Holy Spirit (see 1 Jn 4:8).

the church,"[26] has bemoaned a later patristic "mysticizing" of the kiss which to her mind left the kiss "withered" and "shrivelled."[27] Careful exegesis of the scriptural texts, however, reveals a startling amount of meaning present in the holy kiss from the very beginning, meaning that would be faithfully explored and developed by the Church fathers.

THE EARLY CHURCH

Although we cannot determine with certainty whether the holy kiss was a regular feature of the Eucharistic liturgy during the apostolic age, we do know, based on the evidence just surveyed, that it was a well-established Christian ritual, that is, a practice with distinct religious meaning for those within the Church. Phillips, for instance, even suggests that the Pauline blessing, "the grace of the Lord Jesus Christ be with your spirit," was the formula used when giving the holy kiss, which is why Paul treats one as a metonymy for the other.[28] It is therefore not surprising that the first post-biblical appearance of the kiss should be in connection to the liturgy. The *First Apology* of St. Justin Martyr (100–165), written about AD 150, states that "when we have finished the prayers, we greet each other with a kiss."[29] Justin's remark occurs

---

26   Peter C. Erb, response to Eleanor Kreider, "Let the Faithful Greet Each Other: The Kiss of Peace," in *Conrad Grebel Review* 5 (1987) 153–156, at 155.

27   Eleanor Kreider, "Let the Faithful Greet Each Other: The Kiss of Peace," in *Conrad Grebel Review* 5 (1987) 29–49, at 38, 40 (respectively). Kreider's thesis is significantly flawed even on her own terms. She faults the fourth-century Peace of Constantine for "numenizing the kiss" and then is left unable to explain "this spiritualizing, mysticizing tendency" in the second-century author Clement of Alexandria (38). Her hermeneutic of rupture evinces no awareness of the mystical (hidden) and spiritual (pneumatological) dimensions in Paul's writings that are in continuity with the writings of the Church fathers. Such misreadings are potentially dangerous because they, as in Kreider's case, lead to faulty prescriptions for change.

28   Phillips, *The Ritual Kiss in Early Christian Worship*, 9–10, 12–13.

29   Justin Martyr, *First Apology* 65,2 (ed. Miroslav Marcovich, Patristische Texte und Studien 38 [Berlin–New York: Walter de Gruyter, 1994] 125. Translations from Greek and Latin sources are my own, unless otherwise noted.

after a description of a baptism and before an account of the Eucharist, thereby implying that the kiss functioned liturgically as a seal or consummation of prayer. This function would be made explicit approximately fifty years later by Tertullian, who calls the kiss of peace the *signaculum orationis* and asks, "What prayer is complete when divorced from the holy kiss?"[30] And even after the church in Rome moved the kiss from before the anaphora to after the consecration and Lord's Prayer, a point to which we shall return later, it continued to regard the kiss in this light.[31]

The Spirit

Understanding the kiss as a *signaculum*, however, did not preclude other meanings, of which there were several. First among these is again the pneumatic. Justin's placement of the kiss after baptism anticipates the *Apostolic Tradition*, which instructs the bishop to kiss the neophyte after baptizing and anointing him and to say, "The Lord be with you," to which the neophyte responds, "And with your spirit."[32] As we shall see in a moment, this is the first holy kiss that the believer receives, holy because it is filled with the Spirit and confers the Spirit. Consequently, the neophyte's response, "et cum spiritu tuo," is not an empty Hebraicism, but a theological acknowledgment of the spirit which abides with the bishop and which has just been given to him.[33] The *Apostolic*

---

30   Tertullian, *De oratione* 18 (PL 1:1282): "Quae oratio cum divortio sancti osculi integra?" The translation is taken from *Tertullian's Treatises: Concerning Prayer, Concerning Baptism*, trans. Alexander Souter (New York: Macmillan, 1919) 33.

31   See Innocent I, *Epistola* 25,1,4 (PL 20:553).

32   *Apostolic Tradition* 21,23 (Paul F. Bradshaw, Maxwell E. Johnson, and L. Edward Phillips, *The Apostolic Tradition: A Commentary*, Hermeneia [Minneapolis: Fortress Press, 2002] 118).

33   See Phillips, *The Ritual Kiss in Early Christian Worship* 18–19. Kreider, "Let the Faithful Greet Each Other," 33, is wrong to opine that because this was not the kiss of peace, it was "merely the oriental greeting of the times." Aside from the basic consideration that very little in the church's symbolic worship can ever be soundly prefaced with the restrictive qualifier "merely," Kreider overlooks the fact that the liturgical kiss of peace and the holy kiss are not synonymous but rather the former is a species of the latter genus.

Tradition, true to its name, keeps intact the Pauline link between kissing and holiness-as-spirit-filled. Indeed, the same document treats both Christian breath and saliva as holy because they contain in some way the Holy Spirit.[34]

While no doubt surprising to the modern mind, such depictions are consistent with what we may call a biblical metaphysics. When, for instance, Jesus commissions the seventy disciples to go into the nearby towns, he says: "Into whatsoever house you enter, first say: "Peace be to this house." And if the son of peace be there, your peace shall rest upon him; but if not, it shall return to you (Lk 10:5–6)."[35] As David Yeago notes, Christ describes the peace bequeathed to his disciples not in metaphorical terms but "with utter substantial realism," as "a concrete reality" which "confers the gift of which it speaks" and has the power to return to the giver if the recipient is unworthy.[36] That "utter substantial realism" applies not only to the peace the seventy were commissioned to give and retract but, *mutatis mutandis,* to the holy kiss and liturgical kiss of peace as well. As James Perella notes in his magisterial study, *The Kiss Sacred and Profane,* for Church fathers such as Sts. Cyril of Jerusalem (315–386) and John Chrysostom (347–407), "the kiss exchanged by the brethren is more than just a symbol:" it is the actual mixing of souls,[37] the movement of souls towards "a mutual intercourse."[38]

---

34   See *Apostolic Tradition* 41–42 (ed. Bradshaw, Johnson, and Phillips, 194–202 and 216); Phillips, *The Ritual Kiss,* 18. The *Apostolic Tradition* also provides an early witness of the kiss's common appearance at ordinations, again because of its association with the Spirit. See *Apostolic Tradition* 4,1 (ed. Bradshaw, Johnson, and Phillips, 38); *Canons of Hippolytus* 3,17 (Patrologia Orientalis 31:2, 352); *Constitutiones Apostolorum* 8,5,10 (SC 336:149).

35   The unsurpassed accuracy of the RSV translation notwithstanding, this essay employs the Douay-Rheims translation for direct quotations of the Bible. I am partial to the Douay-Rheims's literary resonance and elegance, and none of the passages I have quoted are defective in their translations. When citing passages, however, I adhere to the modern system of biblical titles and abbreviations.

36   Yeago, "Unfashionable Thoughts on Sharing the Peace," 292.

37   Perella, *The Kiss Sacred and Profane,* 24. Perella cites Cyril, *Catechesis* 23,3 (PG 33:1112). Of course, the accuracy of Perella's statement depends on what is meant by symbol. If symbol is taken to mean a mere convention that points to something

The bold contentions of Cyril and Chrysostom, together with the exalted view of the holy kiss held by the early Church as a whole, rest on a biblically-inspired ontology that understands sensible phenomena to be participating in greater intelligible realities. By virtue of this participation, there is a connatural affinity between spirit and kiss, since kissing generally involves or simulates a communication of breaths, and breath (linguistically, scripturally, and even metaphysically) is linked to the immaterial soul or spirit. As Perella observes, both the Latin *spiritus* and *anima* "carry an earlier meaning of breath but also the significance of the immaterial stuff of spirit and soul."[39] Similarly, Genesis 2:7 describes man's "living soul" as the direct product of God's breath. Little wonder, then, that St. Ambrose (340–397), who interprets the passionate kisses of lovers as attempts to "pour their spirit/breath (*spiritum*) into each other," designates the holy kiss as a means through which the spirit of the divine bestower of kisses (God the Word) is truly poured forth into the soul of the believer.[40]

Christ Incarnate

Ambrose's reflections on the essence of soul and spirit also intimate a link between the holy kiss and the incarnate Word. Paul denotes Jesus Christ as the incarnation of peace between Jews and Gentiles, the cornerstone of the city of God (Eph 2:14–20). Developing this line of thought, Augustine observes that a cornerstone joins two different walls together, not unlike the kiss of peace that

---

else without also either making that to which it points truly present or without participating in the essence of that to which it points, then the statement is accurate.

38   John Chrysostom, *Hom.* 30 (PG 61:606); see *In Ep. II ad Cor.* 30,2 (PG 61:607). And if the kiss produces united souls, it also produces one body; see John Chrysostom, *In Ep. I ad Cor.* 44,4 (PG 61:376).

39   Perella, *The Kiss Sacred and Profane*, 45.

40   Ambrose of Milan, *De Isaac et anima* 3,8 (PL 14:531–532): "Per hoc osculum adhaeret anima Deo Verbo, per quod sibi transfunditur spiritus osculantis: sicut etiam ii qui se osculantur, non sunt labiorum praelibatione contenti, sed spiritum suum sibi invicem videntur infundere." See Augustine, *Sermo* 267,4,4 (PL 38:1231), where he argues that the relationship between an individual's soul and his body is a microcosm of the relationship between the Holy Spirit and Christ's Body, the Church.

unites believers into one visible body.[41] Indeed, a kiss is itself a kind of incarnation: just as the very notion of a Word or Logos includes a making audible or visible a meaning that is intelligible and immaterial, so too does a kiss make carnal or tangible the invisible motions of the heart. Origen thus speaks of the holy kiss between Christians as a figure of the bridegroom's kissing his bride in the Song of Songs.[42]

Nor, it should be noted, is there a contradiction or obfuscation in seeing the kiss as both pneumatological and Christological. As Perella concludes from his study of patristic sources, "whenever the kiss image appears having Christian symbolic value, Christ *and* the Spirit are present."[43] In the succinct words of Ambrose: ". . . he who receives the Spirit kisses Christ."[44] Chrysostom, working with the Pauline description of the body as a temple of the Holy Spirit, refers to the body as the temple of Christ and to the mouth as the door of the temple. Hence, when Christians kiss, they are kissing the "vestibule and entrance" through which Christ has entered.[45] St. Cyprian of Carthage (d. 258) develops his Christocentric interpretation of the kiss eschatologically. "Present to the Lord with all your heart and with contempt for the things of the present," he writes, "you think only of the things that are to be, so that you may be able to come to the fruition of the eternal kingdom and to the embrace and kiss and sight of the Lord."[46]

Paschal Mystery

Both the pneumatological and Christological are present and unified in one particularly dramatic moment of the Paschal Mystery.

---

41   Augustine, *Sermo* 204,2 (PL 38:1037).
42   Origen, *In Canticum Canticorum* prol.,1,1 (PG 13:86).
43   Perella, *The Kiss Sacred and Profane*, 23, original emphasis.
44   Ambrose of Milan, *Ep.* 41,15 (PL 16:1165): "Te Scriptura docet, quod osculetur Christum, qui accipit Spiritum."
45   John Chrysostom, *Hom.* 30 (PG 61:606).
46   Cyprian of Carthage, *Ep.* 81,4 (PL 3:0428): "Toto corde ad Deum prompti, contemptu praesentium futura tantummodo cogitatis, ut ad fructum regni aeterni et ad complexum et osculum Domini et conspectum venire possitis."

On the evening after his resurrection, our Lord greeted the apostles by saying "Pax vobis," and breathed onto them the Holy Spirit (Jn 20:22). John 20 is the passage that Ambrose has in mind when he says, as noted earlier, that receiving the Spirit is kissing Christ, for as we have again already seen, breathing is evocative of kissing and vice versa.[47] For the Church fathers, Christ's Easter insufflation was thus a mystical kiss,[48] a kiss that brings the fruits that come from his paschal victory over death. Augustine eloquently compares this paschal kiss to God's breathing of a rational soul into man in the book of Genesis: just as the Lord vivified Adam, made from the slime of the earth, so too does Jesus vivify the apostles, enabling them to rise from the slime and to renounce slimy works.[49] Nor is this figurative interpretation exegetically defective: the verb in John 20:22 that is usually translated as "breathing on," *enephusésen*, means "to breathe into."[50] The kiss of peace which relays the Holy Spirit is thus the same kiss that the risen Christ gave his Church.

Peace

As a communication of the spirit of Christ, the holy kiss infuses the faithful with Christ himself, who is not simply the bringer of peace (*pacifer*) but the peace itself (*pax*). Significantly, the "cornerstone" passage in Ephesians that Augustine explicated also contains the declaration that Christ "is our peace" (2:14). The total identification of Christ and authentic peace explains why Church figures as early as Tertullian call the holy kiss the kiss of peace (*osculum pacis*)[51]

---

47   According to a sermon sometimes ascribed to Augustine, when Christ breathed on the apostles, he in some [mystical] way placed his mouth on theirs: *Sermo* 42,8, *De Elisaeo*, II (PL 39:1830).

48   See Caesarius of Arles, *Sermo* 128,8 (CCL 103:1008). In Migne this sermon is listed under "Auctor incertus (Augustinus Hipponensis?)," PL 39:1830.

49   Or more accurately, worthless deeds. Augustine, *In Io. Ev. Tract.* 32,6 (PL 35:1645): ". . . ut a luto exsurgerent, et luteis operibus renuntiarent."

50   Phillips, *The Ritual Kiss in Early Christian Worship*, 13.

51   Tertullian, *De oratione* 18 (PL 1:1282). A similar sentiment is found in Cyprian of Carthage, *Ep.* 15,3 (PL 3:267): "Sufficiently blessed are those who, passing through these paths of glory, have already withdrawn from this world and, having

and why the *Passion of Saints Perpetua and Felicity* (c. 203), in a usage that would be widely followed, simply refers to it as the *pax*.[52] This idiom is not simply a convenient abbreviation but an apt testimony to the substantial realism undergirding the practice: since the kiss of peace truly communicates Christ, it is more than a dramatization or even a conduit of peace: it is an actualization of it. As Perella explains, the kiss "is a symbol in the truest sense of the word: it is itself what it signifies—a fusional or unifying action."[53]

Family Ties

Drawing from Paul's reference to the brethren and from the biblical and cross-cultural association of kissing with familial intimacy, the early Church also understood the kiss of peace as a family affair, an act proper only to the members of one's spiritual household. Like most other kinds of kissing, the liturgical kiss was a token of intimacy, the kind of thing one would do only within the circle of one's loved ones. Hence, the Christian kiss was not given to non-family members such as heretics and schismatics or even to would-be family members like catechumens; nor was it given to the black sheep in the family guilty of mortal sin. Such rules were fairly easy to follow even in liturgical settings, for the Church's discipline of the secret (*disciplina arcani*) ensured that the uninitiated were dismissed from the Eucharistic sacrifice prior to the rite of peace, while public penitents, whose sin had severed their friendship with God and destroyed their holiness, were seated in a separate part of the church or even outside it.[54]

---

traversed the way of virtue and faith, have come to the embrace and kiss of the Lord, with the Lord himself rejoicing" ("Beati satis qui, ex vobis per haec gloriarum vestigia commeantes, iam de saeculo recesserunt, confectoque itinere virtutis ac fidei, ad complexum et osculum Domini, Domino ipso gaudente, venerunt").

52 See *Passio Sanctarum Perpetuae et Felicitatis* 4,2 (PL 3:44), where the action is called "pacem facere."

53 Perella, *The Kiss Sacred and Profane*, 26.

54 See Antonio Santantoni, "Reconciliation in the First Four Centuries," in *Handbook for Liturgical Studies, Vol. 4: Sacraments and Sacramentals*, ed. Anscar J. Chupungco (Collegeville, MN: Liturgical Press, 2000) 93–104, at 95–101.

Part of the motivation behind this discriminating usage, as
Michael Penn has argued extensively,[55] was to mark the boundaries of the religious community: since one would not give the
kiss to an "outsider" within or without Mass, the kiss in the fourth
century and beyond became a sociological tool for demarcating
the line between orthodox and heterodox. But the theological animus should not be overlooked either. For example, rather than
cementing social inequalities that were otherwise tolerated, the
Church allowed Christian slaves to kiss and be kissed every bit as
much as their masters—a markedly different practice from the rest
of the Greco-Roman world.[56] Indeed, for John Chrysostom, the
holy kiss was the great social leveler, making no distinction
between lowly and great.[57] Moreover, the custom of reserving the
kiss for those in a state of grace illustrates the extent to which early
Christians truly viewed the kiss as holy. If, as Paul implies, the kiss
is the Breath or Spirit of God, it cannot be given willy-nilly but
only to those who breathe as one in the mystical Body of Christ.
Again the *Apostolic Tradition* is a valuable witness to the early
Church's underlying theology of the kiss. The neophyte receives
the holy kiss only after being baptized by the bishop because, prior
to his sanctification in the laver of regeneration, he is neither holy
nor Spirit-filled. As a catechumen, he is thereby theologically inca-
pable of receiving or relaying the holiness of the kiss. To borrow
the terminology from Luke 10:5–6, he is no son of peace until he

---

55   See Penn, *Kissing Christians*, and idem, "Ritual Kissing, Heresy and the
Emergence of Early Christian Orthodoxy," in *Journal of Ecclesiastical History* 54 (2003)
625–640.

56   See Penn, *Kissing Christians*, 33. Penn's conclusion is based mostly on a
lack of evidence to the contrary, but his reasoning is persuasive nonetheless, especially
in light of the single text he does cite: *Passio Sanctarum Perpetuae et Felicitatis* 6,4 (PL
3:56), in which we learn that Perpetua and her companions (which included the slave
Felicity) kissed one another "in order to consummate their martyrdom with the offering (*solemnia*) of peace."

57   John Chyrsostom, *Catechesis ultima ad baptizandos* 11,32–34, *Varia graeca
sacra: Sbornik grečeskikh neisdannikh bogoslovskikh tekstov I–IV věkov*, ed. Athanasios
Papadopoulos-Kerameus (St. Petersburg: Kirshbauma, 1909) 174–175.

is an initiated believer, and hence the spirit of peace cannot abide with him. As for heretics, schismatics, and those in a state of mortal sin, they were once filled with the Spirit by virtue of their baptism but have since cut themselves off from the Body of Christ. The spirit of life, Augustine soberly notes, is not to be found in an amputated limb,[58] nor do those who lacerate the Church possess true peace.[59]

Forgiveness

Communal unity, however, must either presuppose or cause reconciliation among estranged members. One of the most readily recognized meanings of the kiss of peace is forgiveness. In his mystagogical lectures, Cyril of Jerusalem tells his neophytes that the kiss of peace "reconciles souls to each other," that it "promises to them that injuries will be wiped from every memory."[60] The kiss of peace, Cyril concludes, does not just reconcile; it actually constitutes a reconciliation,[61] one that is derived from Matthew 5:23–24: "If therefore thou offer thy gift at the altar, and there thou remember that thy brother hath any thing against thee; Leave there thy offering before the altar, and go first to be reconciled to thy brother: and then coming thou shalt offer thy gift." Cyril is not alone in linking Christ's words in the Sermon on the Mount to the kiss of peace. According to an ancient tradition preserved by Eusebius of Caesarea (260–341) and credited to Clement of Alexandria (d. 215), the man who had accused St. James the Lesser of being a Christian was himself converted and given the same death sentence. As the two were being led away to their execution, the man asked for forgiveness from James, who then looked at him for a moment, said "Peace be with you" and kissed him.[62]

---

58   Augustine, *Sermo* 267,4,4 (PL 38:1232).

59   Augustine, *In Io. Ev. Tract.* 6,4 (PL 35:1427): "Illi habent veram pacem, qui Ecclesiam non laniaverunt."

60   Cyril of Jerusalem, *Catechesis* 23,3 (PG 33:1112).

61   Ibid.

62   Eusebius of Caesarea, *Ecclesiastical History* 2,9,2 (PG 19:157).

Holy Communion

Forgiveness, moreover, comes with love, the ultimate agent of union. "What is love but somehow life joining together or yearning to join together in some way two things, namely, the lover and his beloved?"[63] Augustine asks. The kiss of charity is a glue that unites the family of God, and it is also, we have seen above, a union between God the Lover and his beloved. Because of this union of God, self, and brother, Church fathers saw the kiss of peace as an ideal preparation for the reception of Holy Communion, in which the communicant is further incorporated into the Body of Christ by Christ's own sacramental entrance into the communicant. As Pseudo-Dionysius (fl. early sixth century) explains, we cannot participate in the one true God when we are divided within ourselves or alienated from our brethren. The kiss of peace, which "joins like to like and turns the fragmented away from the divine and unique visions," thus fulfills the conditions for our "peaceful union with the One."[64] So strong was the association of the kiss with the Eucharist that the former was used in preparation for the latter even outside the liturgy. The *Dialogues* of Pope St. Gregory the Great (r. 590–604) recount the story about a group of monks who, convinced they were about to be shipwrecked, exchanged the kiss of peace before receiving the sacrament, which they had brought with them.[65] And St. Mary of Egypt (344–421), it is reported, would give the kiss of peace to the monk who brought her the Eucharist.[66] Indeed, because of this natural bond between the *pax* and Holy Communion, the kiss was restricted to communicants in some parts of Europe during the Middle Ages,[67] a fact that also explains his-

---

63   Augustine, *De Trinitate* 8,10,14 (PL 42:960). See *De ordine* 2,18,48 (PL 32:1017).

64   Ps.-Dionysius, *De ecclesiastica hierarchia* 3,3,8 (PG 3:437), trans. Colm Luibheid, *Pseudo-Dionysius: The Complete Works* (New York: Paulist, 1987) 218.

65   Gregory the Great, *Dialogi* 3,36 (PL 77:307); also *Hom.* 37,9 (PL 76:1281).

66   Sophronius, *Vita s. Mariae Aegypti* 22 (PL 73:87).

67   See Josef Andreas Jungmann, *The Mass of the Roman Rite*, trans. Francis A. Brunner (New York: Benziger, 1951–1955) vol. 2, 323–325.

torically its omission from the one common Mass in which the faithful did not communicate, namely, the Requiem.[68]

Moreover, the Eucharist itself was understood as an even more intimate kiss between Christ and the communicant. For Ambrose, Holy Communion occurs when Christ says to the believer, in the words of the Song of Songs, "Let him kiss me with the kisses of his mouth;" and the believer, in turn, replies: "May Christ plant a kiss on me!"[69] For Chrysostom, the kiss of peace is the kissing of the brethren that sets the stage for a kiss from the Master,[70] while Theodoret of Cyrrhus (393–457) writes: "when it is time for the sacrament (*mustike kairô*), we receive the members of the Bridegroom and we kiss and embrace him . . . and we picture with our heart and mind a certain nuptial embrace" by which we are united to him.[71]

Treacherous Kissing

Both union and communion also presuppose a harmony of gesture and sentiment, an integrity of external deed and internal disposition. Referring to the Middle Ages, Jean-Claude Schmitt writes that "gestures figured, or better, *embodied* the dialectic *intus*

---

68   Adrian Fortescue, *The Mass: A Study of the Roman Liturgy* (Boonville, NY: Preserving Christian Publications, 2007) 372.

69   Ambrose of Milan, *De sacramentis* 5,2,7 (PL 16:447): "Osculum mihi Christus infigat!"

70   John Chrysostom, *Baptismal Instruction* 11, trans. Paul W. Harkins, Ancient Christian Writers 31 (Westminster, MD: Newman, 1963), 171–172; for the original Greek, see Papadopoulos-Kerameus, 154–183.

71   Theodoret of Cyrrhus, *Expl. in Cant. Cant.* 25 (PG 81:53). For other texts that link or somehow associate the kiss of peace with the Eucharist, see Ambrose, *Ep.* 41,14–18 (PL 16:1117–1118); Cyril of Jerusalem, *Mystagogiae* 5,3 (PG 33:1111); Origen, *Comm. in Cant. Cant.* 1,1,13 (PG 13:39–40); John Chrysostom, *In Ep. II ad Cor.* 30:2 (PG 61:607); Augustine, *Sermo* 227 (PL 38:1101), *Contra litteras Petiliani* 2,23,53 (PL 43:277); Jerome, *Ep.* 82,3 (PL 22:737); *Testamentum Domini* 2,9 (in *Testamentum Domini*, ed. Ignatius E. Rahmani [Mainz: Kirchheim, 1899] 131); Innocent I, *Ep.* 25,1 (PL 20:553); Theodore of Mopsuestia, *On Eucharist and Liturgy* 5 (in *Commentary of Theodore of Mopsuestia on the Lord's Prayer and on the Sacraments of Baptism and the Eucharist*, ed. Alphonse Mingana [Cambridge: Heffer, 1933] 230–232).

and *foris* since they were supposed to express without the 'secret movements' of the soul within;" but he could just as easily have been speaking of the early Christian era.[72] If the kiss came to assume a place of great prominence in Christian thought, it was by virtue of what it both signified and effected rather than its physicality per se. Specifically, a kiss bestowed without the love of God and neighbor, however well executed physically, is not a kiss but a despicable lie, despicable because it distorts and deceives about something so important and good.[73] "In the same way that your lips are exhibiting peace," Augustine admonishes, "may it be so in your conscience; that is, just as your lips approach the lips of your brother, so too may your heart not withdraw from his."[74] Elsewhere Augustine asks,

> Who would not get angry watching men praise God with their mouth and deny him with their practices? Who would not get angry watching men renounce the world with their words and not with their deeds? Who is there who would not get angry watching brothers plotting against brothers, not keeping true to the kiss that they give during the divine mysteries?[75]

The kiss of peace, then, is not only something that must be given in good faith but kept in good faith long after: it must be both a pledge and a consequence of true Christian living. Or to borrow again from Augustine, it must follow the example of doves, which are sweet and chaste kissers, and not the example of ravens, which have a reputation for violent osculation:

> If someone has the Holy Spirit, he ought to be innocent like a dove, to have true peace with his brothers, which is what the

---

72   Jean-Claude Schmitt, "The Rationale of Gestures in the West: Third to Thirteenth Centuries," in *A Cultural History of Gesture*, 59–70, at 60.

73   Ambrose, *Ep.* 41,16 (PL 16:1117).

74   Augustine, *Sermo* 227 (PL 38:1101): "Sicut ostendunt labia, fiat in conscientia. Id est, quomodo labia tua ad labia fratris tui accedunt, sic cor tuum a corde eius non recedat."

75   Augustine, *Enarr. in Ps.* 30,2,2,3 (PL 36:240).

kisses of doves signify. For ravens have kisses, but in ravens there is a false peace: in a dove there is true peace. Not everyone, then, who says, "Peace be with you," is to be heeded like a dove. Then how do we distinguish the kisses of ravens from the kisses of doves? Ravens kiss, but they mutilate: the nature of doves is free from mutilation. Therefore, where there is mutilation, there is no true peace in the kisses.[76]

The human paragon of such a "ravenous" perversion is Judas Iscariot, who served as a chilling counterexample for the early Church of how not to give the kiss of peace. Commenting on Judas' infamous kiss in the Garden of Gethsemane (Mt 26:49), Ambrose remarks that he offered a kiss but not the "mystery of a kiss" (*osculi sacramentum*).[77] Leaving the meaning or *sacramentum* out of the kiss is gutting it of its most important component, for what is sought after is not "a kiss of the lips" but a kiss of "the heart and mind."[78] Therefore, someone who lacks good faith and charity lacks the capacity to kiss, "for with a kiss the force of love is imprinted upon another."[79] Augustine offers a similar note of caution: "Don't be a Judas: Judas the traitor kissed Christ with his mouth, and ambushed him in his heart."[80] And the fourth-century *Apostolic Constitutions* solemnly warns against kissing with deceit or hypocrisy, "as Judas betrayed our Lord with a kiss."[81]

Judas' kiss of betrayal had a profound impression on the Church fathers. Ambrose calls Judas a "kind of marvel" (*prodigii genus*) for devising such a perverted sign that would use "the pledge of peace for the discharge of cruelty," a sign that can only be called a "bestial yielding of the mouth" (*bestialis oris obsequium*).[82] This bestial act is one of the reasons why the kiss of peace

---

76   Augustine, *In Io. Ev. Tract.* 6,4 (PL 35:1379).
77   Ambrose of Milan, *Ep.* 41,16 (PL 16:1117).
78   Ibid.: "Osculum non labiorum quaeritur, sed cordis et mentis."
79   Ibid. 41,17 (PL 16:1118).
80   Augustine, *Sermo* 229,3 (PL 46:836, which catalogs this sermon as *Sermo* 6 of the *Sermones inediti*). See Origen, *Comm. in Ep. ad Rom.* 10,33 (PG 14:1282–1283).
81   *Constitutiones Apostolorum* 2,5,17 (SC 320:319).
82   Ambrose of Milan, *Hexaemeron* 6,9,68 (PL 14:270).

was not given during the Maundy Thursday or Good Friday liturgies, as the bitter aftertaste of the traitor's kiss was too fresh, too
vivid, for those reliving our Lord's last hours.[83]

Concupiscent Kissing

From Augustine's account, and those of many others, we also
learn that the kiss of peace was a full, labial act. In the second century and most likely earlier, this kiss was exchanged between
members of the opposite sex as well as between members of the
same sex. Athenagoras, writing around AD 176, commends Christians' self-control in kissing each other; yet he is also concerned
about the ongoing purity of this practice. "The kiss . . . ought to
be used with the utmost caution," he warns, "[for] it excludes us
from eternal life if it is polluted even a little by our thoughts."[84]
Part of Athenagoras' anxiety was theological: if Christians are truly
brothers and sisters in Christ, then their introduction of a lascivious
element into the holy kiss would be not only a sin of lust, but a
crime of spiritual incest.

Even by itself, concupiscence was dangerous enough, especially when surreptitiously co-opting the sacred. Clement of
Alexandria, writing several decades later, was livid about what had
become of the holy kiss:

> There are those who do nothing else except disrupt the churches
> with their kisses, since they do not have inward friendship itself.
> And indeed, this disgraceful matter arouses suspicion and slan-
> der; what they impudently use for a kiss ought to be a mystery
> (*mustikon*). Having tasted of the kingdom worthily, let us dis-
> pense our soul's good will with a mouth chaste and closed,

---

83   Tertullian states that the *pax* was not given during the *Pascha* (Good Friday), but he does not state why; *De oratione* 18 (PL 1:1282). A later tradition, at least,
would later understand this omission with reference to the Judas kiss; see Berno, abbot
of Reichenau, *De rebus ad missam spectantibus*, ch. 7: "In parasceve, ait, ab osculo
abstinemus propter Iudae traditoris exemplum, qui per simulatae pacis osculum tradidit
Dominum Iesum Christum" (PL 142:1079).

84   Athenagoras, *Legatio pro christianis* 32,5,8 (PG 6:963–964).

through which a gentleness of manners is chiefly expressed. But there is another kiss as well: unchaste, filled with poison, counterfeiting holiness. Or do you not know that spiders, even if they touch with the mouth only, cause men serious pain? Kisses, moreover, often inject the venom of sexual impurity. "For this is the love of God," says John, "that we keep his commandments"—not that we stroke each other on the mouth.[85]

The problem was eventually solved in the third century by prohibiting the two sexes from giving the kiss to each other. The *Apostolic Tradition* is our earliest testament to this shift,[86] and it would be followed by others.[87] Admonitions from an appropriate authority were also useful, ranging from indirect references to the importance of chaste kisses[88] to explicit rejections of holy-kissing between men and women.[89] By the Middle Ages, both East and West appear to have cemented this policy by segregating the sexes to different sides of the nave. Despite its eventual decline in the early modern period, it is interesting to note that the custom of separating men and women was still being recommended in the Latin West as recently as the 1917 Code of Canon Law[90] and that a number of Eastern-rite parishes, both Catholic and non-Catholic, continue to observe it.

---

85   Clement of Alexandria, *Pedagogus* 3,110 (PG 8:659–862).

86   *Apostolic Tradition* 18 (ed. Bradshaw, Johnson, and Phillips, 100).

87   See *Constitutiones Apostolorum* 2,5,17 (SC 320:319), 8,11,9 (SC 336:175); Ps.-Clement, *Ep. II ad Virgines* 2 (PG 1:421).

88   See Origen, *Comm. in Ep. ad Rom.* 10,33 (PG 14:1282–1283).

89   E.g., Amalarius of Metz, *De ecclesiasticis officiis* 3,32 (PL 105:1153): "Carnales amplexus, quibus iunguntur saepissime viri et feminae, vitandi sunt in ecclesiae conventu." See also William Durandus, *Rationale divinorum officiorum* 4,53,9 (CCCM 140:546)

90   *Codex Iuris Canonici* (Vatican City: Typis Polyglottis Vaticanis, 1958) can. 1262, § 1: "Optandum ut, congruenter antiquae disciplinae, mulieres in ecclesia separatae sint a viris."

THE MIDDLE AGES AND THE PASCHAL KISS

Evolving Practices

At the same time that the multitudinous meaning of the *pax* was being unfolded, its practice continued to evolve. One of the most significant developments was a gradual shift in the kiss's administration. We have already seen that after AD 200 it was considered more appropriate for men and women not to administer the holy kiss to each other. Later on, the *Apostolic Constitutions* and several other sources add that the clergy should only give the kiss to each other, just as men should only give it to other men and women to other women.[91] This was often done with the lesser ministers giving the kiss to the greater. In the *Apostolic Constitutions*, "the clergy salute the bishop,"[92] and in *Ordo Romanus I*, "the archdeacon gives the peace to the first bishop."[93] The laity, in turn, "kiss each other,"[94] usually at the prompting of the deacon. Whether this was a spontaneous kiss of one's neighbor or something more organized is difficult to say. Judging from the indeterminate language, the former is more likely, yet it would be presumptuous to arrive at any unassailable conclusions. For most of the twentieth century, according to Paul Bradshaw, many liturgical scholars have relied on two unwarranted assumptions borrowed from Edmund Bishop and Anton Baumstark: 1) that the forms of early Christianity serve as the best model for contemporary worship, and 2) that "the oldest forms were always simple and austere compared with

---

91   *Constitutiones Apostolorum* 8,11,9 (SC 336:175). See *Testamentum Domini* 1,23 (ed. Rahmani, 36); Innocent I, *Ep.* 25,1 (PL 20:553), Ps.-Dionysius, *De ecclesiastica hierarchia* 6,3,4 (PG 3:536); Theodore of Mopsuestia, *On Eucharist and Liturgy* 5 (ed. Mingana, 230–232).

92   *Constitutiones Apostolorum* 8,11,9 (SC 336:175).

93   *Ordo Romanus I*, 96 (ed. Michel Andrieu, *Les Ordines Romani du haut moyen âge*, vol. 2, Spicilegium Sacrum Lovaniense 23 [Louvain: Peeters, 1948] 98).

94   See Augustine, *Sermo* 227 (PL 38:1101).

later developments."⁹⁵ Both assumptions could easily skew one's
judgment of how best to construe the scanty details of the primitive *pax*.

What we can say with greater certainty, at least with the
churches that followed or were significantly influenced by the
Ordines Romani, is that after the eighth century, the sequence of
the *pax* changed. *Ordo I* states that "the archdeacon gives the peace
to the bishop first, then to all the others in order (*per ordinem*), and
the people do the same."⁹⁶ Later manuscripts, however, have the
deacon give the kiss "to the others in order and to the people."⁹⁷
As Josef Andreas Jungmann explains, "Thus the kiss of peace is
made to proceed from the altar and, like a message or even like a
gift which comes from the Sacrament, is handed on."⁹⁸

One of the effects of this move was to begin the kiss not with
the deacon but with the principal celebrant, who eventually would
receive it from Christ himself. Twelfth-century manuals show the
celebrant first kissing the altar, the host, the chalice, the book, or
the crucifix;⁹⁹ he would then pass the peace on to the deacon, who
in turn passed it on to the lesser ministers and the congregation.
We will examine the full significance of this development later.

Second, the location of the kiss in the liturgy was changed.
While all the Eastern rites and most Western rites, such as the
Ambrosian and Gallican, placed the kiss before the offertory, the
churches in Rome and North Africa, some time before the reign
of Pope Innocent I (401–417), placed it after the canon and before
Holy Communion. It is generally held now that the Roman inno-
vation had something to do with the *fermentum*, the part of the
host that was consecrated by the pope during the stational liturgy

---

95   Paul Bradshaw, "The Genius of the Roman Rite Revisited," in *Ever Directed Towards the Lord: The Love of God in the Liturgy of the Eucharist Past, Present, and Hoped For*, ed. Uwe Michael Lang (London: T&T Clark, 2007) 49–61, at 53.

96   *Ordo I*, 96 (ed. Andrieu, vol. 2, 98).

97   See Jungmann, *The Mass of the Roman Rite*, vol. 2, 326, citing Mabillon (PL 78:945).

98   See ibid., 326.

99   See ibid., 326–327.

and sent to the title churches (*tituli*) in the city of Rome. According to recent speculation, the priests in these *tituli* were not allowed to celebrate the Eucharistic liturgy on their own because of a commitment to the ancient principle of one Mass, celebrated by the bishop, per city. The *tituli* presbyters therefore led a sort of Liturgy of the Word at their churches and waited for the pope's *fermentum* to arrive. When it did, they put it in a chalice of wine or perhaps touched it to pieces of bread, an action which was believed to consecrate by contact, that is, "ferment," these elements and make them suitable for Holy Communion. The kiss of peace normally would have taken place between the prayers of the faithful and the anaphora, but since there was no anaphora, the service went directly from the kiss of peace to Holy Communion. The association of the *pax* and Holy Communion that was strengthened by this proximity ensured the retention of the practice even after Eucharistic liturgies were eventually allowed in all parts of the city of Rome.[100]

Another distinctive factor of the papal liturgy was the use of the *sancta*, fragments of the consecrated species of bread reserved from a previous Mass. A powerful symbol of "the unity of the sacrifice, to make, as it were, a continuation from one Mass to the next,"[101] the *sancta* were also commingled with the chalice. Over time, then, there appear to have emerged two comminglings: the first commingling of the *sancta* before the peace and the second commingling of the *fermentum* afterwards. These two comminglings were duly recorded in the Roman *ordines* that made their way to Charlemagne's kingdom in the eighth and ninth centuries, but since the Franks had neither the *sancta* nor the *fermentum* (indeed, they were probably confused about what these terms meant), they eventually chose the location of the former. This

---

100   See Bradshaw, "The Genius of the Roman Rite Revisited," 60–61; John F. Baldovin, "The *Fermentum* at Rome in the Fifth Century: A Reconsideration," in *Worship* 79 (2005) 38–53. This theory does not, however, explain the origin of the custom in North Africa, which had no *fermentum*.

101   Fortescue, *The Mass*, 366–367; see Jungmann, *The Mass of the Roman Rite*, vol. 2, 312.

meant that the fraction and commingling would precede the words, "Pax Domini sit semper vobiscum," and the kiss of peace. Jungmann speculates that "allegorical considerations" were "a determining factor in this decision,"[102] just as they were in fixing the place of the formula, "Haec commixtio. . . ."[103] It is to these considerations, then, that we now turn.[104]

The Paschal Kiss

Regardless of the reasons for its historical development, the distinctive ordering of the *pax* in the Roman Mass set the conditions for a distinctive theological appropriation of the patristic heritage in the Western Church. Specifically, and this, as far as I can tell, is a simple but crucial fact that has been generally overlooked: while the pre-anaphoral placement of the *pax* lends to it a predominantly "conciliatory" meaning based on Matthew 5:23–24, the post-anaphoral and post-fractional placement of the *pax* lends to it a predominantly "paschal" meaning based on John 20:21–22.[105] That is, while exchanging the kiss before the offertory and consecration is strongly evocative of the admonition in the Sermon on the Mount to be reconciled to one's brother before offering one's gift, the exchange of the kiss after the consecration and fraction is strongly evocative of an entirely different scriptural model, the mystical kiss of the risen Jesus to his apostles. It is this paschal model that proved to be the decisive hermeneutic for the liturgical kiss in the Roman Rite and for its further development.

---

102   Jungmann, *The Mass of the Roman Rite*, vol. 2, 314.

103   Ibid., 318–319.

104   We should also note that the prayer *Domine Iesu Christe* begins to be used between the *Pax Domini* and the giving of the peace in the eleventh century. This prayer, which is meant to build up to the performance of the peace, is the first prayer in the Ordinary of the Mass to address the Son of God—a fitting distinction given the nature of the *pax*; see Jungmann, *The Mass of the Roman Rite*, vol. 2, 330–331.

105   The one possible exception is Dominic E. Serra's "The Greeting of Peace in the Revised Sacramentary: A New Pastoral Option," in *Liturgy for the New Millennium: A Commentary on the Revised Sacramentary*, ed. Mark R. Francis and Keith F. Pecklers (Collegeville, MN: Liturgical Press, 2000) 97–110, at 110.

It will be recalled that the Church fathers saw Christ's paschal insufflation in the Gospel of John as a kiss. It should also be noted that Luke relates an equally important resurrection account with the disciples of Emmaus (Lk 24:13–43). Christ appears to the two men on the road and explains to them the meaning of the Scriptures. They then stop for supper, and in Jesus' act of breaking bread they recognize him. Significantly, the text does not state that they ate the bread but that they immediately hurried back to Jerusalem to tell the apostles: "Now whilst they were speaking these things [about how they knew him in the breaking of the bread], Jesus stood in the midst of them, and saith to them: 'Peace be to you'" (Lk 24:35–36). In order to prove that he is not a ghost, Christ then eats some fish and honeycomb and gives it to the others to take and eat. The story of the disciples of Emmaus, then, recapitulates the traditional Roman Order of Mass, from the Liturgy of the Word to the *fractio panis* to the Rite of Peace to Holy Communion. Some medieval commentators, such as Amalarius of Metz (d. 850), detected the similarity and therefore interpreted the *Agnus Dei* after the *pax* in terms of "the joys of the resurrection" experienced by the disciples of Emmaus, "who knew the risen Lord in the breaking of the bread."[106]

Further, the medieval Roman post-fractional sequence recapitulates Gideon's sacrifice to the Lord in Judges 6:17–24, where, first, Gideon sacrifices flesh and unleavened cakes to God and second, God, accepting them through his angel (see the *Supplices te rogamus* in the Roman Canon), says to Gideon, "Peace be with you" (6:23). It is the first time in the Bible that God is said to have used this formula. A grateful Gideon goes on to build an altar to the Lord and calls it *YHWH-shalom*, "The LORD is Peace." This appellation is typologically significant, for according to an old tradition the holy name YHWH designates not simply God but God the Son.[107] And as we have already noted, Christ is our peace.

---

106   Amalarius of Metz, *De ecclesiasticis officiis* 3,33 (PL 105:1153).

107   See the Great Antiphon for Vespers on December 18, "O Adonai," in which Christ is addressed as he who appeared in the burning bush.

These biblical associations are reflected in the medieval tradition of mystical or allegorical interpretations of the Mass.[108] Just as the consecration was generally seen to signify not simply the Last Supper but the various stages of our Lord's passion, the kiss of peace was invariably tied to the glory of the first Easter Sunday. "Peace be with you," as St. Thomas Aquinas (1225–1274) notes, is the Lord's signature greeting only after his resurrection. Hence, whatever peace Christ promised his apostles at the Last Supper,[109] a promise repeated verbatim by the priest at this point in the Mass,[110] is provided only through his rising from the dead. Aquinas so interprets the three signs of the cross made by the priest when he says "May the peace of the Lord be ever with you" immediately before the commingling as a representation of the resurrection on the third day.[111] According to Honorius of Autun (fl. 1106–1135), "By sharing the *pax*, [the priest] denotes the peace given after Christ's resurrection and our participation in its joy."[112]

Reinforcing this allegorical reading is the fact that in the traditional Roman Rite the *fractio panis*, or breaking of the host, and the subsequent commingling of a particle of the host with the Precious Blood take place immediately before the peace. The medieval doctors were quick to see in the fraction of the host "the rending of Christ's body" during the Passion[113] or the separation of his soul from his body at the moment of his death. Similarly, they noted how the commingling of the species aptly signifies the resurrection, for the mixing of the sacred Body and Blood calls to mind the Easter reunion of all that had been sundered on Good Friday.[114] It is reasonable, then, that the peace,

---

108   For a defense of this form of exegesis, see Michael P. Foley, "The Mystic Meaning of the *Missale Romanum*," in *Antiphon* 13 (2009) 103–125.
109   See Jn 14:27.
110   The prayer, *Domine Iesu Christe, qui dixisti Apostolis tuis.*
111   Thomas Aquinas, *Summa theologiae* III, q. 83, a. 5, ad 3.
112   Honorius of Autun, *Gemma animae* 1,83 (PL 172:570).
113   Thomas Aquinas, *Summa theologiae* III, q. 83, a. 5, ad 7.
114   See Amalarius of Metz, *De ecclesiasticis officiis* 3,35 (PL 105:1154).

which represents the fruits of the resurrection, take place immediately following that part of the Mass which mystically signifies
the resurrection itself.

The paschal connotations of the kiss also gave it the character
of a moment marked by the deep, personal intimacy of Mary
Magdalene with the risen Christ on the morning of the resurrection, as we find in the thirteenth-century *Ancrene Wisse*, or
"Anchoresses' Guide:"

> [At the *pax*,] you should forget the world. There be entirely out
> of the body. There in shining love embrace your beloved, who
> has come into your heart's bower from heaven, and hold him
> close until he has granted you all you ask.[115]

Simply put, if the kiss in the Eastern rites is a conciliatory kiss with
pneumatological and paschal corollaries, the kiss in the Roman
Rite is a pneumatological and paschal kiss with conciliatory corollaries, a kiss that, while effecting the reconciliation of estranged
brethren, is nonetheless ordered primarily to the grace of the risen
Christ and his bestowal of the Spirit. Such a differentiation of liturgical practices does not imply that the two are mutually exclusive
or that one is superior to the other, but it does suggest that they
are not synonymous or interchangeable.

But, it may well be asked, does this Latin medieval appropriation of the kiss do justice to the manifold meanings attached to
the kiss by the New Testament and the early Church? Judging
from the writings of medieval liturgical commentators, the answer
is in the affirmative. William Durandus (1237–1296), who begins
his exposition of the kiss of peace with an account of John 20, goes
on to compare the giving of the peace by the priest to the people
to the actions of the risen Christ "who, having overcome the devil,
gave peace and other gifts to men;" he then artfully lists and coor-
dinates virtually all of the patristic meanings we enumerated ear-

---

115   *Ancrene Wisse*, pt. 1. The translation is taken from Mark Amsler, "Affective
Literacy: Gestures of Reading in the Middle Ages," in *Essays in Medieval Studies* 18
(2001) 38–110, at 89.

lier.[116] Similarly, Peter the Chanter (d. 1197) draws from patristic theologies of the peace to explain its association with the mission of the Holy Spirit and the Incarnate Word.[117] It is worth pointing out here that Jungmann's description of the Roman *pax* as relaying a message is only half-right. It is not a message that is being relayed; it is the Logos himself. Further, medieval practices kept intact patristic teaching on the scope of the kiss, preserving it for the practicing faithful who were in a state of grace.[118] In some cases, the Roman Rite departed from the letter of the early Church in order to preserve the spirit. Omitting the kiss of peace from the Maundy Thursday liturgy and from Masses for the dead may be a departure from patristic precedent, but it also marks a deeper appropriation of the patristic teaching, a point to which we shall return later.

A more fundamental answer, however, is to be given to this question. As Augustine says in one of his sermons, *magnum sacramentum osculum pacis*—"the kiss of peace is a great mystery."[119] This being the case, it is impossible to give equal weight to all of its different dimensions at the same time and in the same way. It is appropriate, therefore, that one particular meaning should serve, at least in the practical context of the liturgy, as an ordering principle for the others, not in order to suppress the subalternated meanings but in order to organize and relate them to each other. Note, for instance, that regarding the kiss as a paschal moment does not preclude the teaching of the Sermon on the Mount about reconciliation, for John 20 also treats the theme of forgiveness. Nor is seeing the kiss as a "seal" or consummation of prayer, as in Tertullian and Innocent I, contradictory to viewing it as a preparation for Holy Communion; for as Alcuin (735–804) explains, "the peace of Christ, which has no end, is the completion of every pious act"[120] as well as an apt act of preparation. Further, it is

---

116   See William Durandus, *Rationale divinorum officiorum* 4,53,1–7 (CCCM 140:543–545).

117   Peter the Chanter, *Verbum abbreviatum* 29 and 110 (PL 205:104 and 294).

118   Ibid. 50 (PL 205:158).

119   Augustine, *Sermo* 6,3 (PL 46:836).

120   Alcuin, *De divinis officiis* 40 (PL 101:1270; the author is listed as uncertain).

appropriate that different quarters of Christendom should elect to have a different architectonic principle and thereby highlight a different aspect of the same *sacramentum*. Indeed, it is from the various practices of the apostolic churches, living in the healthy diversity of Pentecost morning, that the greatness of the mystery of the holy kiss is more fully fathomed.[121]

A Roman Theology

We are now in a position to summarize the uniquely Roman theology of the kiss of peace that has both followed from and affected its gradual development. In the beginning, God kissed Adam, breathing in him the spirit of life, and placed him in a garden of peace. That peace was broken by acquiescence to the serpent, which may be understood as a sort of satanic mockery of the kiss of peace: rather than peace flowing from God to the man to the woman to the beasts, rebellion proceeded from the beast to the woman and from the woman to the man, the forbidden fruit functioning as a kind of demonic pax-brede. So God kissed the world again through the Incarnation of his Son: as Peter the Chanter puts it, the Word assuming human nature is like the mouth that is kissing (*os osculans*) while the human nature being assumed is like the mouth that is being kissed (*os osculatum*).[122] From this results a new and successful alloy of peace (*electrum effectivum pacis*) between God and mankind in the person of Christ Jesus.

The ancient serpent, however, tried to destroy this peace as well with a similar ploy as before in the Garden of Gethsemane; he enters that garden through Judas, who was filled with Satan (Lk 22:3). Judas' kiss was literally an act of betrayal but it can also be read as an allegory of Judas' trying to exhale the evil spirit into Christ. But Jesus Christ, the new Adam, refuses it; instead he holds his breath, as it were, until the moment of his death, when he gives up his spirit (*expiravit*) (Lk 23:46). On Easter Sunday his spirit

---

121   If this is true, however, then it entails a duty to preserve a distinctive tradition rather than abandon it for another.

122   Peter the Chanter, *Verbum abbreviatum* 110 (PL 205:294).

returns to his broken body, and the risen Christ shares his Holy Spirit with the apostles through a kiss-like insufflation (Jn 20:22). It is that kiss that all united Christians share until God breathes his Spirit into the bodies of the dead at the end of time.

And it is that very kiss which is eventually enshrined in the Roman Mass after the consecration and the commingling of species. Rather than nullify any of the meanings attached to the *pax* by the Church fathers, this placement establishes the Paschal Mystery as the center to which its other meanings relate as so many radii. The kiss interpreted primarily in light of the Paschal Mystery is essentially Johannine, based as it is on John 20:21–22, but it also echoes Luke's account of the disciples on the road to Emmaus and Gideon's sacrifice to the Lord God.

THE LATE MIDDLE AGES AND THE TRIDENTINE ERA

The kiss of peace continued to retain its relevance and multi-valent significance throughout that "culture of gestures" known as the Middle Ages.[123] Outside the liturgy, the kiss performed a wide array of social functions, such as bestowing knighthood, acknowledging feudal loyalties, sealing contracts and agreements, and, perhaps most importantly, brokering peace. Kiril Petrov has catalogued the astonishing extent to which the non-liturgical holy kiss was used in public peacemaking, in private acts of reconciliation between two warring parties known as "love days,"[124] and in contract law; he has also explored how these conventions went on to influence social ties and patterns of behavior. Willem Frijhoff, somewhat tongue-in-cheek, speaks of "the kissing-eager Middle Ages,"[125] yet this eagerness, it should be noted, was owed in part to the precedent set by the Church's liturgical life. As Jean-Claude Schmitt remarks, "everyone [in the Middle Ages] belonged to an

---

123   Schmitt, "The Rationale of Gestures in the West," 59.

124   See Josephine Waters Bennett, "The Mediaeval Loveday," in *Speculum* 33 (1958) 351–370.

125   Frijhoff, "The Kiss Sacred and Profane," 213.

ordo, a word with a non-coincidental reference to the ritual *ordines* of liturgy" (61). Specifically, the gestures of the liturgical *ordo* informed those of the civil and social orders.

Inside the liturgy, paschal dimensions of the kiss incorporated the themes of love, unity, spirit, forgiveness, sincerity, peace and, above all, Christ himself. It continued to be a contact of lips between members of the same sex after the fraction and before communion, and it continued to be an intimate act for only those who were in good spiritual standing. Indeed, as the reception of Holy Communion became less frequent in the Middle Ages, the kiss's various spiritual meanings and value were cherished all the more.

Starting in the mid–1200s, however, the kiss began to fall into disuse both inside and outside the Church, although no one is certain why. Theories, of course, abound, including the claim that it was an unintended casualty of the Church's renewed rejection of homosexual activity. We do know, however, that at this time in some places the Church tried to sustain the rite of peace by substituting for the liturgical kiss a wooden or gilt tablet called a "pax-brede," "pax-boarde," or *instrumentum pacis*. This object, similar in appearance to a communion-plate, would be kissed by the priest, then the ministers, and then the laity, in order of rank. Eventually, perhaps because of disputes within the congregation over who outranked whom, the use of the pax-brede was restricted to only the most notable dignitaries present.[126]

The traditional kiss, however, was never abrogated, although it became limited to the priest and his ministers in the sanctuary and was not extended to the Low Mass or the *Missa cantata*. And, some time in the Middle Ages, the kiss underwent a gradual modification, becoming, in a certain sense, less like a kiss. By the time that Pope St. Pius V (r. 1566–1572) codified the *Missale Romanum* in 1570, labial contact had ceased to be a part of the rite. The giver

---

126   In the rubrics of the 1962 Missal, the pax-brede is limited to "lay persons of high rank;" see John Berthram O'Connell, *The Celebration of Mass*, 4th ed. (Milwaukee: Bruce Publishing Co., 1964) 430.

of the peace bowed to the recipient and placed his hands on the other's shoulders. He leaned forward towards the recipient's left cheek and said "Pax tecum," to which the recipient replied, "Et cum spiritu tuo." The rubrics actually state that the cheeks of the giver and recipient should "lightly touch," though rubricians interpreted this as "a moral, not a physical touch;"[127] hence no cheek-to-cheek contact was necessary.

While the Tridentine kiss may seem rather rarified (it has been described as "stilted," "somewhat ceremonious,"[128] and "some curious species of shadow-boxing"[129]), it nevertheless maintains the basic phenomenology of a kiss at the same time that it circumvents all of a kiss's potential drawbacks, such as the moral dangers that we noted earlier of men and women passing the peace with their lips touching or the recurring concern of the Church, not without good reason, for physical hygiene and contagion. Indeed, the word "accolade," which originally could be either an embrace or a kiss marking the bestowal of knighthood, comes from the Latin *ad collum*, to the neck,[130] because the act of "falling on" someone's neck betokens a kiss. Luke, for example, writes that the father of the prodigal son ran out of his house and "fell upon his [son's] neck and kissed him" (Lk 15:20).[131] Perella, after analyzing the writings of the Church fathers, concludes that they "plainly indicate that whatever form the Christian holy kiss was taking—for example, an embrace and a light cheek-to-cheek press—the notion behind it implied mouth-to-mouth contact."[132] This is important, for in preserving the outline of a kiss, the Roman rite of peace was still able to evince the rich scriptural, patristic, and medieval traditions from which it was derived.

---

127   Ibid., 499, n. 11. The rubrics are to be found in the *Caeremoniale Episco-porum* II,viii,75.

128   Woolfenden, "Let us offer," 239.

129   "Liturgical Briefs," in *Orate Fratres* 16 (1942) 177–185, at 181.

130   See *The Oxford English Dictionary*, 2nd ed. (Oxford: Clarendon Press, 1989) s.v. "Accolade," and "Accoll."

131   See Gen 33:4; Tob 7:7; Acts 20:37.

132   Perella, *The Kiss Sacred and Profane*, 27.

Moreover, the Tridentine accolade, as I will call it to distinguish it from labial kissing, preserved an already centuries-old tradition of ordered administration. In the traditional form of the Roman Rite the priest kisses the altar near where the sacred host lies (earlier rubrics have him kissing the host itself or the lip of the chalice) and then "kisses" the deacon who in turn "kisses" the subdeacon and so on. No one can give the peace who has not received it from someone else, including the priest, who has received it from Christ himself. The symbolism is both beautiful and clear. All true peace comes from Christ through the ministration of his Church. Grace cascades from the Eucharistic sacrifice through Christ's ministers to his people, forming what several Western rites aptly called a "chain of peace and charity" that both binds together and elevates.[133]

The hierarchical distribution of the kiss of peace thus reinforces a central truth of Christianity, that it is not by the will of the flesh nor by the will of men but by God alone that we become part of his Mystical Body (Jn 1:13). This is reinforced in the protocols governing the ritual. Although it is common in the Tridentine form of the rite to bow to one's ecclesiastical superior at incensations and similar moments, one does not acknowledge the rank of the giver of the peace before it is administered, for, as the *Caeremoniale Episcoporum* puts it, "there is consideration not for the minister bringing it but for the Peace [itself], which is conveyed to him from the Sacrifice of the altar."[134] The giver of the peace, in other words, represents not himself but Christ, for the peace that he gives *is* Christ (see Eph 2:19).

---

133   Along with the "Pax Domini sit semper vobiscum," several medieval missals include the blessing: "Habete vinculum pacis et caritatis, ut apti sitis sacrosanctis mysteriis;" see Jungmann, *The Mass of the Roman Rite*, vol. 2, 332, n. 61.

134   *Caeremoniale Episcoporum* I,xxix,8: "Quia ante non habetur consideratio ipsius ministri deferentis, sed Pacis, quae a Sacrificio altaris ad illum defertur."

THE TWENTIETH CENTURY

As a result of the Liturgical Movement of the nineteenth and twentieth centuries, there arose a growing desire to return the laity to a more vibrant participation in the *pax*.[135] Authors who wished to see "a much more harmonious and communal spirit than now exists"[136] looked to the rite of peace as a means of "breaking down . . . isolated individual worship"[137] and of recalling "the social significance of the Sacrament."[138] Some indulged in rhetorical exaggeration, ominously claiming that the kiss of peace "was the last expression left of Christian fellowship at the Lord's Supper" and that "we have done all we could [to suppress] all demonstrations of brotherly love" since "the beginning of Christ's religion."[139] Occasionally an author would recommend the use of several small crosses or "pax tablets,"[140] but more often than not the handshake was deemed an acceptable substitute for the antiquated and potentially prurient kiss and the Tridentine accolade, with honorable mention made of the double hand-clasping of the Malankarese rite.[141] However, it was generally envisioned that the handshake would take place within a hieratic framework. One author conjectured that the servers could receive the *pax* from the priest, "go down the center aisle rapidly, and be back at the altar in ample time for the preparation of Holy Communion."[142] Potential draw-

---

135   The liturgical congresses at Maria Laach (1951), Mont Saint-Odile (1952), and Lugano (1953) resolved to "find a way to have the congregation participate in the Pax." Hans Ansgar Reinhold, *Bringing the Mass to the People* (Baltimore: Helicon, 1960) 105.

136   Thomas E. Cassidy, "A Modern 'Kiss of Peace'?" in *Orate Fratres* 14 (1940) 283–284, at 283.

137   Ibid.

138   "Liturgical Briefs," 181.

139   Walter Lowrie, "The Kiss of Peace: A Declaration of *Koinonia*," in *Theology Today* 12 (1955) 236–242, at 236, 237.

140   See Reinhold, *Bringing the Mass to the People*, 96–97.

141   "Liturgical Briefs," 181.

142   Cassidy, "A Modern 'Kiss of Peace'?" 284. See Lowrie, "The Kiss of Peace," 240.

backs were rarely mentioned, and if they were, it was to minimize their danger. "No harm could be done by trying it," opined Thomas Cassidy, "and the only trouble caused would be the slight confusion in starting the observance which is so strange to us."[143] Indeed, several parts of Europe in the 1930s were already attempting to revive the practice.[144]

Moreover, the prominent liturgical scholar Josef Andreas Jungmann, whose authority would carry much weight before, during, and immediately after Vatican II, expressed dissatisfaction with the state of the fraction, commingling, and peace in the 1570 Missal. Ever since the disappearance of the *fermentum*, the rite, he claimed, "has lost some of its significance." Jungmann makes this judgment on the assumption that the *tituli* churches had a complete Eucharistic liturgy of which the *fermentum* was a part, but this has since been called into question, as has the meaning of the *Haec commixtio* presumed by Jungmann.[145] Jungmann also laments "the later contraction and compression" of the fraction and commingling, although it is difficult to see how things would have developed differently after the *sancta* and the *fermentum* were dropped and the large loaves of bread, which necessitated a lengthy fraction, were replaced by small individual hosts.

Jungmann also states that the "rite has hardly any purpose at all, since it is perceptible only to those close to the altar."[146] Curiously, he does not mention the rite's aural cues, such as the iteration of the *Pax Domini*, that would alert the congregation to what is transpiring. Nor does he address the way in which the rite's "imperceptibility" might enhance its symbolic meaning. If the purpose of the commingling, for instance, is to betoken the resurrection (an event that was not witnessed by human eyes), then "hiding it" would actually constitute a more powerful symbol. This, of course,

---

143   Cassidy, "A Modern 'Kiss of Peace'?" 284.

144   See Pius Parsch, *Volksliturgie: Ihr Sinn und Umfang* (Klosterneuburg: Volksliturgischer Verlag, 1940) 18, 224.

145   See Paul Bradshaw, "The Genius of the Roman Rite Revisited," 60–61; Baldovin, "The *Fermentum* at Rome in the Fifth Century," 38–53.

146   Jungmann, *The Mass of the Roman Rite*, vol. 2, 321.

presupposes the value of symbolic meaning, but I submit that since the fraction and commingling have had no practical value for one thousand years, symbolic meaning is all that we have left.

Finally, Jungmann speculates that the hierarchical passing of the *pax* from person to person would have entailed "disturbance and confusion"—unlike, he conjectures, when it was "merely exchanged between neighbors."[147] Forty years of experience, however, have shown otherwise.

Throughout this period of scholarship, the pneumatological and paschal dimensions of the *pax* were generally ignored or, if they were acknowledged, dismissed as groundless "allegorizing."[148] Many liturgical scholars, in a drive to disambiguate Christian emblems and deeds and to return the Church to a more primitive and pristine condition, had contradistinguished "symbol" and "allegory," extolling the former and condemning the latter.[149] Whether this divorce of the two is actually consistent with the New Testament and early Christian writings is debatable, especially in the light of the patristic understanding of *sacramentum* or *mysterium*. In any event, the first scholarly, systematic study of the symbolism of the kiss that could have challenged such a contention, James Perella's aforementioned *Kiss Sacred and Profane*, was not published until 1969, by which point the *Novus Ordo Missae* was already in its final stages.[150]

---

147   Ibid., vol. 2, 326.

148   Twentieth-century liturgiology tends to contrast patristic and medieval models of worship. Kenneth Stevenson, for instance, differentiates the "unitive piety" of the early Church with the "representational piety" of the medieval Church, favoring the former and criticizing the latter; see *Jerusalem Revisited: The Liturgical Meaning of Holy Week* (Washington, DC: Pastoral Press, 1988) 9–10. Because the idea that the Mass is somehow a "re-enactment" or mimesis of the passion is frowned upon today, allegorical interpretations of liturgical rituals are approached with heightened suspicion.

149   See Crispino Valenziano, "Liturgy and Symbolism," in *Handbook for Liturgical Studies, Vol. 2: Fundamental Liturgy*, ed. Anscar J. Chupungco (Collegeville, MN: Liturgical Press, 1998) 29–44, at 32; Reinhold, *Bringing the Mass to the People*, 75, nn. 2 and 3.

150   Twentieth-century liturgists may also have been eager to simplify the meaning of the peace on the assumption that its allegorical potency was allowing the

The Rite of Peace in the Pauline Missal

The Second Vatican Council's Constitution on the Sacred Liturgy *Sacrosanctum Concilium* does not mention the kiss of peace, let alone call for its restoration, although it does robustly affirm the Mass as "a sacrament of love, a sign of unity, a bond of charity, a paschal banquet,"[151] characterizations which elide well with what became the Roman Rite's paschal understanding of the *pax*.

In addition to significantly increasing its use,[152] the *Missale Romanum* of 1970 mandated a number of alterations to the *pax*. First, a new location, between the *Pax Domini sit semper vobiscum* and the *fractio panis*, was assigned. This restores the order that is given in the older Roman *ordines*, yet it should be recalled that this order was shaped by the use of the *fermentum*, the *sancta*, and the time-consuming breaking of consecrated loaves. Significantly, Roman liturgies that did not have the *fermentum* and *sancta*, that is, the non-papal, non-stational liturgies in Rome, were known to place the fraction *before* the *Pax Domini* and kiss of peace.[153] There-

---

kiss to be used as a substitute for the reception of Holy Communion; see Robert Cabié, "Le rite de la paix," in *Les combats de la paix: Mélanges offerts à Réné Coste*, ed. Pierre Colombani (Toulouse: Bayard, 1996) 47–71, at 65. These scholars, following their medieval counterparts, may have overestimated the frequency of Holy Communion in the patristic era and hence set up a false dichotomy. As John Baldovin writes, "It may be necessary to revise our romantic notions of a time when the eucharist enjoyed a kind of organic integrity. It may be that not many baptized Christians at all ever participated regularly in holy communion—at least not until the encouragement of frequent communion by Pope Pius X at the beginning of the twentieth century." "The *Fermentum* at Rome in the Fifth Century," 52–53.

151   Second Vatican Council, Constitution on the Sacred Liturgy *Sacrosanctum Concilium* (4 December 1963) no. 47.

152   As mentioned at the beginning of the article, the *Missale Romanum* of 1970 stipulates that the rite of peace should take place *pro opportunitate*—when it is appropriate. Some liturgists, however, argue that this rubric applies only to the text, "Offerte vobis pacem," and that the gesture itself "is *always* to be exchanged among the faithful as part of the communion rites at every Eucharist." Jan Michael Joncas, "Musical Elements in the *Ordo Missae* of Paul VI," in *Handbook for Liturgical Studies, Vol. 3: The Eucharist*, ed. Anscar J. Chupungco (Collegeville, MN: Liturgical Press, 1999) 209–244, at 236, emphasis in the original.

153   See Jungmann, *The Mass of the Roman Rite*, vol. 2, 309, n. 34.

fore, had the location of the kiss in the *Missale Romanum* of 1570 been maintained, it would have retained an ancient patristic practice, one that had not "suffered from the intrusion of anything out of harmony with the inner nature of the liturgy."[154]

Regarding the current location, whereas Eleanor Kreider sees in it a "clearing up" of "medieval confusion and incoherence,"[155] Graham Woolfenden concludes that the arrangement makes "it more difficult for a congregation to relate the Eucharistic Prayer to the receiving of Communion."[156] "So many words are [now said aloud] and so much action takes place," Woolfenden explains, "that it is difficult to sustain any level of interest that has been built up in the Eucharistic Prayer."[157] Neither author mentions, however, a more fundamental complication: that placing the kiss before the fraction and before the commingling blurs and confuses the figurative significance of this part of the liturgy. According to the *Instrumentum laboris* of the 2005 Synod, the *fractio panis* still "denotes the Body of Christ broken for us;"[158] similarly, the commingling is still a *typos* or *figura* of the resurrection (the synod's *lineamentum* on the commingling ends with the exclamation "Now Christ is risen!").[159] Consequently, under the current arrangement, the sign of the risen Christ's peace is now being

---

154   *Sacrosanctum Concilium*, no. 21.

155   Kreider, "Let the Faithful Greet Each Other," 48.

156   Woolfenden, "Let us offer," 242.

157   Ibid. Woolfenden in particular finds redundant the prayer, "Lord, Jesus Christ," which was kept at the insistence of Pope Paul VI (ibid., 249).

158   2005 Synod, *Instrumentum laboris*, no. 50, available at http://www.vatican.va/roman_curia/synod/documents/rc_synod_doc_20050707_instrlabor-xi-assembly_en.html.

159   2005 Synod, *Lineamenta*, no. 42, available at http://www.vatican.va/roman_curia/synod/documents/rc_synod_doc_20040528_lineamenta-xi-assembly_en.html. The revised General Instruction of the Roman Missal (Institutio Generalis Missalis Romani [henceforth: IGMR]) 2002, no. 83 explains the commingling as the unity of "the living and glorious Body of Jesus Christ" ("ad significandam unitatem. . . . Corporis Christi Iesu viventis et gloriosi"). For a comparison of the different editions of the IGMR, see Maurizio Barba, *Institutio Generalis Missalis Romani: Textus, Synopsis, Variationes*, Monumenta Studia Instrumenta Liturgica 45 (Vatican City: Libreria Editrice Vaticana, 2006).

exchanged *before* the sign that Christ is risen from the dead; the people of God are savoring the joys of the resurrection while Christ still lies mystically suffering and dying on the altar.[160] *Sacrosanctum Concilium* stipulates that the liturgy should be restored in such a way that its texts and rites "express more clearly the holy things which they signify.[161] The rite of peace in the *Missale Romanum* of 1970 does not meet this standard; it obfuscates the paschal meaning of the *pax* by placing a sign of Christ's joyful resurrection immediately before a sign of his dolorous death.

The economy of the *pax* itself is also different in the renewed Missal. The priest or deacon is instructed to turn to the people and say, "Offerte vobis pacem" ("Offer one another the peace"). According to the rubrics, the following then happens: "And all signify to each other peace and charity, in accordance with local custom. The priest gives the peace to the deacon or server."[162] The imperative that is new to the Roman liturgy, "Offerte vobis pacem," is redolent of the pre-anaphoral "Offerte nobis pacem" of the Ambrosian rite, which also contains a rubric instructing the priest to say to the server while giving him the *pax*: "Habete vinculum pacis et caritatis ut apti sitis sacrosanctis mysteriis Dei" ("Take hold of the chain of peace and charity, that you [plural] might be fit for the sacred mysteries of God"). But by not having

---

160   If St Thomas's interpretative framework is maintained (which can be justified in light of the paschal interpretation of the commingling in IGMR 2002, no. 83), the congregation is spending several moments offering each other the peace and joy of the Pasch while the two species remain separated on the altar in sorrowful commemoration of Christ's agony and death. In the *Missale Romanum* of 1962 the statement that evokes Christ's signature greeting on the day of his resurrection, "Pax Domini sit semper vobiscum," also takes place before the commingling, but it is also being said while the priest makes the preliminary action of the commingling, the three signs of the cross with the Particle over the Chalice. Hence the *Pax Domini* functions as a prolepsis that strengthens rather than dilutes the paschal significance of the sacramental reuniting of the Body and Blood.

161   *Sacrosanctum Concilium*, no. 21.

162   *Missale Romanum* 1970, no. 129 (p. 473): "Et omnes, iuxta locorum consuetudines, pacem et caritatem sibi invicem significant; sacerdos pacem dat diacono vel ministro."

this latter rubric and mentioning the priest's actions after those of the people, the new Mass does not presuppose a tangible causal relation between the peace announced by the celebrant and that which is exchanged by the congregation: instead of a hierarchical cascading of peace from the altar of the risen Lord, an exchange of peace occurs simultaneously in the pews.[163]

Even aside from the emotional excesses that, according to Pope Benedict XVI, have tended to come from this arrangement, it again becomes more difficult to trace the connection between the risen Christ in the Eucharist and the peace he diffuses through and to his Church, for there is no longer a demonstrative link, a conspicuous "chain of peace and charity," binding together the Eucharistic offering, altar, ministers, and faithful.[164] Visually and performatively, the vertical mediation of Christ's peace has been replaced by a horizontal immediacy. In the light of this phenomenon, it is not surprising that contemporary liturgical theology tends instead to place weight on the conciliatory function of the peace,[165] thereby conflating the two traditions or discarding its

---

163   IGMR 2002 shows some sense of hierarchy by stipulating that the deacon is to receive the peace from the priest (no. 181), but no mention is made from where the priest obtains the peace. He does not, as in former ages, kiss the host, the lip of the chalice, or the corporal before giving the peace. Further, no. 239, which deals with concelebration, states that the concelebrants give the peace to each other; they do not need to receive it from the principal celebrant if they are not close to him or wait for someone who has received the peace from him.

164   More recent documents, solicitous of maintaining a greater sense of propriety, limit the exchange of peace to one's immediate neighbors and forbid the celebrant from leaving the sanctuary. See IGMR 2002, nos. 82, and 154; also *Sacramentum Caritatis*, no. 49. Nevertheless, restrained simultaneity is not the equivalent of hieratic nexus.

165   See 2005 Synod, *Instrumentum laboris*, no. 50; *Sacramentum Caritatis*, no. 49, n. 150; National Conference of Catholic Bishops, *The Challenge of Peace: God's Promise and Our Response, A Pastoral Letter on War and Peace* (3 May 1983) no. 295, available at http://www.usccb.org/upload/challenge-peace-gods-promise-our-response-1983.pdf; Harbert, "The Church, the Kingdom and the English Mass," 6; Kreider, "Let the Faithful Greet Each Other;" Cochran, "Passing the Peace, Restoring Relationships," 18–19; David Abrahamson, "Making the Ordinary Extraordinary," in *Lutheran Forum* 21 (1987) 26–30, at 30; Sarah Mitchell, "Piecing Together: The Pax as Reconciling Sign for the New Church," in *Worship* 77 (2006) 237–250.

paschal implications, even though the 2004 Instruction *Redemptionis Sacramentum* defends the Roman practice of the peace by stating explicitly:

> According to the tradition of the Roman Rite, this practice does not have the connotation either of reconciliation or of a remission of sins, but instead signifies peace, communion and charity before the reception of the Most Holy Eucharist.[166]

The lack of hierarchical movement in the renewed Missal's rite of peace has been enthusiastically welcomed by scholars who see it as a return to a more primitive—and hence wholesome—practice. Robert Cabié laments that with the first historical mention of the kiss occurring *per ordinem*, "the expression of brotherhood is on its way to losing the character of equality."[167] Cabié does not deny the hierarchical character of the assembly, but he seems uncomfortable with it, as is evident by his putting "hierarchical" in quotation marks.[168] And he is quick to characterize the "excessive ritualization" of the traditional kiss as "a devaluing of the primitive usage."[169]

Yet Cabié appears unaware of the fact that the same "primitive" era serving as his *aliquid quod maxime est* saw no contradiction between hierarchy and the equalizing quality of the *pax*. Chrysostom, whom we cited earlier commending the kiss as a social leveler, states in the same passage that the kiss drives away resentment between the lowly and the great, not that it eliminates the difference between them.[170] Theodore of Mopsuestia (350–428) regards

---

166   Congregation for Divine Worship and Discipline of the Sacraments, Instruction on Certain Matters to be Observed or to be Avoided Regarding the Most Holy Eucharist *Redemptionis Sacramentum* (25 March 2004) no. 71: "Iuxta enim traditionem Ritus romani hic usus notam habet nec reconciliationis nec peccatorum remissionis, sed potius pacis, communionis et caritatis ante sanctissimae Eucharistiae receptionem significandae." The instruction goes on to state that it is the penitential rite at the beginning of Mass which denotes fraternal reconciliation.

167   Cabié, "Le rite de la paix," 63–64.

168   Ibid., 66.

169   Ibid.

170   John Chrysostom, *In Ep. ad Rom.* 21,4 (PG 60:671).

the laity's kiss as an act of obedience to clerical hierarchy that makes possible reconciliation with each other.[171] Instead of presaging the assumption of Jean-Jacques Rousseau (1712–1778) in his *Second Discourse* that inequality is essentially synonymous with injustice and oppression, the early Church understood hierarchy as a great and sacred chain of being that elevates and joins, lifting up the downtrodden and compelling the mighty to be responsive to them. When animated by love, a hierarchy becomes, as Pseudo-Dionysius teaches, the conduit for "a unifying and co-mingling power which moves the superior to provide for the subordinate, peer to be in communion with peer, and subordinate to return to the superior and the outstanding."[172] "The goal of a hierarchy," he concludes, "is to enable beings to be as like as possible to God and to be at one with him."[173] True hierarchy, a word coined by Pseudo-Dionysius, is a ladder to, rather than a ceiling obstructing, human solidarity and holiness.

Multiplication of Meanings

Further, with the contemporary displacement of the paschal meaning of the *pax* has come a tendency to ascribe or call for the ascription of new meanings to the kiss of peace. The bishops of the United States define the rite of peace not only as "an authentic sign of our reconciliation with God and with one another," in contradiction of *Redemptionis Sacramentum*, no. 71, but as "a visible expression of our commitment to work for peace as a Christian community."[174] Judging from the context of the document, the "peace" mentioned here is not the peace "which the world cannot give," the peace unique to the City of God, but the civic and social peace of our local communities. Christians, of course, as Augustine famously reminds them in the *De civitate Dei*, are committed to

---

171   Theodore of Mopsuestia, *On Eucharist and Liturgy* 5 (ed. Mingana, 230–232).

172   Ps.-Dionysius, *De divinis nominibus* 4,15 (PG 3:713), trans. Luibheid, 83.

173   Ps.-Dionysius, *De caelesti hierarchia* 3,2 (PG 3:165), trans. Luibheid, 154.

174   *The Challenge for Peace*, no. 295.

the latter peace as well as to the former, but whether this is the meaning of the kiss in the sacred liturgy, East or West, is another matter.

The American bishops, however, may be said to be accurately drawing out implications from the General Instruction of the Roman Missal. Despite variations in wording, all three typical editions of the General Instruction describe the rite of peace as an imploration of peace and unity for the Church *and* for the whole human family.[175] As my added emphasis is meant to show, it is the inclusion of the latter group that is curious, since the prayer linked to the rite of peace, the *Domine Iesu Christe*, mentions peace and unity for the Church but not for humanity as a whole, and the scriptural verse which inspires it contrasts the peace which Christ alone gives to the peace which the world provides (Jn 14:27). There is obviously nothing wrong with praying for all mankind: indeed, as Pope Benedict XVI points out, "the Church has become increasingly conscious of her responsibility to pray insistently for the gift of peace and unity for herself and for the whole human family."[176] Yet the question again remaining is whether the liturgical *pax*, formed in the crucible of family identity, is meant to discharge such a responsibility. On the one hand, this novel interpretation of the *pax*, even though it is not justified by the prayer texts, expands the wishes of peace in a heartfelt and poignant way to all of humanity. By that very fact, on the other hand, it also unwittingly undermines the kiss of peace as an intimate and unique act of the Christian family.

The Question of Recipients

Similarly, while the General Instruction describes the rite as proper to the faithful (*fideles*), no mention is made of how heretics,

---

175   See IGMR 1970, no. 56b: ". . . quo fideles pacem et unitatem pro Ecclesia et universa hominum familia implorant." The slightly revised version of IGMR 2002, no. 82 reads: ". . . quo Ecclesia pacem et unitatem pro se ipsa et universa hominum familia implorat."

176   *Sacramentum Caritatis*, no. 49.

schismatics, unbelievers, or catechumens will be excluded from the peace or whether believers in a state of mortal sin should be excluded as they once were. The result is that the liturgical peace as it was so carefully developed in the patristic age, the age considered paramount or "golden" by Vatican II when undertaking liturgical revisions,[177] has been transformed from a preserve of the orthodox in a state of grace to a good indiscriminately exchanged between faithful and non-faithful. This may seem an insignificant detail or even a welcome development, especially in light of the Church's ecumenical aspirations, but it has the drawback of diluting the *pax*'s meaning. If the peace is a preparation for Holy Communion, why is it being extended to those who cannot receive Holy Communion? If it is a seal of the Eucharistic prayer, how can it be enacted by those who do not agree with the prayer or with the community professing it? If it is a sign of reconciliation, how can be it offered to those who are not reconciled with the see of Peter or with God? And if it is Christ himself, who is our peace, then how can this holy thing be given, to borrow his own startlingly blunt language, to dogs and swine (see Mt 7:6)?

Graham Woolfenden remarks that the kiss of peace is "a good thing in itself; it should not need to be used in a manipulative fashion for any other purpose, no matter how well-intentioned."[178] Others, following the trajectory opened by this new strain of interpretation, would strongly disagree. Sarah Mitchell, looking for "new beginnings in a church where meaning must be sought in the cracks and interstices of a tired liturgy,"[179] would like to see the *pax* become a conduit for not only social justice, but for hospitality, inclusivity, "becoming the other,"[180] and affirming "MAD-ness"—multiplicity, ambiguity, and diversity.[181] Mitchell welcomes the egalitarian and unstructured format of the contem-

---

177   See ibid., no. 50.
178   Woolfenden, "Let us offer," 251.
179   Mitchell, "Piecing Together," 240.
180   Ibid., 247.
181   Ibid., 248.

porary rite of peace, for it liberates believers, especially women, from the "difficulties of priestly dominance, discipline and control"[182] and allows the faithful to embrace chaos,[183] a necessary precondition for creativity.[184]

Shifts in Language

Another change to the peace in the Ordinary Form of the Roman Rite is the manner in which it is discussed. As noted earlier, the early Church consciously referred to the kiss of peace as "the peace," designating it not as a mere convention or construct but as an actualization or conferral of Christ himself. This usage is retained in the 1970 Missal's instruction "Offerte vobis pacem" and in some of the new rubrics,[185] but more often than not, it is replaced by the language of symbolism. The "rite of peace" (*ritus pacis*)[186] or "sign of peace" (*signum pacis*)[187] is used instead of "the peace" (*pax*), while the verbs *exprimere* (express)[188] and *significare* (signify)[189] are preferred to *dare* (give, bestow). In the approved English translations, this nomenclature is then applied to all other instances in which the peace is mentioned so that the residual references to the *pax simpliciter* are removed entirely in the vernacular. *Pacem dare*, for example, is translated as "giving a sign of peace" rather than "giving the peace,"[190] and the imperative in the Mass,

---

182   Ibid., 245.
183   Ibid., 247.
184   Ibid., 245.
185   See IGMR 2002, no. 154: "Sacerdos pacem potest dare ministris, semper tamen intra presbyterium remanens, ne celebratio turbetur. Item faciat si e rationabili causa aliquibus paucis fidelibus pacem dare velit. Omnes vero, iuxta ea quae a Conferentia Episcoporum statuta sunt, pacem, communionem et caritatem sibi invicem significant. Dum pax datur, dici potest: Pax Dómini sit semper tecum, cui respondetur: Amen." See also nos. 181 and 239.
186   See IGMR 1970, no. 56b; IGMR 2002, no. 82.
187   See IGMR 2002, no. 82.
188   See IGMR 1970, no. 56b; IGMR 2002, no. 82.
189   See IGMR 2002, no. 82; also *Redemptionis Sacramentum* 71.
190   See IGMR 2002, no. 154, and the translation in *The Roman Missal: Renewed by Decree of the Most Holy Second Ecumenical Council of the Vatican, Promul-*

"Offerte vobis pacem," is rendered, "Let us offer each other the sign of peace"[191] instead of "Offer to one another the peace."

There is, it must be stressed, nothing doctrinally erroneous in this linguistic shift, since Catholic theology distinguishes without divorcing a sign from its referent and understands signs as a "making present" of the signified. When, for example, a husband kisses his wife and means it, his kiss is both an indication and an instance of his love. Further, the term "sign of peace" is not a neologism but one that has roots in patristic and medieval writings.[192]

Yet the danger of understanding the peace primarily as a sign—particularly in an age that has ideologically closed itself off to a non-empiricist ontology of participation—is the loss of a sense of what Yeago calls "utter substantial realism," the fact that the kiss of peace is not simply an affirmation, demonstration, or celebration of the "peace and friendship that already exists among the congregation,"[193] but an increase or conferral of a divine peace that readies them, in this case, for the awesome act of receiving God sacramentally. A sense of this increase, this gift, is lost when the nomenclature of realism is completely superseded by a nomenclature of symbolism. And it is also lost when the *pax* is characterized predominantly as a petition or prayer for peace (the "not yet") or as a celebration of the "already here;" in both cases the kiss itself is demoted from agent to metaphor.[194] This demotion may be evinced in the liberal use of

---

gated by Authority of Pope Paul VI and Revised at the Direction of Pope John Paul II, English translation according to the third typical edition (Totowa, NJ: Catholic Book Publishing, 2011).

191   *Roman Missal* 2011, no. 128.

192   See Augustine, *Sermo* 207 (PL 38:1101). That said, the term is less frequent than *pax* or *osculum*. In *Sermo* 207 Augustine is characterizing the kiss as a sign of peace, not designating a new term: "Post ipsam dicitur, Pax vobiscum: et osculantur se Christiani in osculo sancto. Pacis signum est: sicut ostendunt labia, fiat in conscientia." For the medieval use of the term, see William Durandus, *Rationale divinorum officiorum* 4,53,1 (CCCM 140:543).

193   Harbert, "The Church, the Kingdom and the English Mass," 3. Harbert does, however, also speak of the rite's eschatological anticipation of the Kingdom of God.

194   It may be objected that referring to the *pax* as "the peace" instead of "the sign" or "rite" of peace is awkward in English and should therefore be avoided. This,

quotation marks by some contemporary liturgists when they describe the "giving [of] the *pax*" or the *pax*'s being "brought" from the altar to the people,[195] a use which implies skepticism about the reality of what the Fathers claimed was transpiring and which creates a critical and alienating distance between the modern worshipper and early Christian self-understanding.

This subtle demotion is at least potentially reinforced by describing the *pax* chiefly as an *expression* of mutual charity[196] or as an *exchange* of some sign of peace. While examples of both phrases, especially the latter, abound in patristic literature, they are apt to suggest to the modern mind that has not been properly nourished on sound metaphysics, or that harbors skepticism about the reality of immaterial being, a reciprocal transaction of pre-existing love or a peace generated between two or more parties rather than the new and adventitious reception of a gift over and above what each congregant currently has. Here, as in the previous cases, the important point remains to achieve a certain balance in terminology which suitably reflects the reality of what is transpiring.

Finally, the occasional designation of the peace as a "greeting"[197] restores to some degree the language of the New Testament but without Paul's strongly implied pneumatology to guide its appropriation or without having taken into consideration the *non*-liturgical context of its original usage. "Greeting"—as opposed to the more archaic (and hence less colloquial) "salutation"—also has an informal, casual connotation in contemporary English,

---

however, may be precisely why it is so useful. Its jarring and peculiar quality alerts the reader or listener to the fact that this act within the sacred liturgy is not ordinary but distinctive and unusual. This may even explain why the Latin and Greek Fathers chose to adopt the unusual usage in the first place.

195   See Robert Cabié, *The Church at Prayer: An Introduction to the Liturgy. Vol. 2: The Eucharist*, trans. Matthew J. O'Connell (Collegeville, MN: Liturgical Press, 1986) 165; Joncas, "Musical Elements in the *Ordo Missae* of Paul VI," 236.

196   See IGMR 1970, no. 56b; IGMR 2002, no. 82. The 2005 Synod goes so far as to describe this not as "mutua caritas" but "mutuus amor" (*Lineamenta*, no. 42).

197   See 2005 Synod, *Lineamenta*, no. 42: "oblatio vel salutatio pacis." "He gives the greeting of peace" is the official (and reasonable) English translation of "pacem annuntiat" from IGMR 2002, no. 154.

which could, if not nuanced properly by magisterial and pastoral instruction, serve to obfuscate the great sacramental mystery of the *pax*[198] by replacing it with a chipper, shallow disposition. In other words, a disproportionate emphasis on the concept of greeting, at least in the context of a deformalized and egalitarian age, can easily engender the kind of amiable and insouciant distortions that the pope and the synod lament.

Local Custom

Another significant change to the new rite of peace is the decision to let its specific form be guided by local custom.[199] The General Instruction stipulates that this gesture is to be established by the conferences of bishops.[200] *Redemptionis Sacramentum* adds that the bishops' decision must receive the *recognitio* of the Holy See.[201] No episcopal conference to my knowledge, however, has ever made such a determination or sought such a *recognitio*.

The result, as one would expect given the diversity of local customs worldwide, has been varied. The Tridentine accolade survives in some religious orders and papal liturgies, albeit in a modified and unstructured form impishly described by a former rector of the English College in Rome as a "sort of bear-hug" while "grinning like Cheshire cats."[202] The Missionaries of Charity, adapting a custom common in Indian culture, fold their hands and bow gracefully to each other in silence. One unforeseen consequence of this rubric, especially when coupled by a lack of specific guidance from the episcopate, is that some of the abuses bewailed by Clement of Alexandria have resurfaced after over 1,800 years. I have personally seen osculatory signs of peace between couples that have not only left me ill-prepared for the *Panis angelicus* but for earthly sustenance as well.

198   See Augustine, *Sermo* 207 (PL 38:1101).
199   *Missale Romanum* 1970, no. 129 (p. 473): "iuxta locorum consuetudines."
200   IGMR 1970, no. 56, and IGMR 2002, no. 82.
201   *Redemptionis Sacramentum*, no. 72.
202   See Woolfenden, "Let us offer," 239.

For most of the West, however, it is the handshake that has come to dominate. As a recognizable sign of peace, this is not an unreasonable choice. The right hand is the hand that bears arms, and so an extended and empty right hand signifies, for the moment at least, an absence or cessation of hostility.[203] It is easy to see how the handshake became a popular gesture for greeting and departing in social circles, especially in democratic societies that eschew gestures of rank or subservience.[204] And it is easy to see how a handshake came to signify the ratification of a contract or agreement in the world of business and politics. One sees this even in the New Testament: after acknowledging Paul's *bona fides*, the apostles Peter, James, and John offered him and Barnabas the "right hands of fellowship" as a way of ratifying their decision that the latter "should go unto the Gentiles" and the former "unto the [people of the] circumcision" (Gal 2:9).[205]

Yet it is precisely the meaning of the handshake in these spheres that calls into question its suitability as a token for the peace that is Christ. Shaking hands is a sign not of eternal but of temporal peace, or more properly, of a truce: it is tailored for transactions in the city of man, not worship in the city of God. For although a handshake may indeed signify a union of wills or genuine friendship, it is not first and foremost a sign of love or intimacy, and thus it is less capable of expressing the charity that the Holy Spirit pours forth into our hearts.

Further, even if it were chiefly a sign of love, because a handshake is not a kiss or even, as in the case of the Tridentine accolade, the cousin of a kiss, its liturgical use nevertheless marks a break with a previously unbroken apostolic custom. The ongoing wit-

---

203   This is a biblical presumption as well. Had the guards of Eglon, the king of Moab, searched the ambidextrous Hebrew assassin Aod before his audience with their lord, they would not have thought of checking his right thigh, where Aod had strapped the dagger that he would plunge into Eglon's stomach (Judg 3:15–22).

204   Bowing and doffing one's hat before one's superior, for example, stands in sharp contrast to the egalitarian shaking of hands.

205   Similarly, the rite of marriage, borrowing from Roman law, still has the *dextrarum iunctio* as a sign that a binding contract or covenant is being freely made.

ness of the Eastern churches serves as an important reminder of the irreplaceable significance of the holy kiss to living tradition. When Pope Benedict XVI and Ecumenical Patriarch Bartholomew I met at Rome for the Feast of the Sts. Peter and Paul in 2008, they framed their meeting in terms of the practice and meaning of the kiss. After the pope's welcoming address, in which he expressed his "joy of once again having the happy opportunity of exchanging the kiss of peace with" the patriarch, Bartholomew described the traditional Byzantine icon of Sts. Peter and Paul, in which the two are shown kissing. He then went on to say: "It is indeed this kiss that we have come to exchange with you, Your Holiness, emphasizing the ardent desire and love in Christ, things which are closely related to each other."[206] The year before in another part of the world, the unity of an ancient church had even been restored with a holy kiss. When the Patriarch of Moscow, Alexy II, head of the Russian Orthodox Church, signed an agreement with Metropolitan Laurus, head of the Russian Orthodox Church Outside of Russia (the branch that had broken off when the mother church failed to oppose the communist government of the Soviet Union), "the two elderly, bearded clerics in sparkling headgear" sealed their rapprochement by bending "to kiss each other's cheeks." When this occurred, "worshippers crossed themselves and shed tears," an indication that the power of the kiss of peace is not lost on a modern audience.[207]

More specifically, the abandonment of an apostolic custom is a serious matter not because it violates a nostalgic antiquarianism, but because it more often than not alienates us from the rich cluster of denotations and connotations that came with that custom. Regarding the *pax*, David Yeago is right when he asserts:

> It is not true that the handshake is our cultural equivalent to the ancient kiss of greeting. We have no equivalent in our culture

206   *Patriarch's Homily for Feast of Sts. Peter and Paul, With Benedict XVI's Introduction* (30 June 2008), available at https://zenit.org/articles/patriarch-s-homily-for-feast-of-sts-peter-and-paul/.
207   "Russian Churches End Rift," Associated Press, 17 May 2007.

to the seriousness with which the ancients took ceremonies of greeting and friendship; the kiss of greeting had a solemnity even in purely secular use which is not all reproduced in a modern handshake.[208]

Part of this seriousness, especially after its Christian transformation, is the association of the kiss with intimate family love, the insufflation of the Holy Spirit, and the paschal banquet. And part of it is also the foreboding counterexample of Judas' perfidious greeting and the continuity with the New Testament's holy kiss. These meanings are no doubt shaped by human convention, but it is equally important to note (as we have already) that they are also grounded in a phenomenology of nature. The association of the mouth and lips with breathing and with the word, for example, is natural and reasonable, and kissing is universally recognized as a sign of some form of love, even by the cultures that disapprove of it, as will be discussed later. The kiss, simply put, is irreplaceable: even the lovely bow of the Missionaries of Charity, it must candidly be admitted, is the gesture favored by polite strangers, not brothers and sisters.[209]

Finally, unlike the Roman kiss and virtually every other sacred gesture in the liturgy, the handshake and the like have undergone no modification or transformation that would mark them as distinctive from their "profane" or non-sacred counterparts. This is a crucial failing, for in retaining its worldly form, the handshake retains its worldly resonance. Yeago writes of the importance of emphasizing and dramatizing "with all the verbal and ceremonial means at our disposal the specialness, the transcendence, the more-than-natural quality of what goes on in the service of worship."[210] Even Sarah Mitchell, whose exotic thoughts on inclusivity and chaos we mentioned earlier, writes that when the "peace becomes an opportunity for a civil greeting," it not only loses its theological

208   Yeago, "Unfashionable Thoughts on Sharing the Peace," 293.
209   Syro-Malabar and Syro-Malankara families in the Kerala region of India customarily give the peace to each other with the double handclasp, both within the liturgy and without.
210   Yeago, "Unfashionable Thoughts on Sharing the Peace," 293.

meaning, but it may even lose its civic function, since "without its theological content, the exchange of the Peace becomes even emptier than a social, civil greeting."[211] Romano Tommasi no doubt is too harsh, but he has a point when he argues that the mundane handshakes, waves, nods, and smiles used as signs of peace today render the rite "a meaningless *liturgical* gesture."[212]

Further, having an action that is distinct from what is found *pro fano*, outside the temple, is especially important when the reality of Christian peace is at stake, for the peace of Christ is not only profoundly different from that which the world gives but in a real sense opposed to it. In the words of René Girard:

> Jesus distinguishes two types of peace. The first is the peace that he offers to humanity. No matter how simple its rules, it "surpasses human understanding" because the only peace human beings know is the truce based on scapegoats. This is "the peace such as the world gives." It is the peace that the Gospel revelation *takes away from us* more and more. Christ cannot bring us a peace truly divine without first depriving us first of the only peace at our disposal.[213]

Moreover, it is precisely when the two types of peace are confused or conflated that the worst political theologies have historically emerged, invariably harming both the ecclesial and civic realms.

The Universality of Kissing?

It may be objected, however, that if there is indeed no real substitute for the kiss or the kiss-like accolade, then the *pax* is

---

211   Mitchell, "Piecing Together," 242.

212   Romano Tommasi, "The Construction of the New Mass, Part II: Some Funny Things Happened Near the Roman Forum," in *The Latin Mass* 11 (Summer 2002) 32–35, at 34, emphasis in the original.

213   René Girard, *I See Satan Fall Like Lightning*, trans. James G. Williams (Maryknoll, NY: Orbis, 2001) 186. Girard's anthropological account of the crucifixion can also be used to illuminate the *pax* in the Roman Rite, for it reinforces the Girardian notion of the resurrection as the definitive unveiling of Satan's false peace and the true peace which follows as a result.

doomed to failure. Willem Frijhoff writes that the taboo in northern Europe against "the sacred kiss is so strong that most northern Europeans cannot imagine that the rules of conduct of their cultural systems once resembled those of the present-day Mediterranean nations."[214] Other parts of the world view any public display of kissing as lewd. William Lowrie, in justifying his support of the liturgical handshake in 1955, wrote that "today a great proportion of mankind, the 600 million Chinese, and in Japan and elsewhere an equal number who are under the influence of Confucius, have been taught to regard the kiss as an exhibition of sexual love exclusively."[215] Such conventions are still in force, as actor Richard Gere recently learned when he kissed an Indian actress on the cheek and found himself shortly thereafter being burned in effigy by angry mobs in Bombay.[216]

Yet as we have already seen, the Roman form of the kiss can hardly be considered lascivious by even the most stringent or offish of cultures, especially since according to the rubricists of the Tridentine era not the even the cheeks of the participants need touch. Moreover, the Roman accolade intersects in interesting ways with a little-known form of kissing approved by several African and Asiatic peoples. The so-called "sniff-kiss" involves two individuals first approaching and, as the name would suggest, sniffing each other. Not only is there a morphological similarity between the two gestures, since the sniff-kiss is usually made next to the hair and shoulder,[217] but there is even some overlap in significance. The word that the Vedic poets of ancient India used for a kiss can mean either "smell" or "breath," thus opening up the gesture to a

---

214   Frijhoff, "The Kiss Sacred and Profane," 213. Frijhoff is mostly speaking of the veneration of objects rather than people, yet his point about the less demonstrative traits of non-Mediterranean Europeans still stands.

215   Lowrie, "The Kiss of Peace," 240. Also Frijhoff, "The Kiss Sacred and Profane," 213.

216   "Gere Kiss Sparks India Protests," BBC News, 16 April 2007.

217   At least this is the case in Thailand. The main physical difference between the Roman accolade and the sniff-kiss is that the former is an exhalation and the latter an inhalation.

pneumatological reading, and indeed there is a "mystic doctrine of breaths" going back to the Upanishads that links sniffing at someone with long life and health.[218] The sniff-kiss even holds special meaning as an affirmation of family identity: just as a cow recognizes its calf by smelling, so too, maintain the ancient *Domestic Regulations*, should the father of a newborn sniff three times at the child's head as an act of official recognition.[219] Notably, the first time that a kiss is explicitly mentioned in the Old Testament is when a blind Isaac kisses Jacob and smells him as a means of recognition (Gen 27:26).[220] The traditional Roman accolade may be more capable of global acceptance than is apparent at first blush, thus preserving one of the goals of Vatican II: the substantial unity of the Roman Rite.[221]

Derestricted

The final way in which the sign of peace was modified in the *Missale Romanum* of 1970 is that it is no longer omitted in the Holy Thursday Mass and Masses for the dead. If the kiss of peace is truly instrumental in preparing the believer for Holy Communion, then one can see why it would be especially appropriate for the feast that celebrates the institution of the Eucharist. Similarly, if a Mass for the dead is truly a "requiem" Mass, that is, a Mass that imprecates eternal rest, then one can see why the source of that rest, the Peace that is Christ, would be shared.

On the other hand, the spiritual underpinnings of the traditional practice are not without their merit. Omitting the kiss on Holy Thursday has a threefold effect. First, it paradoxically enables the faithful to enter into the scriptural narrative of the Lord's Passion and into the mystery of the Paschal Triduum more deeply by having them pointedly refrain from imitating the

218   Edward Washburn Hopkins, "The Sniff-Kiss in Ancient India," in *Journal of the American Oriental Society* 28 (1907) 120–134, at 121.
219   Ibid.
220   Of course in this case, the act proved to be deceptive, albeit providential.
221   *Sacrosanctum Concilium*, no. 38.

external actions of Judas the traitor on this holy, if ominous, night. Giving the kiss of peace with Judas' betrayal so fresh on one's mind is as palatable as eating a grilled sausage after meditating on the martyrdom of St. Lawrence.[222] Respecting this psychological sensitivity encourages the faithful to be more attuned to the sacred qualities of the day, an important component to their spiritual exercise. Second, the Holy Thursday omission vividly teaches the foulness of kisses of peace that are robbed of their true Christian meaning; hence it silently admonishes the faithful to align *intus* and *exterius*, the motions of their heart with those of their body. Third, it underscores the great importance of the kiss, for paradoxically, it is by occasionally removing a sacred thing from our midst that the Church reminds us of its value.[223] Since the typical Eucharistic liturgy during the course of the year will not have specific mementos about, for example, the evils of hypocritical kissing, having an annual lesson such as this becomes all the more useful.[224]

The omission of the *pax* at Masses for the dead, on the other hand, arises from a different set of considerations. Without denying the enormous spiritual benefits that a Requiem Mass affords to all who are present, especially those who are grieving, its primary objective is not grace for the living but repose for the soul or souls of the departed. Theologically, this is echoed in other features of the traditional Requiem Mass, such as the priest not bless-

---

222   Which is why, incidentally, there is an old folk tradition of not eating cooked foods on the feast of St. Lawrence. As for the memory of Judas' betrayal, while it is true that the Gospel reading for Holy Thursday does not include an account of the kiss, it does mention Judas' early departure from the Last Supper in order to betray Jesus (Jn 13:1–15). Moreover, the details of the Passion should be so well known by Catholics that anyone participating in the liturgy on Holy Thursday evening would be cognizant of what transpired in Gethsemane that night.

223   The veiling of sacred images during Passiontide would be another example of this principle, as well as abstinence from flesh meat on Fridays.

224   A fourth reason may be adduced from Tertullian, namely, that it is acceptable to omit the kiss during times of public fasting, such as Good Friday (and, later, Holy Thursday). Tertullian, *De oratione* 18 (PL 1:1282) only disapproves of declining the kiss when one is fasting privately, for it pharisaically calls attention to oneself.

ing himself at the introit, kissing the Missal after the Gospel, or saying the prayer "Per evangelica dicta. . . ."[225]

Yet the souls of the departed, as the medieval liturgist William Durandus notes, "are no longer in the tumult of this world, nor will they ever be," and hence it is not necessary to give them the kiss, "which is a sign of peace and concord."[226] Nor is it possible: the *pax*, as we have seen from the patristic authors, is the union of two bodies that unites two souls; therefore, if the recipient's soul is absent from his body, it cannot receive the spirit of peace from the kiss. Kissing the body of a deceased loved one remains a touching and appropriate gesture, but as a sign of reverence and affection, not as a spiritual communication. The living at a Requiem Mass could, of course, offer the peace only among themselves, but again, this particular votive Mass is neither about them nor for them: hence the change in the *Agnus Dei* from the refrain, "Have mercy on *us*," to "Grant peace to *them*." Omitting the *pax* for the living, together with other omissions and changes, aptly directs their attention, and Christ's peace, towards the main objective of the Mass, namely, supplication for the dead. And it is in keeping with the mournful tone of such a Mass that the *pax* is understandably not given, for the peace is a sign of irrepressible joy.[227]

CONCLUDING REFLECTIONS

Whether the kiss of peace in the Extraordinary Form of the Roman Rite should be amended is an interesting and, at least to my mind, open question. Extending the Roman accolade to the *Missa cantata* and the Low Mass is certainly feasible for the minis-

---

225   "By these evangelical sayings, may my sins be blotted out" (my translation). I say "theologically" because the historical reasons for this anomaly are different from their eventual theological rationale.

226   William Durandus, *Rationale divinorum officiorum* 4,53.8 (CCCM 140:546). Some religious apparently took this principle quite far, for in the same passage Durandus mentions that the kiss is not given to monks, "who are reckoned as dead to the world."

227   *Rationale* 53.6.

ters in the sanctuary, although acclimatizing the congregation to it would take time and effort, especially given the fact that most devotees of the Extraordinary Form are resistant to change. The pax-brede would be easier to implement and is already allowed in the *usus antiquior*, be it Low Mass or High Mass,[228] although it is technically reserved to "lay persons of high rank."[229] Nevertheless, Robert Cabié makes a valid albeit exaggerated point when he asserts that with the pax-brede the rite of peace loses "its expressive character,"[230] and there are valid hygienic concerns about its use in large congregations.

The *pax* as a whole, either as an accolade or with the brede, could be reinstated beyond the sanctuary without the laity's late medieval spats over pecking order by simply having it proceed from the first pew to the last in the manner of the Eastern churches. Perhaps a new generation of rubricists could boldly propose that the instruction *leviter tangant* does indeed suggest more than a moral touch, at least for the cultures amenable to such contact. But a restored mouth-to-mouth kiss in either form of the Roman Rite would, in my opinion, be imprudent. In addition to issues of hygiene, kissing between members of the opposite sex would return the age-old risk of substituting *cupiditas* for *caritas*, and there currently seems to be little impetus for re-segregating the sexes to different sides of the nave. Physical kissing between members of the same sex, on the other hand, would prove difficult to implement, especially in non-Mediterranean cultures; and it would be dogged in this oversexualized era by homoerotic construals. If such concerns were enough to derail the platonic labial kiss in the twelfth century, it is not difficult to imagine what might happen today.

The more fundamental problem, however, is that any attempt to increase congregational participation in the traditional *pax* must first confront the matter of giving the peace to non-Catholics,

---

228   Except, of course, Requiem Masses and the Mass of Holy Thursday.

229   O'Connell, *the Celebration of Mass*, 430.

230   Cabié, *The Eucharist*, 165. It would be more accurate to say that with the brede the *pax* loses *some* of its expressive character, although not enough to disqualify it, as we see in the case of the handshake, from an authentic kissing ritual.

who are of course permitted to attend the entire liturgy nowadays and are more likely to do so in our pluralistic era. The question then becomes in what way the peace ought to be reserved for the faithful without causing undue offense to separated brethren or nonbelievers, not to mention Catholics in a state of mortal sin. We could, of course, depart from this ancient prescription and let the peace be given to all as a sign of eschatological hope for full reunion, but if we do so, we again run the risk of diluting the meaning of the peace as a genuine actualization of familial concord and of total unity in Christ's mystical body. Perhaps the solution, whatever it may be, would somehow incorporate the lessons of Luke 10:5–6, in which the peace is given to those who are unworthy, but with no derogation from the sacred.[231]

The issue of familial membership applies to the celebration of Mass according to 1970 Missal as well; yet that is not its most pressing problem. Putting the matter somewhat dramatically, we may argue that the Roman kiss of peace as it is typically practiced in the Ordinary Form today is neither historically Roman nor a species of kiss nor, judging by the most popular gestures, an instance of uniquely Christian peace. The renewed Missal, therefore, would benefit considerably from: 1) a restoration of the paschal meaning of the Roman kiss, 2) a reuse of the Roman accolade, and 3) a reconsideration of the location of the *fractio panis*.

Regarding the first point: as we have already seen, *Sacrosanctum Concilium* gives eloquent testimony to the Paschal Mystery re-presented (i.e., literally made present again) in every Mass, and this paschal account elides perfectly with the traditional significance of the kiss (indeed, it is almost as if the council fathers had it in mind). Rediscovering the relation of the kiss to the risen Christ and the breath of the Holy Spirit would militate against confusion about its position in the Mass, and this in turn would inform the proper ethos in which the kiss is to be administered. On the other hand, moving the peace to another part of the Mass would obfuscate these

---

231   See our remarks on this passage above and Yeago's reading of its "utter substantial realism."

dimensions by subordinating them to the conciliatory meaning prevalent in pre-anaphoral signs of peace. This meaning is, I repeat, equally beautiful and important, but this fact should not be used to destroy the unique testimony that the traditional Roman Rite gives to the paschal aspect of the kiss. On the contrary, since it is by looking to the traditions of both East and West that the full meaning of the holy kiss may be found, the unique tradition of the Roman church should be fostered every bit as much as those of the Ambrosian, Byzantine, Maronite, and other rites.

Second, replacing the horizontally spontaneous handshake with the vertically mediated paschal embrace would: 1) preserve the phenomenological essence of the liturgical kiss without incurring any of the moral or hygienic risks of labial kissing and without scandalizing non-Western believers; 2) "re-sacralize" a part of the Mass currently prone to banality and abuse; and 3) remind the faithful of the mediatory nature of the Church and her grace, the dynamic of the Holy Spirit, and the uniqueness of the peace that comes from our risen Lord alone. Indeed, helping the new form of Mass rediscover rather than reinvent or relocate the kiss could be one of the greatest gifts of the *usus antiquior* to the Ordinary Form. In this way, it would contribute substantially to Benedict XVI's goal of the two missals mutually enriching each other.[232]

Third, the paschal meaning of the Roman *pax* would be all the more manifest if the *fractio panis* were to occur not in its most primitive position (before the *pax*), but in the position accorded it by the gradual and organic development of a living tradition. This would be in compliance with the Second Vatican Council's *Sacrosanctum Concilium*, which encourages change only if it is truly necessary,[233] and with *Mediator Dei*, in which Pius XII warns against

---

232   See Benedict XVI, Letter to the Bishops Accompanying the Motu Proprio *Summorum Pontificum* (7 July 2007).

233   See *Sacrosanctum Concilium*, no. 23. The constitution also states that elements should be changed that "have suffered from the intrusion of anything out of harmony with the inner nature of the liturgy" (no. 21), but as this essay demonstrates, the Roman *pax* as it developed during the Middle Ages is in harmony with patristic practice and theology, even when some of its external forms and orders occasionally vary.

the error of archeologism, the choosing of the older over the newer simply because it is older, as if an authentic development of pious praxis were absent or impossible.[234]

Not all of these changes would prove easy to implement, but they are preferable to the option of changing the kiss of peace from a pre-communion to a pre-anaphoral rite. This would effectively destroy the only witness to the paschal, as opposed to conciliatory, meaning of the *pax* that remains in the liturgies of the historic, apostolic churches. According to Dominic Serra:

> The idea that the greeting of peace ought to be placed elsewhere in the liturgy because it distracts the participants from the true meaning of Communion is supported neither by our tradition nor by the Roman Rite Eucharistic Liturgy. To move it for this reason would be a mistake and another capitulation to a Eucharistic spirituality the conciliar reforms declared to be misguided.[235]

Finally, it must be added that an enrichment such as the one we have been discussing is sorely needed, for behind the current crisis in the *pax* is more than deviations from apostolic tradition or failures to be adequately prepared for the reception of the Eucharist, as grave as both these matters are. In the words of David Yeago, what is also at stake is a sound ecclesiology:

> On the one side, there are those who confess the church as a mystery of the last days, as the messianic community in whose midst there occur great deeds of God, holy and wonderful, though visible as such only to faith. On the other side, there are those for whom the church is a voluntary association for the pursuit of religious self-expression, personal well-being, and better human relationships. Inevitably these two understandings of the nature of the church imply two entirely different systems of liturgics. The question of the right practice of the Sharing of

234   See Pius XII, Encyclical on the Sacred Liturgy *Mediator Dei* (20 November 1947) nos. 62–64.

235   Serra, "The Greeting of Peace in the Revised Sacramentary," 109.

the Peace is an important one, because it sets us squarely before
these two alternatives and demands that we choose.[236]

While the manner in which Yeago, a Lutheran theologian, for-
mulates the two alternatives may be slightly different from our
own, his diagnosis of the significance of the *pax* is worth our consideration. For ultimately, how we practice and understand the
kiss of peace both reflects and shapes our beliefs regarding the
nature and character of Christ's mystical body and the life we share
in him.

---

236   Yeago, "Unfashionable Thoughts on Sharing the Peace," 294.

Eucharistic Fasting: A Review of Its Practice and Evaluation of Its Benefit

MADELEINE GRACE, CVI

INTRODUCTION

Fasting was firmly established within the Judeo-Christian tradition long before its connection to the sacrament of the Eucharist. In the Old Testament, it is seen as a token of sorrow rather than an ascetical practice. In the New Testament, Jesus fasted forty days before beginning his ministry. One may recall from the example of Paul and Barnabas, among others, that fasting with prayer is seen as a means of seeking divine assistance.

Fasting prior to reception of the Eucharist was quite widespread by the fourth century. In fact, St. Augustine of Hippo (354–430) assumed that its almost universal practice must have been divinely inspired.[1] By the Middle Ages it had become universal, as verified by the Council of Constance in 1418, which declared that the Eucharist may not be received by anyone who has not fasted, except in case of necessity.[2] St. Thomas Aquinas (1225–1274) gave credence to the value of fasting, pointing out that this practice enables the mind to arise more freely to the contemplation of heavenly things.[3] Pope Pius XII (1939–1958)[4] declared in 1953

---

1   Augustine of Hippo, *Ep.* 54,8 (CCSL 31:232).

2   Council of Constance (1414–1418), Session XIII (June 15, 1415), in *Enchiridion symbolorum definitionum et declarationum de rebus fidei et morum*, ed. Heinrich Denzinger and Peter Hünermann, 43rd ed. (San Francisco: Ignatius Press, 2012) no. 1198.

3   Thomas Aquinas, *Summa theologiae*, II-II, q. 147, a. 1.

4   Dates given for all pontiffs reflect the years served within the pontificate.

that water and medication did not break the fast. Four years later he reduced the fast from midnight to three hours, which Pope Paul VI (1963–1978) further reduced in 1964 to one hour. It is widely recognized that the changes brought about by Pius XII and Paul VI were due to the social and economic conditions of modern society. By the same token, it must be pointed out that these changes have led to a decline in the importance of the Eucharistic fast. Some perceived these changes as making St. Pius X's (1903–1914) ideal of frequent communion a reality.[5] The following study places the events in this chronology within the context of the challenge to catechesis in preparing those approaching reception of this sacrament, so central to our faith.

FASTING WITHIN THE SCRIPTURES

The practice of fasting is well known within Judaism. The Day of Atonement presumed a refraining from food. Within the Old Testament, fasting is connected with mourning and repentance (1 Sam 7:5). It accompanies prayer in a time of great need. Christ refused to allow his followers to enter into the exaggerated fasts prescribed by Jewish rabbis. Fasting was not appropriate during a time of joy, as it was considered to be a sign of mourning, inappropriate when the Bridegroom is present (Lk 5:33–35). Jesus presumes that the disciples would fast, but they were meant to conceal this practice. This was to avoid the dangers of formalism and pride. Later his disciples would fast in imitation of Christ (Mt 4:2), specifically referring to the forty-day Lenten fast. After fasting and prayer, Paul and Barnabas received a special blessing before beginning Paul's first missionary journey. The writings of Paul give evidence that he engaged in the penitential practice of fasting all of his life (2 Cor 6:5, 11:27).

---

5   Berard L. Marthaler, OFM Conv., "The Eucharistic Fast: A Long Past into the Present," in *Reclaiming Catholicism: Treasures Old and New*, ed. Thomas H. Groome and Michael J. Daley (Maryknoll, NY: Orbis, 2010) 224–227, at 227.

FASTING WITHIN ANTIQUITY

The *Didache* (AD 70) conveys that fasting was practiced on Wednesdays and Fridays.[6] Fasting is tied with almsgiving among the early Church fathers, as illustrated in the writings of St. John Chrysostom (347–407). This Eastern father states in his *Homilies on Matthew* that fasting without almsgiving was no fast at all.[7]

One finds within the early Church that fasting[8] was practiced immediately prior to the feasts of saints, and specifically of martyr saints. Filastrius, bishop of Brescia, c. 385, reports that there is a fast before Christmas, but not one preceding the Epiphany, which signifies the greater dignity given to the feast of Christmas. The second fast he states is *in pascha*. He defines it as *quadragesimae*. The third fast is in preparation for the feast of the Ascension, which is the fortieth day after *pascha*. The fourth fast appears to reflect two different practices. The first is a fast from the Ascension to Pentecost. The second is a fast after Pentecost.[9] Until the liturgical changes of Vatican II, fasting was required on the vigils of Christmas, Pentecost, the Assumption and All Saints.[10]

The practice of observing Rogation Days had its origin in the second half of the fifth century, when the people of Vienne were experiencing many calamities. They had just been conquered by the Burgundians, and were fearful of God's anger for their transgressions. St. Mamertus, bishop of Vienne, prescribed three days of public atonement for sin, during which the faithful were to give themselves to penance, and walk in procession while chanting

---

6   *Didache* 8,1 (SC 248:172).

7   John Chrysostom, *In Matt.* 77,6 (PG 58:710).

8   Originally the fast endured till after Vespers; it was then shortened till after None, then till noon. By the sixteenth century, the main meal plus two light collations was permitted; practice was to a great extent determined by monastic custom. See *New Catholic Encyclopedia*, 2nd ed. (Detroit–Washington, DC: Thomson/Gale–Catholic University of America, 2003) s.v. "Fast and Abstinence."

9   Thomas J. Talley, *The Origins of the Liturgical Year* (New York: Pueblo, 1986) 147.

10   *Saint Joseph Daily Missal* (New York: Catholic Book Publishing Co., 1956) Fasting and Abstinence Days, 16.

appropriate psalms. The three days preceding the Ascension were the days chosen. In addition to avoiding the chastisements which sin deserved, the intent of the Rogation Days was to draw God's blessings upon the fruits of the earth. The churches of Gaul adopted the devotion, as is apparent from the canons of the Council of Orleans, which was held in 511. Abstinence from flesh meat as well as fasting was required. Masters were required to dispense their men from work, as the events took up most of the three days. The Council of Tours in 567 imposed this obligation of fasting. The major part of the rite consisted in singing in procession canticles of supplication (hence *rogare*, meaning to ask) as they passed from place to place. St Caesarius of Arles states that the processions lasted six hours. When the clergy became tired, the women took up the chanting. Individuals received ashes on their heads prior to the procession,[11] as now is the practice on Ash Wednesday. The collect *post nomina* from the first Rogation Mass on Monday in the *Missale Gothicum*, a witness to the ancient Gallican tradition, notes that the participant desires that the practice of fasting may lead to a "rest from sin," which of course is a fitting preparation for the Eucharist.

> It is from thee, O Lord, we receive the food, wherewith we are daily supported; to thee also do we offer these fasts, whereby, according to thy command, we put upon our flesh the restraint from dangerous indulgence. . . . Vouchsafe to bless and receive this our offering of a three days' penitential fast and mercifully grant, that while our bodies abstain from gratification, our souls also may rest from sin.[12]

All of the Western Church adopted the Rogation Days; however, the fasting that was so much a part of the practice in Gaul was

---

11   Prosper Guéranger, OSB, *The Liturgical Year*, trans. Laurence Shepherd, OSB, 15 vol. (Westminster, MD: Newman Press, 1948–1950) vol. 9, 130–135.

12   *Missale Gothicum (Vat. Reg. lat. 317)*, ed. Leo Cunibert Mohlberg, OSB, Rerum Ecclesiasticarum Documenta, Series Maior, Fontes V (Rome: Casa Editrice Herder, 1961) XLV. Missa prima die in rogationibus, no. 329 (p. 83); translation from Guéranger, *The Liturgical Year*, vol. 9, 151.

not adopted in Rome yet even though abstinence was observed.[13]

Ember Days (Wednesday, Friday, and Saturday) are connected with the fast of the Four Seasons or *Quattuor Tempora*, commemorated four times a year. The *Liber Pontificalis* attributes to St. Callistus (217–222) the addition of a Saturday fast to each of the four seasons.[14] The practice may be seen as coming from the synagogue: Zechariah writes of the fasts of the fourth, fifth, seventh, and tenth months (Zech 8:19). Its introduction into Christianity is seen very early, as testified by Pope St. Leo the Great, St. Isidore of Seville, and other ancient writers. The purpose was to consecrate by penance the four seasons of the year to God. Leo the Great (440–461) gives evidence of their practice in his sermons:

> . . . the solemn fast of the tenth month, which is now to be kept by us according to yearly custom because it is altogether just and godly to give thanks to the Divine bounty for the crops which the earth has produced for the use of men under the guiding hand of supreme Providence. And to show that we do this with ready mind, we must exercise not only the self-restraint of fasting, but also diligence in almsgiving, that from the ground of our heart also may spring the germ of righteousness and the fruit of love. . . . On Wednesday and Friday next, therefore, let us fast. . . .[15]

A second intention for these Ember Days is the obtaining of worthy ministers for the sacrament of ordination.[16] Pope Gregory VII (1073–1085) actually fixed the Ember Days on the modern calendar:[17] for the Wednesday, Friday, and Saturday after December 13 (St. Lucy), after Ash Wednesday, after Whitsunday (Pentecost),

---

13   See Guéranger, *The Liturgical Year*, vol. 9, 134.

14   See Geoffrey G. Willis, *Essays in Early Roman Liturgy*, Alcuin Club Collections 46 (London: SPCK, 1964) 51.

15   Leo the Great, *Tractatus* XVII,1, 4 (CCSL 138:68, 71); translation from *Nicene and Post-Nicene Fathers, Second Series. Vol. 12: Leo the Great, Gregory the Great* (New York: Christian Literature Company, 1895) 126, 127.

16   Guéranger, *The Liturgical Year*, 1:218–220.

17   Ibid., 5:156.

and after September 14 (Exaltation of the Holy Cross). Emphasis
on the fast is readily seen in the Masses on these Ember Days, and
prepares one for reception of the Eucharist, as illustrated in the
Secret for the Ember Saturday in Lent: "We beseech Thee, O Lord,
sanctify our fasts by these present sacrifices, that what our observance shows forth outwardly, may be accomplished inwardly."[18]

Bearing in mind the prescriptions of the Universal Norms for
the Liturgical Year and the General Roman Calendar, "On Rogation and Ember Days the practice of the Church is accustomed to
entreat the Lord for the various needs of humanity, especially for
the fruits of the earth and for human labor, and to give thanks to
him publicly,"[19] the General Instruction of the Roman Missal indicates: "In the drawing up of the calendar of a nation, the Rogation
and Ember Days should be indicated (cf. no. 373) as well as the
forms and texts for their celebration."[20] Pope Paul VI told the Bishops' Conferences to arrange the Ember Days on their own calen-
dars.[21] The American bishops have not yet complied with this
directive. They have designated the anniversary of Roe vs. Wade
(January 22) as a day of prayer and penance, but the term fasting
is not used in the document, nor is this annual observance understood as either an Ember Day or a Rogation Day.[22] Consequently,
the vast majority of American Catholics practicing the Ordinary
Form of the Roman Rite are ignorant of Ember and Rogation
Days, and those among them who are familiar with their observance have no assigned date on which to keep them.

18   *Saint Joseph Daily Missal*, Ember Saturday in Lent, 160.
19   *The Roman Missal: Renewed by Decree of the Most Holy Second Ecumenical
Council of the Vatican, Promulgated by Authority of Pope Paul VI and Revised at the Direction
of Pope John Paul II*, English translation according to the third typical edition (Totowa,
NJ: Catholic Book Publishing, 2011) Universal Norms for the Liturgical Year and the
General Roman Calendar, no. 45; these norms were first published in 1969.
20   *Roman Missal*, General Instruction of the Roman Missal, no. 394.
21   *General Norms for the Liturgical Year and the Calendar* (21 March 1969), nos.
45–46, as referenced in *Documents on the Liturgy 1963–1979, Conciliar, Papal and Curial
Texts* (Collegeville, MN: Liturgical Press, 1982) nos. 3811–3812 (p. 1161).
22   *Roman Missal*, General Instruction of the Roman Missal, no. 373 (US
edition).

THE PRE-BAPTISMAL FAST LEADING TO THE LENTEN FAST

The *Didache*, which is considered the oldest manual of Christian instruction, conveys the practice that the catechumen, as well as priest and family, enter into fasting as preparation for the sacrament of baptism.[23] Fasting was perceived as a means of disposing oneself to the forgiveness of all sin, in addition to making oneself available to the grace of the sacrament of entry into the Church. Fasting practiced beyond the catechumenate enabled others to renew their resolve to live the Christian life in a time of persecution. St. Justin Martyr (c. 100–165), like other Church fathers, writes of the pre-baptismal fast in his *First Apology*. He notes that the reason for the practice is the forgiveness of past sins.[24]

In medieval times, Thomas Aquinas identifies fasting as an act of virtue that is directed by reason to some virtuous good. Fasting is seen as a virtue when it is practiced for a threefold purpose: as a means of enabling chastity, fostering the contemplation of heavenly things, and atoning for sin.[25]

The pre-baptismal fast made way for the Lenten season. It lasted for about two and a half weeks in Rome. The monastic-ascetic movement of the fourth century encouraged the faithful to join the catechumens in this pre-baptismal fast and attend the instructions as a means of strengthening their own faith. St. Athanasius (296–373), in a letter to his flock in 336, urges a fast of forty days. Rome seemed to be observing a six-week fast in 339. Pope St. Leo the Great (440–461) preached a six-week fast in his Lenten sermons in 450. Not until the seventh century was the full total of forty days of actual fasting observed in Rome, with the addition of Ash Wednesday. The imposition of ashes began in Gaul in the sixth century. It spread to England and Rome in the ninth or tenth century, and then to Germany, southern Italy, and

---

23   *Didache* 7,4 (SC 284:172).
24   Justin Martyr, *First Apology* 61:2–3 (ed. Miroslav Marcovich, Patristische Texte und Studien 38 [Berlin–New York: Walter de Gruyter, 1994] 118).
25   Thomas Aquinas, *Summa theologiae*, II-II, q. 147, a. 1.

Spain.[26] This earlier distribution of ashes is usually connected with admission to the penitential state. Aelfric, in his *Lives of the Saints* at the beginning of the eleventh century, relates that on Ash Wednesday all the faithful were to participate in a ceremony that included the imposition of ashes. At the end of that same century, Pope Urban II, at a synod at Benevento in 1091, ordered the general imposition of ashes on that day.[27] Gregory Dix maintains that Lent does not originate as a commemoration of the Lord's fasting in the desert or even as a preparation for Holy Week and Easter but rather as a "private initiative of the devout laity in taking it upon themselves to share the solemn preparation of the catechumens for the sacraments of baptism and confirmation."[28] Lent was seen as a corporate effort of the whole Church. In looking back over the time period, it may be noted that Athanasius' fast of forty days does not mention Lent, as it immediately follows upon the feast of the Epiphany. However, the *Canons of Hippolytus* relate the forty days of fasting to an imitation of Christ. In addition, Bishop Peter of Alexandria issued a series of canons in 305, one of which provides a forty-day fast in imitation of Christ for those *lapsi* who had completed their penitence for three years. It is maintained here that Lent developed from an earlier pre-Paschal fast in imitation of the Lord's forty-day fast in the desert.[29]

As hinted at above, the character of Lent changed with the changes in sacramental practices. In the fourth century, with the great number of adult converts to Christianity, Lent was an intense preparation for baptism. Later, when infant baptism became normative, reconciliation of penitents became the focus of Lent. When public penance ceased, this season became a time of repentance, conversion, and penance for all. The expectation

26   Gregory Dix, *The Shape of the Liturgy* (London: Dacre Press, 1964) 354–357.

27   Talley, *The Origins of the Liturgical Year*, 224.

28   Dix, *The Shape of the Liturgy*, 356.

29   Talley, *The Origins of the Liturgical Year*, 189–194, and Lauren Pristas, *The Collects of the Roman Missals: A Comparative Study of the Sundays in Proper Seasons Before and After the Second Vatican Council* (London: Bloomsbury, 2013) 113.

was that all Christians would participate in the Lenten observance, as the death and resurrection of Christ provided redemption for all.[30]

The Lenten fast, as practiced for centuries in the Church, was
mitigated by Pope Paul VI through his Apostolic Constitution
Paenitemini issued February 17, 1966. Essentially, it maintained the
penitential character of the season, but lessened the gravity
through the observance of only two fast days, Ash Wednesday and
Good Friday (ages 18–59), and abstinence reserved for Ash
Wednesday and Fridays during Lent (ages 14–59). The pontiff
invited "everyone to accompany the inner conversion of the spirit
with the voluntary exercise of external acts of penitence."[31] The
same document reiterates that all Fridays are days of abstinence.[32]
However, the American Bishops' Conference asked and received
permission (in 1966) from the Holy See for Catholics in the United
States to substitute a penitential or charitable act of their choosing.
Members of the National Conference of Catholic Bishops pointed
out that "renunciation of the eating of meat is not always and for
everyone the most effective means of practicing penance. Meat
was once an exceptional form of food; now it is commonplace . . .
the spirit of penance primarily suggests that we discipline ourselves
in that which we enjoy most. . . ."[33]

EARLY EUCHARISTIC FAST

For the first three centuries, there was no fixed practice of
abstinence from food for a definite time before receiving Holy
Communion. This celebration of the Eucharist was often pre-

---

30   Talley, *The Origins of the Liturgical Year*, 222–225, and Pristas, *The Collects
of the Roman Missals*, 114.

31   Paul VI, Apostolic Constitution on Fast and Abstinence *Paenitemini* (17
February 1966) Chapter III.

32   Ibid., Chapter III, no. II.2.

33   National Conference of Catholic Bishops, *Pastoral Statement on Penance and
Abstinence: A Statement issued by the National Conference of Catholic Bishops* (November
18, 1966) nos. 19–20.

ceded by a meal; on the other hand, the *Apostolic Tradition*[34] records that presbyters, virgins and widows were urged to fast frequently. The bishop could not fast except when all the laity fasted; there may be times when someone wishes to offer a meal to the church, a practice known as the *chaburah* meal, and this individual could not be denied. Thus the text notes that fasting was observed as a private devotion.[35] A century and a half later, however, St. Augustine gives evidence that the Eucharist was being celebrated in the morning and that fasting before communicating was a universal practice: "Should the whole Church, nonetheless, be made the subject of slander because it always receives when fasting?"[36]

EUCHARISTIC FAST DURING MEDIEVAL TIMES

According to St. Thomas Aquinas, the Eucharistic fast in his day was adhered to strictly. One could be prevented from receiving the Eucharist due to unworthiness or breaking the fast. Fasting before communion was observed out of respect for the sacrament, because the spiritual nourishment of Christ should take precedence over any bodily nourishment, and to prevent accidental profanation by vomiting because of overindulgence in food.[37] As mentioned earlier, Aquinas reminds his readers that fasting can be a means of atoning for and preventing sin and of raising one's mind to spiritual things. Everyone is bound to practice this as far as necessary for these purposes.[38]

---

34   On the uncertainty about the date, origin, and authorship of the work known as *Apostolic Tradition*, see Paul F. Bradshaw, Maxwell E. Johnson, and L. Edward Phillips, *The Apostolic Tradition: A Commentary*, Hermeneia (Minneapolis: Fortress Press, 2002) 2–15.

35   *Apostolic Tradition* 23 (ed. Bradshaw, Johnson, and Phillips, 138–139).

36   Augustine of Hippo, *Ep.* 54,8 (CCSL 31:232); trans. Roland Teske, SJ, *Letters 1–99*, The Works of Saint Augustine: A Translation for the 21st Century, II/1 (Hyde Park, NY: New City Press, 2001) 213.

37   Thomas Aquinas, *Summa theologiae*, III, a. 80, a. 8.

38   Ibid., II-II, q. 147, a. 1 and 4.

The Council of Constance (1414–1418) declared that the Eucharistic fast from midnight was the universal law of the Church. The discipline was made universal due to the erroneous teachings of Jan Hus and others.[39] With little variation, this universal law remained intact until the mid-twentieth century.

CHANGES IN EUCHARISTIC FAST: TWENTIETH CENTURY

Pope St. Pius X (1903–1914), known as the "Pope of the Eucharist," urged a more frequent reception of the sacrament through the decree *Sacra Tridentina*, issued on December 20, 1905, and designed in part to correct the errors of Jansenism.[40] While this document did not address the Eucharistic fast, the pontiff's compassion for the sick made way for the following addition in the 1917 code:

> Those who have been sick lying down for a month, however, without a certain hope of a speedy recovery, with the prudent advice of a confessor, can take the most holy Eucharist once or twice in a week even if beforehand they have taken some medicine or some liquid as a drink.[41]

In general, the 1917 Code of Canon Law confirmed the Eucharistic fast from midnight.[42] During the Second World War, on December 1, 1940, Pope Pius XII issued his Motu Proprio *Cum bellica conflictio*, which granted a general concession of the fast in anticipation of the Christmas Midnight Mass to the afternoon of Christmas Eve.

---

39   Council of Constance (1414–1418), Session XIII (15 June 1415), Decree *Cum in nonnullis*, in Denzinger–Hünermann, *Enchiridion symbolorum*, no. 1198, and Thomas Francis Anglin, *The Eucharistic Fast: An Historical Synopsis and Commentary* (Washington, DC: Catholic University of America Press, 1941) 42.

40   Sacred Congregation for the Council, Decree on Frequent and Daily Reception of Holy Communion *Sacra Tridentina* (20 December 1905).

41   *The 1917 Pio-Benedictine Code of Canon Law*, in English translation with extensive scholarly apparatus, ed. Edward N. Peters (San Francisco: Ignatius Press, 2001) can. 858, §2.

42   *1917 Code of Canon Law*, can. 858, §1.

The faithful were allowed to communicate provided they had fasted four hours from food and drink prior to the reception of Communion, while the priest was to fast four hours from the time of Mass. This concession was granted due to the blackouts during the war. The text does not permit Communion on Christmas Day to those who communicated at the anticipated Midnight Mass.[43]

Midnight Mass has enjoyed its own tradition, recorded since the time of the pilgrimage of Egeria to Jerusalem in the late fourth century. She provides testimony in her diary of a Vigil Mass for the Epiphany with a procession from Jerusalem to Bethlehem to the Church of the Nativity and back.[44] The Gelasian Sacramentary gives evidence of this practice in the West.[45] When Masses began at midnight or shortly thereafter, a fast of some hours was required. Thus in 1885, in the case of a pilgrimage, Pope Leo XIII granted the privilege of saying Mass at the church in Lourdes immediately after midnight, provided that the priests celebrating fasted from all food and drink for four hours. This fast was not required, however, for the Masses of Christmas Eve that were celebrated at midnight.[46] Further clarification came about when evening Masses appeared in the mid-twentieth century.[47]

---

43   See T. Lincoln Bouscaren, SJ, "Midnight Mass, in Countries Where 'Black-Out' Is Ordered by Law During War (December 1, 1940)," in *The Canon Law Digest. Vol. 2: 1933–1942* (Milwaukee: Bruce Publishing Co., 1949), on can. 821.

44   Egeria, *Itinerarium* 25,6–7 (SC 296:250).

45   *Liber Sacramentorum Romanae Aeclesiae Ordinis Anni Circuli (Cod. Vat. Reg. lat. 316/Paris Bibl. Nat. 7193, 41/56) (Sacramentarium Gelasianum)*, ed. Leo Cunibert Mohlberg, OSB, Rerum Ecclesiasticarum Documenta, Series Maior, Fontes V, 3rd ed. (Rome: Casa Editrice Herder, 1981) I,i–iv (pp. 7–10). For further study of the Christmas Mass sets, see Bernard Moreton, *The Eighth-Century Gelasian Sacramentary: A Study in Tradition* (London: Oxford University Press, 1976) 25–39.

46   Anglin, *The Eucharistic Fast*, 41.

47   *1917 Code of Canon Law*, cans. 808 and 858, §1: When the Vigil Mass begins at midnight, it is not an "evening" Mass, and the Eucharistic fast is governed by the usual regulations. This was determined by the Holy Office (modifying the terms of the Eucharistic fast for the experimental Easter Vigil) on April 7, 1954. See *The Rites of Holy Week: Ceremonies, Preparations, Music, Commentary*, ed. Frederick McManus (Paterson, NJ: Saint Anthony Guild Press, 1956) 14, n. 20.

On January 6, 1953, Pius XII proclaimed in his Apostolic Constitution *Christus Dominus* that neither water nor medicine would break the fast. In this document the pontiff also pointed out that the Eucharistic fast is based on very serious reasons. Abstaining from food and drink is a sign of deep reverence for Christ, whom we are about to receive. When we consume the Eucharist before any other nourishment, we testify that the Eucharist is the most excellent of nourishments. This practice also fosters devotion and can be an aid to holiness.[48] Further, when the body is not burdened with food, "the mind reacts with more agility and is inspired to meditate with greater fervor on that hidden and sublime mystery which is enacted in the temple of the soul to the increase of divine charity."[49] Yet the pontiff pointed out that notable changes had been introduced into the social and economic conditions of modern society.[50] Pius XII refers to the shortage of priests and the burden put on them in offering Mass at a later hour and two or three times a day. He relates that priests may have to travel many miles to the place of worship. This is also the case for the faithful in missionary countries. School children, on the other hand, who wish to receive Communion and then return home for a meal before going to school may have difficulty doing so. It would be a significant benefit for those who attend religious celebrations later in the day to have the Eucharistic sacrifice available to them. The pontiff also writes that the wars of the twentieth century had weakened the physical constitution of many. He believes that a mitigating of the Eucharistic fast may be a further way to renew piety in the sacrament. Petitions from bishops had become more frequent, and more such dispensations were granted.[51] Within the same docu-

---

48   John C. Ford, SJ, *The New Eucharistic Legislation: A Commentary on the Apostolic Constitution Christus Dominus and on the Instruction of the Holy Office on the Discipline to be Observed Concerning the Eucharistic Fast* (New York: P. J. Kenedy & Sons, 1953) 4–5.

49   Pius XII, Apostolic Constitution Concerning the Discipline to be Observed with Respect to the Eucharistic Fast *Christus Dominus* (January 6, 1953) no. 6.

50   Ibid., no. 11.

51   Ibid., nos. 12–20.

ment this pontiff permitted a limited use of evening Masses after 4:00pm, requiring only a three-hour fast from solid food and alcoholic drink, and a one-hour fast from non-alcoholic drink.[52]

In his Motu Proprio *Sacram Communionem* of March 25, 1957, Pope Pius XII granted two requests from a number of bishops: that evening Masses be celebrated on a daily basis, and that the three-hour fast from food and one hour fast from drink excluding alcohol be extended to all morning Masses. This fast must be observed by those who receive Communion at midnight or in the first hours of the day.[53]

HOLY WEEK SERVICES

The change in the Eucharistic fast brought its own adjustments to the celebration of Holy Week, which has enjoyed a long and venerable history within the Church. One may note from the *Didascalia Apostolorum* in the early fourth century that the Pascha was celebrated in the third hour of the night, meaning 9:00 pm. The fast was to be maintained till this third hour.[54] This Easter Vigil service is likewise recorded by Egeria in her diary.[55]

As Pope Pius XII mentioned in his decree issued on November 16, 1955, "in the beginning the rites of Holy Week were celebrated on the same day of the week and at the same hours of the day at which the sacred mysteries took place." In the Middle Ages, however, for various reasons, the time for these liturgies began to be anticipated to such a degree that toward the end of the medieval period, all liturgical services of Holy Week had been pushed back to the morning, thereby "creating confusion between the Gospel accounts and the liturgical representations referring to them." Holy Saturday, by way of example, lost its sorrowful character as

52   Ibid., no. 29.

53   Pius XII, Motu Proprio on Laws of Fasting and the Evening Mass *Sacram Communionem* (19 March 1957).

54   *Didascalia Apostolorum* 21 (Corpus Scriptorum Christianorum Orientalium 407: 214 [Syriac original] and 408:199 [English translation]).

55   Egeria, *Itinerarium* 38 (SC 296:291).

the commemoration of the Lord's burial. For centuries, Thursday, Friday, and Saturday had been included among the festive days, enabling Christians to be present at these ceremonies. However, by the seventeenth century, this practice no longer existed, meaning that attendance necessarily decreased. Pius XII restored the liturgy of Easter Vigil in 1951 on an experimental basis. Requests were then made by ordinaries that a similar liturgical restoration taken place for the other days of Holy Week. This permission was granted on November 16, 1955, and took effect on March 25, 1956. The Mass of the Lord's Supper was to be celebrated between 5:00 and 8:00 pm. The liturgical service of Good Friday was to take place in the afternoon, at approximately 3:00 pm but not after 6:00 pm. The abstinence and fast of Lent would cease on Holy Saturday at midnight.[56] It is to be recalled that the three-hour fast from food and one hour fast from drink was already in place from *Christus Dominus*.

ONE-HOUR FAST

Pope Paul VI, in his Motu Proprio *Pastorale Munus* of 1963, allowed the bishop to permit priests to take liquid between Masses even if one hour had not elapsed.[57] On November 21, 1964, at the end of the third session of the Second Vatican Council, Paul VI issued a statement reported in the *L'Osservatore Romano* stating that the Eucharistic fast would be reduced to one hour before the reception of Communion.[58] As the pontiff stated,

In view of the difficulties felt in many places regarding the Eucharistic fast, Pope Paul VI, acceding to the requests of the

---

56   Pius XII, Instruction for the Proper Celebration of the Restored Order of Holy Week (16 November 1955) as found in McManus, *The Rites of Holy Week*, 137–146.

57   Paul VI, Motu Proprio on the Powers and Privileges Granted to Bishops *Pastorale Munus* (30 November 1963) I.3.

58   Paul VI, "Eucharistic Fast Reduced to One Hour," in *L'Osservatore Romano* (December 4, 1964) 2, as recorded in *The Canon Law Digest. Vol. 6: 1963–1967* (Milwaukee: Bruce Publishing Co., 1994) 566.

bishops, grants that the fast from solid foods is shortened to one hour before Communion in the case of both priests and faithful. The concession also covers use of alcoholic beverages, but with proper moderation being observed.[59]

Further, a priest who celebrates Mass two or three times on the same day may take something before the second or third Mass even if the period of one hour does not intervene. All of this legislation is found in the 1983 Code of Canon Law. In 1973, the Sacred Congregation of the Sacraments issued the instruction *Immensae Caritatis*, which permits those who are ill to receive the Eucharist after only a fifteen-minute fast.[60] However, can. 919 does not view this fifteen-minute fast as necessary: "The elderly, the infirm and those who care for them can receive the Most Holy Eucharist even if they have eaten something within the preceding hour."[61]

Care that the seriously ill receive the viaticum can be seen from antiquity, even when the Eucharistic fast was not firmly in place. The Council of Nicaea in 325 affirmed that *lapsi* could receive on their deathbed, even if their penance was not completed.[62] Prior to the pontificate of Pius X (September 7, 1897), exceptions were being made for the ill, as seen in the permission granted for someone with a chronic illness to take something "*per modum potus*, that is a mixture having the nature of a liquid food."[63] On March 25, 1946,

---

59   Paul VI, *Concession on the Eucharistic Fast*, announced at a public session of Vatican Council II, November 21, 1964, as referenced in *Documents on the Liturgy*, no. 2117.

60   Sacred Congregation of the Sacraments, Instruction on Facilitating Sacramental Eucharistic Communion in Particular Circumstances *Immensae Caritatis* (25 January 1972) no. III.

61   *New Commentary on the Code of Canon Law*, ed. John P. Beal, James A. Coriden, Thomas J. Green (New York: Paulist Press, 2000) can. 919.

62   Henry Joseph Schroeder, OP, *Disciplinary Decrees of the General Councils* (St. Louis: Herder, 1937) 42, citing the Council of Nicaea (325), can. 13.

63   T. Lincoln Bouscaren and James O'Connor, SJ, "Eucharistic Fast: *Per Modum Potus* (September 7, 1897)," in *The Canon Law Digest. Vol. 4: 1953–1957* (Milwaukee: Bruce Publishing Co., 1958) 268–269.

the ordinaries of the United States were granted permission to dispense from the Eucharistic fast for those who are hospitalized.[64]

FASTING TAKEN IN PERSPECTIVE

It is apparent from the preceding historical survey that fasting has been seen as integral to growth in the spiritual life, and was quite often directly related to sacramental reception. Recall that the catechumen as well as his family and the priest were to fast in preparation for the sacrament of baptism. The primary intention of the Embertide fasts was the consecration of the four seasons to God, and their secondary intention was obtaining ministers worthy of the sacrament of ordination.

The fasting of Rogation Days, on the other hand, had as their original intent the avoidance of the anger of God through natural calamities and, eventually, a petition for blessings upon the harvest. These fasts, however, are all but forgotten today.

The obligation of a penitential practice on every Friday remains, yet poor catechesis has given many Catholics the understanding that the Friday abstinence has been removed, and with it any trace of penance. In the same document, Pope Paul VI maintains that during the Lenten season, everyone should accompany an inner conversion of the spirit with the voluntary exercise of external acts of penitence. While Lent has been extolled from antiquity as a time of prayer, fasting, and almsgiving, one may wisely ask whether a true appreciation of fasting during this holy season, as one prepares for the gift of redemption, has been practiced. There is tremendous opportunity for catechesis in the preparation for baptism, the Ember observances, and the Friday abstinence. The removal of the obligation to fast provides an opportunity for extolling the benefits of fasting. Thomas Aquinas viewed fasting as a virtue that strengthened the

---

64   T. Lincoln Bouscaren and James O'Connor, SJ, "Faculty to Dispense Persons Hospitalized, So that They May Take Drink or Medicine," in *The Canon Law Digest. Vol. 3: 1942–1953* (Milwaukee: Bruce Publishing Co., 1956) 366–367.

Christian in numerous ways on his journey, including in the practice of prayer.

Pope Benedict XVI distinguished between a hermeneutic of discontinuity and rupture and a hermeneutic of reform in his December 22, 2005 address to the Roman Curia. While the hermeneutic of discontinuity and rupture has "frequently availed itself of the mass media and also one trend of modern theology," the hermeneutic of reform has provided opportunity for renewal within the Church. Certainly a discontinuity can be seen in the elimination of the obligation of fasting in each of the practices mentioned above. Within this same document, however, Pope Benedict pointed out that "it is precisely in this combination of continuity and discontinuity at different levels that the very nature of true reform consists." Those who have uttered a "fundamental yes" to the modern era have underestimated the inner tensions and contradictions in this era, and likewise the perilous frailty of human nature.[65] Is it not strange that fasting, which has been extolled and constantly practiced as a means of spiritual growth since the birth of Christianity and even before, remains nearly absent from contemporary Church observance? Is there not a misreading of the nature of the human person and his basic reliance upon the strength of the grace of the Lord? In an era that has become increasingly secular, the benefits of fasting could well strengthen soft spiritual muscles.

EUCHARISTIC FASTING

It would be difficult to state that the present one-hour fast prior to reception of Holy Communion is a fast at all. There is little opportunity to call to mind the need for food or drink within that brief single hour. In that sense, the current practice may therefore be seen as a discontinuity from a long and esteemed practice

---

65   Benedict XVI, *Address to the Roman Curia Offering them his Christmas Greetings* (22 December 2005). See Esther Mary Nickel, RSM, "Rogation Days, Ember Days, and the New Evangelization," in *Antiphon* 16 (2012) 21–36 for greater background on Rogation and Ember Days.

of the Eucharistic fast. The fast is not divine law but Church law, and therefore could readily be adjusted. Consequently, varied writers have brought forth their own solutions.

Robert Bubel, in his thesis on the Eucharistic fast, states that the beauty of the current rule is that it is "frequent, simple, uncomplicated and keepable."[66] The intent of the Eucharistic fast is to raise one's heart and soul to God to prepare oneself to receive the sacrament.[67] Bubel recommends that the fast be one hour before Mass begins. Ultimately, he believes, this practice would make a greater impression on Catholics. Fasting has its own way of disciplining the will and is not easily replaced. As Bubel states, the reception of Communion presumes a self-offering in preparation. Fasting as an act of penance and self-denial begins this process of offering oneself to God. A physical fast creates hunger, and thus a greater desire to be fed by the Eucharist.[68]

Edward Peters, on the other hand, promotes a restoration of the three-hour Eucharistic fast, clarifying that if there is to truly be a fast, it must be one that is experienced by the individual. With a fast of one hour there would even be opportunity for eating and drinking while commuting toward Church for the celebration of the Eucharist. Since the fast is calculated till the time of Communion, individuals can be distracted by calculating the time of the homily. A fast oriented only toward reception of the Eucharist diminishes appreciation of the Liturgy of the Word.[69]

In looking more deeply at the benefit of fasting, it must be acknowledged that the near vanishing of fasting before Communion has been attributed to pragmatic concerns. There is no question that pontiffs who have fostered and brought about this mitigation of Eucharistic fasting perceived a convenient practice as a means

---

66   Robert Bubel, "The Eucharistic Fast: An Important Form of Reverence and Preparation for Holy Communion" (unpublished master's thesis, St. Joseph's Seminary, Yonkers, NY, 2008) 47.

67   Ibid., 56.

68   Ibid., 52.

69   Edward N. Peters, "The Communion Fast: A Reconsideration," in *Antiphon* 11 (2007) 234–244.

of drawing more individuals to the reception and frequent reception of the sacrament. These pontiffs had also witnessed years of petitions from local ordinaries requesting exception from the Eucharistic fast for specific reasons. Fr. Thomas Anglin devotes two chapters of his dissertation on the Eucharistic fast to dispensations from the fast and penalties against priests who violate the fast.[70]

It is quite apparent that in our own times many members approach the altar for the Eucharist yet seldom approach the sacrament of penance for the forgiveness of sin. Could there a connection? Fasting has readily been practiced as an atonement for sin, whether as a focus during the Lenten season, a personal practice taken on as a means of releasing one's hold on sin, or as a penance drawing from the sacrament of reconciliation itself. Fasting in this light draws attention to the gift of redemption and the bountiful love of the Lord. Fasting in a penitential light as an atonement of sin necessarily leads to the gift of Eucharist, but it leads to the gift with an investment made, a deep appreciation of Who one is to receive. When penance is seldom practiced, reflection on the tremendous selfless love of a redeeming God may be absent from one's life. This absence can in turn lead to a more casual approach to the altar.

While the popes in the twentieth century have made the Eucharistic fast remarkably simple to observe, the challenge of internal preparation for the gift of the Eucharist increases. In a certain sense, that internal preparation can be focused by choosing to take on the three-hour fast from food and one-hour fast from drink before Mass begins. This time frame orders one's day more readily toward Holy Communion. The opportunity of reflecting upon the gift to be received is apparent. The inconvenience of the fast is a testimony to an appreciation of the gift. Eucharistic fast of this nature speaks counter-culturally to a society prone to instantaneous gratification. One is called to wait and to search out one's desires for the Lord. It is an excellent time to evaluate spiritual priorities in light of the current culture. Ample opportunity for catechesis from the pulpit and classroom is apparent in all of these endeavors.

---

70   Anglin, *The Eucharistic Fast*, 141–163.

Interior preparation for reception of the Eucharist certainly cannot be legislated. Yet, it has been a constant urging among spiritual writers. For a final resource, let us turn to the writings of Pope Benedict XVI, whose attitude of reverence for the sacrament pervades all of his Eucharistic writings.

FROM THE CHAIR OF PETER—POPE BENEDICT XVI (2005–2013)

The effectiveness of Eucharistic catechesis is seen in an "increased sense of the mystery of God's presence" outwardly expressed in reverence. There is likewise an intrinsic relationship between the celebration and adoration of the Eucharist. Adoration is a natural consequence of the Eucharistic celebration. "Receiving the Eucharist means adoring him whom we receive."[71] Pope Benedict clarified that Eucharistic worship should lead to a "total self-offering made in communion with the whole Church."[72] When the faithful share in the Sacrifice of the Cross, they partake of Christ's self-giving love, which equips them in turn to live that charity with others.[73]

Benedict addressed the awareness of the church as the house of God, noting its continuity with the Jewish synagogue and Temple.[74] The synagogue houses the Torah, the Word of God, whereas the church houses the Eucharist, which leads to the centrality of the tabernacle within the church building. Paul VI reminded us that the tabernacle should be situated "in churches in a most worthy place with the greatest honor."[75] It is a sad com-

---

71   Benedict XVI, Post-Synodal Apostolic Exhortation on the Eucharist as the Source and Summit of the Church's Life and Mission *Sacramentum Caritatis* (22 February 2007) no. 66.

72   Ibid., 70.

73   Ibid., 82.

74   Joseph Ratzinger, *The Spirit of the Liturgy*, trans. John Saward (San Francisco: Ignatius Press, 2000) 62–74.

75   Paul VI, Encyclical on the Holy Eucharist *Mysterium Fidei* (3 September 1965) no. 66, as cited in *Catechism of the Catholic Church*, 2nd ed. (Washington, DC: United States Catholic Conference, 2000) no. 1183.

mentary on American Catholicism that the choice of parish by many families is determined by whether the church dwelling itself is one in which individuals can enter into quiet prayer.

One of the more significant elements of Benedict's discussion pertaining to liturgy centered on his understanding of the term "active participation." The term participation, he stated, "does not refer to mere external activity during the celebration." Rather, active participation "must be understood in more substantial terms, on the basis of a greater awareness of the mystery being celebrated and its relationship to daily life."[76] The Second Vatican Council's Constitution on the Sacred Liturgy urged the faithful to "participate in the sacred action, conscious of what they are doing, actively and devoutly."[77]

A writer frequently quoted by Benedict XVI, Romano Guardini (1885–1968), viewed stillness as essential in preparation for the Eucharist. He described stillness as the tranquility of the inner life, "a collected total presence," a being "all there." Attentiveness is the "clue," as he terms it, to this stillness before God.[78] In addressing composure, he advised that we go to church early "in order to tidy up inwardly." We must frankly face our restlessness, confusion, disorder.[79] We are called to an intrinsic readiness and calm reflection in order to grasp the mystery that is taking place on the altar. This readiness opens the heart to a response of reverence.[80]

Another mentor of Benedict XVI, Louis Bouyer (1913–2004), reminds his readers that prayer is connected with fasting, as seen by the example of Christ himself. There need be some privation of physical food in order to dispose ourselves for spiritual food. Unfortunately, many are so attuned to "the cult of comfort" that the sense in fasting is not seen. To remain hungry on occasion, however, to

---

76   Benedict XVI, *Sacramentum Caritatis*, 52.

77   Second Vatican Council, Constitution on the Sacred Liturgy *Sacrosanctum Concilium* (4 December 1963) no. 48.

78   Romano Guardini, *Meditations before Mass,* trans. Elinor Castendyk Briefs (Westminster, MD: Newman Press, 1956) 5.

79   Ibid., 19.

80   Ibid, 42.

deprive oneself of that which is superfluous and a bit of that which is necessary, is a practice "essential for liberation, [for] it entails a certain stripping of oneself without which one cannot give a certain degree of attention to God."[81] Bouyer emphasized that fasting is an elementary form of that doing without

> . . . which should hold in check the continually threatening unruliness of our desires; it should habitually cut down the idolatry with which all our pleasures, even the most legitimate, are fraught. We need, unwearyingly, to undo that accommodation to the world which here ensnares us and would speedily, if we yielded to it without resistance, stupefy us spiritually.[82]

SUMMARY AND CONCLUSION

In looking back over this study, it is apparent that fasting has been a constant practice of the Church since biblical times. The Old Testament gives evidence of fasting practiced as part of the Day of Atonement. In moving toward the New Testament, Christ preached an appropriate time for fasting, giving emphasis to the reality that fasting is a private act between the individual and his Maker, rather than a matter of show. The awareness of Christ's time spent in the desert gives an example of the spiritual benefit of fasting for fortifying oneself against evil. Moving beyond the Scriptures, the Church fathers preached that fasting has an integral relationship to almsgiving in helping those who are in need. Fasting was practiced to make way for the feasts of significant saints and martyrs.

Fasting cannot be seen apart from its continuous practice of preparation for the sacraments. While Rogation Days wished to ward off natural disasters and Ember Days sought the blessing of the four seasons, the latter are seen in light of worthy candidates for the priesthood. Catechumens took on fasting, with their family

---

81   Louis Bouyer, *Introduction to Spirituality,* trans. Mary Perkins Ryan (New York: Desclee, 1961) 179.
82   Ibid., 180.

and the priest, as a means of disposing themselves to the forgiveness of sin and of strengthening the neophytes as they entered into the Christian way of life. A Lenten fast seeks atonement for sin, and therefore the sacrament of penance, in addition to preparation for the tremendous gift of redemption.

Thomas Aquinas viewed fasting as a virtue that strengthened the Christian in numerous ways on his journey, certainly as a means of focusing one's prayer, which automatically instills that long tradition of reverence before the sacrament, so readily extolled by Pope Benedict XVI.

Eucharistic fasting was observed within the Church when morning Masses became a common practice in the course of the first three centuries. Initially the Eucharist had been preceded by a meal, which was often hosted by a Christian in whose home the Eucharist was being celebrated. The Council of Constance confirmed the universality of Eucharistic fasting, specifying a fast from midnight on. This was maintained until the mid-twentieth century.

While Pope Pius X encouraged frequent reception of the Eucharist, changes leading to the one-hour fast practiced now within Roman Catholicism were actually brought about in the latter part of the twentieth century through Popes Pius XII and Paul VI. One may recall that Bubel sees fasting as frequent, simple, uncomplicated and keepable, and therefore difficult to replace in preparation for reception of the sacrament.

Pope Benedict XVI taught that effective Eucharistic catechesis increases a sense of the mystery of God's presence as outwardly expressed in reverence. He described the Church as the house of God, and therefore a place of prayer, a sacred space. The pontiff further clarified that "'active participation,' rightly understood, brings about a greater awareness of the mystery being celebrated and its relationship to daily life."[83] Guardini brought into focus the great need for internal preparation before approaching the altar to receive. Bouyer recalled the essential irreplaceable nature of the natural fast as a means of focusing one's entire being on the gift to be received.

---

83   Benedict XVI, *Sacramentum Caritatis*, no. 52.

Catechesis today would do well to place emphasis upon a deeper awareness of the sacredness of place, meaning the house of God; sacredness of time, bearing in mind that *kairos*, or liturgical time, embraces the past and the future; and proximate preparations. Spiritual fasting expresses an abstinence from those elements that are ungodlike. Physical fasting disciplines the body, which in turn disciplines the will.

If there is going to be any benefit drawn from fasting, the return to a three-hour fast from food, as ordained by Pope Pius XII, would provide that realization of a physical absence from food which would more readily focus one toward sacramental reception. The catechist, however, as one who extolls the benefit of the fast leading toward sacramental reception, must practice it first. The catechesis needs to begin with oneself.

If legislation regarding the Eucharistic fast is not altered, the benefit of taking on the three-hour fast can be extolled. It is certainly opportune during this time of a casual stance in approaching the Sacrament that catechesis address the motivating force for reception of the Sacrament, that is, a greater realization of the tremendous gift to be received. Spiritual preparation, so essential prior to reception of the Sacrament, would provide a more fruitful possibility of opening the heart to that interior longing for the Lord. This is deepened and focused with the aid of a physical fast. As St. Paul so readily reminds us, we are one whole, body, mind, and spirit (see 1 Thess 5:23). Within this age that gives so much attention to holistic spirituality, a return to a physical fast might bring home the reality of the nature and integration of the human person.

The Order for Blessing Water: Past and Present

DANIEL G. VAN SLYKE

This essay compares and contrasts the current Order for Blessing Water Outside of Mass and its immediate predecessor, with a view to outlining the wider changes that have been made to the blessings of the Roman Rite following the call for liturgical renewal issued by the Second Vatican Council. Because of its previous preeminence among the blessings of the Ritual, the Order for Blessing Water provides a key point of entry for studying the structural and theological differences between the current blessings and those in use before the Second Vatican Council.

BLESSINGS IN ROMAN LITURGICAL BOOKS
AFTER THE COUNCIL OF TRENT

Following the directives of the Council of Trent, the Roman Ritual (*Rituale Romanum*) was revised and promulgated by Pope Paul V on 17 June 1614.[1] The revised Ritual contained only 18 non-reserved blessings—that is, blessings that could be administered by any priest or bishop. The first of these was the *Ordo ad faciendam aquam benedictam* or Order for Blessing Water.[2] Eleven

---

1   *Rituale Romanum Editio Princeps 1614*, Monumenta Liturgica Concilii Tridentini 5, ed. Manlio Sodi and Juan Javier Flores Arcas (Vatican City: Libreria Editrice Vaticana, 2004).

2   In the order in which they appear, the remaining non-reserved blessings follow: (2) blessing of candles; (3) blessing of homes (on Holy Saturday); (4) another blessing of homes (to be used at any other time, with the sprinkling of holy water); (5) blessing of a place; (6) another blessing of a new home; (7) blessing of a bridal

blessings reserved for the bishop followed the non-reserved bless-ings,[3] for a total of 29 blessings.

A brief but very important set of general rules opened Title VII, the section of the Ritual on blessings, and therefore immedi-ately preceded the Order for Blessing Water. The rules stipulated that each blessing should begin with the following dialogue of versicles and responses:

V. Our help is in the name of the Lord (Adjutorium nostrum in nomine Domini).
R. Who made heaven and earth (Qui fecit coelum et terram).
V. The Lord be with you (Dominus vobiscum).
R. And with your spirit (Et cum spiritu tuo).[4]

Then, the general rules continued, the prayer or prayers proper for the thing to be blessed should be said. Each blessing ended with the sprinkling of the object being blessed with holy water and, where indicated, incensation; both of these were done in silence.[5] Thus the post-Tridentine blessings were quite streamlined, con-sisting of two parts following the opening dialogue: (1) prayer or

---

chamber; (8) blessing of a new ship; (9) general blessing of fruits of the earth and vine-yards; (10) blessing of pilgrims setting out to holy places; (11) blessing of pilgrims after returning; (12) blessing of a paschal lamb; (13) blessing of eggs; (14) blessing of bread; (15) another blessing of bread; (16) blessing of new produce; (17) blessing of anything edible; (18) blessing of simple (unmixed) oil.

3   In the order in which they appear, the reserved blessings follow: (1) bless-ing of priestly vestments; (2) blessing of altar linens; (3) blessing of corporals; (4) blessing of a tabernacle; (5) blessing of a new cross; (6) blessing of images; (7) rite of blessing and laying the cornerstone of a church; (8) rite of blessing a new church or public oratory; (9) rite of reconciling a profaned church; (10) rite of blessing a new cemetery (for a priest delegated by a bishop); (11) order of reconciling a pro-faned cemetery.

4   *Rituale Romanum Pauli V Pontificis Maximi jussu editum aliorumque pontificum cura recognitum atque ad normam Codicis Juris Canonici accommodatum: Pii Papae XII auctoritate ordinatum et auctum* (Mechlin: Dessain, 1953) 265, my translation.

5   Ibid.: "Postea rem adspergat aqua benedicta, et, ubi notatum fuerit, pariter incenset, nihil dicendo. Cum Sacerdos aliquid benedicturus est, habeat ministrum cum vase aquae benedictae et adspersorio, et cum hoc Rituali libro, seu Missali."

prayers of blessing, and (2) sprinkling with holy water. Indeed, these parts constituted the entirety of each non-reserved blessing in the Ritual, with the exception of the first, which is under consideration here. The Order for Blessing Water did not end with a sprinkling of holy water on the water being blessed. It was also more complex because salt was used in it, as will be discussed further below.

Because holy water was necessary for every other blessing, the Order for Blessing Water was preeminent among the blessings of the Roman Ritual. It consistently occupied the first place within the section on blessings in the various editions of the Ritual until the Second Vatican Council.[6] Water blessed according to this Order also was reserved at the entrances of churches and sprinkled during pastoral visitations to the sick and at funerals.[7] As the rubrics specifically indicated, the faithful could take it home for sprinkling on sick family and friends, on homes, fields, vines, etc., and for sprinkling themselves daily.[8] The priest also sprinkled this water on the altar, the clergy, and the people while the *Asperges* (or, during Easter, the *Vidi aquam*) was intoned before High Mass.

---

6   Girolamo Baruffaldi [Hieronymus Baruffaldus], *Ad Rituale Romanum commentaria* (Venice: Balleoniana, 1731) XLV, p. 260. Note, however, that there are different kinds of holy water. For a description of four types of holy water found in Tridentine liturgical books—Gregorian water (for consecration of churches), baptismal water, Easter/Pentecost water, and ordinary holy water—see Frederick A. Houck, *Fountains of Joy, or "By Water and Blood,"* 3rd ed. (St. Louis: Herder, 1938) 108–127. What he calls "ordinary holy water" is the topic of the present study. The papal blessing, which is found in the Ritual of 1952, constitutes an exception insofar as it does not make use of holy water: see "Ritus benedictionis papalis super populum elargiendae," and "Formula benedictionis papalis cum indulgentia plenaria," in *Rituale Romanum* (1953), 429–430.

7   On the uses of holy water in liturgy and in devotion, see Henry Theiler, *Holy Water and its Significance for Catholics* (New York: Pustet, 1909) 35–54, and Houck, *Fountains of Joy*, 131–140.

8   *Rituale Romanum* 1953, 268: "Christifideles autem possunt de ista aqua benedicta in vasculis suis accipere, et secum deferre ad aspergendos aegros, domos, agros, vineas, et alia, et ad eam habendam in cubiculis suis, ut ea quotidie et saepius aspergi possint." See Baruffaldi, *Ad Rituale Romanum commentaria* XLV, p. 263: this practice can be traced back at least to the year 890.

Hence it occupied an important place not only in the Ritual, but
also in the Roman Missal, where it immediately followed the calendar in the very first printed editions.[9]

The 29 blessings in the Ritual of 1614 were too few to meet
the pastoral exigencies of all communities; hence the need to add
more blessings arose rather quickly. An edition of Paul V's Ritual
published in 1688 was augmented by a formula for blessing the
people and their fields.[10] It was not placed among the other blessings in the Ritual, but rather at the end of the book, following the
rite of exorcism. Benedict XIV followed such precedents when he
promulgated a new edition of the Ritual on 25 March 1752. An
appendix contained a great number of additional blessings, eventually doubling the length of the original post-Tridentine Ritual.
For ease of use, the blessings were often extracted from the Ritual
and published separately in benedictionals or books of blessing.
Local diocesan rituals and benedictionals developed, especially in
eighteenth- and nineteenth-century France, which gathered blessings absent from the Roman Ritual but deemed fitting for the pastoral needs of the local faithful.[11] These rituals and benedictionals
also opened with the Order for Blessing Water.

---

9   A photographic reprint is provided by Anthony Ward and Cuthbert Johnson, *Missalis Romani editio princeps Mediolani anno 1474 prelis mandata*, Bibliotheca
Ephemerides Liturgicae Subsidia Instrumenta Liturgica Quarreriensia Supplementa
3 (Rome: C.L.V.-Edizioni Liturgiche, 1996) 15–16; for an edited version, see *Missale
Romanum Mediolani, 1474, Vol. 1: Text*, ed. Robert Lippe, Henry Bradshaw Society
17 (London: Harrison and Sons, 1899) xxv–xxvi.

10   *Rituale Romanum Paul V. Pont. Max. jussu editum: Addita formula pro bene-
dicendis populo & agris a S. Rituum Congregatione approbata* (Antwerp: Plantin-Moreti,
1688) 397–408.

11   For a list of printed benedictionals and separately published appendices to
the Roman Ritual in eighteenth- and nineteenth-century France, see Jean-Baptiste
Molin and Annik Aussedat-Minvielle, *Répertoire des rituels et processionnaux imprimés
conservés en France* (Paris: Éditions du Centre National de la Recherche Scientifique,
1984) 559–563; for another example, see *Benedictionale Romanum sive sacrae benedictiones in Rituali romano et in ejus adprobata appendice ac in Missali necnon Pontificali
romano*, 3rd ed. (Ratisbon: Pustet, 1884); see also Pierre Jounel, "Le livre des bénédictions," in *Maison-Dieu* 175 (1988) 27–52, at 39–40.

Pius XI promulgated another edition of the Roman Ritual in 1925. It contained a large appendix of 71 non-reserved blessings and 79 reserved blessings. Fifty-two of these reserved blessings were for the use of particular religious orders. Pius XII promulgated the final edition of the Ritual in 1952, in which the additional blessings were moved from the appendix to Title IX, the section on blessings (*De Benedictionibus*). Although the blessings were substantially re-arranged for ease of use, the Order for Blessing Water remained the first. The Ritual of 1952 contained 179 blessings, 95 of which were reserved.[12]

THE PREVIOUS ORDER

The Order for Blessing Water in Paul V's Ritual remained the same through the various revisions of the Ritual, including that of 1952. It began with an exorcism of salt, followed by a prayer invoking God's blessing and sanctification upon the exorcized salt. For the sake of brevity, analysis of the exorcism and blessing of salt will be omitted from this study. The water itself was subject to one exorcism and one prayer of blessing. Then the salt was mixed with the water, and a final blessing was pronounced over the resulting solution.

The exorcism of water took the following form:

> I exorcize you, creature of water, in the name of God + the Father almighty, in the name of Jesus + Christ his Son our Lord, and in the power of the Holy + Spirit: that you may be water exorcized for putting all strength of the enemy to flight, and that you may be empowered to uproot and cast out the enemy himself with his apostate angels, by the power of the same Jesus

---

12   Jounel, "Le livre des bénédictions," 40–41, and idem, "Blessings," in *The Church at Prayer: An Introduction to the Liturgy, Vol. 3: The Sacraments*, ed. Robert Cabié et al., trans. Matthew J. O'Connell (Collegeville, MN: Liturgical Press, 1988) 263–284, at 275–276. For an overview of the organization of blessings in the Ritual of 1952, see Burkhard Neunheuser, "Evoluzione di mentalità nella prassi delle benedizioni in occidente," *Rivista liturgica* 73 (1986) 213–250, at 206.

Christ our Lord: Who shall come to judge the living and the
dead, and the world by fire. R. Amen.[13]

The exorcism addresses the water itself, or the "creature of water,"
which suggests God's act of creation. One might explain this as
parallel to the manner in which inanimate objects are sometimes
called to praise God in scripture (e.g., Dan 3:60).[14] The priest first
exorcizes the water in the name of the Trinity, then offers a prayer
that Christ might empower the water to drive out the enemy, his
fallen angels, and all of his strength or jurisdiction (*potestas*). The
power (*virtus*) of Christ is mentioned, along with his second coming and the final judgment, which strike terror in the enemy and
his angels.[15] It is important to note that this formula, assuming its
efficacy, not merely exorcizes the water, but also empowers it to
be an instrument of exorcism, in the sense of driving out the
enemy, his companions, and his influence.

---

13   The following Latin text and all those from the pre-Vatican II *Ordo* cited
subsequently are taken from Pius XII's typical edition, *Rituale Romanum* (1953) 266–
268: "Exorcizo te, creatura aquae, in nomine Dei + Patris omnipotentis, in nomine
Jesu + Christi Filii ejus Domini nostri, et in virtute Spiritus + Sancti: ut fias aqua exor-
cizata ad effugandam omnem potestatem inimici, et ipsum inimicum eradicare et
explantare valeas cum angelis suis apostaticis, per virtutem ejusdem Domini nostri
Jesu Christi: qui venturus est judicare vivos et mortuos, et saeculum per ignem. R.
Amen." This translation and those that follow from the Tridentine rite are my own,
although I have consulted two others: Philip T. Weller, *The Roman Ritual: Complete
Edition* (Milwaukee: Bruce Publishing Co., 1964) 396–398, and Theiler, *Holy Water*,
17–22.
14   This is the explanation provided by Pierre-Constant Barraud, "De l'eau
bénite et des vases destinés à la contenir," in *Bulletin monumental*, 4th series 6 (1870)
393–467, at 417–418.
15   At the end of the second century, Tertullian explained the power of Christians over demons as follows in *Apologeticum* XXIII, 15–16 (CCSL 1:132–33), my
translation: ". . . our domination and power over them is possible from the naming of
Christ and from their memory . . . fearing Christ in God and God in Christ, they are
subjected to the servants of God and of Christ. Thus from our touch and breath, with
the contemplation and realization of their punishment of fire, and by our command,
they depart from bodies, unwilling and sorrowing and ashamed before you who are
present."

The prayer over the water continues this theme, invoking God's blessing upon the water so that it may become an instrument for driving away a multitude of evils:

> O God, who for the salvation of the human race have founded all the greatest mysteries (*sacramenta*) in the substance of water: be favorable to our prayers, and pour forth the power of your blessing + upon this element prepared with manifold purifications: so that your creature, serving your mysteries, may take up the effect of divine grace for expelling demons and driving away diseases; so that whatsoever this water sprinkles in the homes or places of the faithful, may be freed from all uncleanness, and delivered from harm: may the pestilential spirit not remain there, nor destroying air: may all snares of the hidden enemy depart; and if there be anything that is hostile towards either the safety or the repose of the inhabitants, let it flee with the sprinkling of this water: so that the well-being asked through the invocation of your holy name may be defended from all that attacks it. Through our Lord Jesus Christ your Son: who with you lives and reigns in the unity of the Holy Spirit, God for ever and ever. R. Amen.[16]

The prayer does not merely ask that the water be blessed, but rather that the water be infused with God's power of blessing. The purpose of this power is once again apotropaic; it is for driving away demons and their snares, disease and all other evils. Expelling evil, however, does not appear as an end in itself: the prayer also

---

16   "Deus, qui ad salutem humani generis, maxima quaeque sacramenta in aquarum substantia condidisti: adesto propitius invocationibus nostris, et elemento huic multimodis purificationibus praeparato, virtutem tuae bene + dictionis infunde: ut creatura tua, mysteriis tuis serviens, ad abigendos daemones, morbosque pellendos, divinae gratiae sumat effectum; ut quidquid in domibus, vel in locis fidelium, haec unda resperserit, careat omni immunditia, liberetur a noxa: non illic resideat spiritus pestilens, non aura corrumpens: discedant omnes insidiae latentis inimici; et si quid est, quod aut incolumitati habitantium invidet, aut quieti, aspersione hujus aquae effugiat: ut salubritas, per invocationem sancti tui nominis expetita, ab omnibus sit impugnationibus defensa. Per Dominum nostrum Jesum Christum Filium tuum: Qui tecum vivit et regnat in unitate Spiritus Sancti Deus, per omnia saecula saeculorum. R. Amen."

requests that safety, repose, and general well-being fill the homes
and places of the faithful sprinkled with this water.

The priest next mixes the exorcized and blessed salt into the
water three times in the pattern of a cross, saying, "May this salt
and water be mixed together, in the name of the Father + and of
the Son + and of the Holy + Spirit," to which the response is
"Amen." The versicle beginning "The Lord be with you . . ." is
repeated,[17] and then the priest utters the last prayer of the Order,
the prayer over the mixture of salt and water:

> O God, source of invincible strength and king of insuperable
> dominion, and ever magnificent triumphant one: you who
> restrain the force of the adversary's dominion: you who over-
> come the savagery of the raging enemy: you who powerfully
> defeat hostile influences: trembling and prostrate we humbly
> beseech and implore you, Lord: that you may look kindly upon
> this creature of salt and water, graciously illumine and sanctify
> it with the dew of your mercy: that wherever it shall be sprin-
> kled, through the invocation of your holy name, every infesta-
> tion of the unclean spirit may be banished: and the terror of the
> venomous serpent may be driven afar: and may the presence of
> the Holy Spirit deign to be everywhere with us, who ask your
> mercy. Through our Lord Jesus Christ your Son: who lives and
> reigns in the unity of the same Holy Spirit, God for ever and
> ever. R. Amen.[18]

---

17   "Hic ter mittat sal in aquam in modum crucis, dicendo semel: Commixtio
salis et aquae pariter fiat, in nomine Pa + tris, et Fi + lii, et Spiritus + Sancti. R. Amen.
V. Dominus vobiscum. R. Et cum spiritu tuo."

18   "Deus, invictae virtutis auctor, et insuperabilis imperii Rex, ac semper
magnificus triumphator: qui adversae dominationis vires reprimis: qui inimici
rugientis saeviam superas: qui hostiles nequitias potenter expugnas: te, Domine,
trementes et supplices deprecamur, ac petimus: ut hanc creaturam salis et aquae
dignanter aspicias, benignus illustres, pietatis tuae rore sanctifices; ut, ubicumque fuerit
aspersa, per invocationem sancti nominis tui, omnis infestatio immundi spiritus
abigatur: terrorque venenosi serpentis procul pellatur: et praesentia Sancti Spiritus
nobis, misericordiam tuam poscentibus, ubique adesse dignetur. Per Dominum
nostrum Jesum Christum Filium tuum: Qui tecum vivit et regnat in unitate ejusdem
Spiritus Sancti Deus, per omnia saecula saeculorum. R. Amen."

This final prayer asks the unconquerable God—for whom the devil is no threat whatsoever—to illumine and sanctify this creature of salt and water. Once again the desired effect is to drive away the infestation of every impure spirit, along with the terror and venom of the ancient serpent. Yet this blessing goes far beyond the apotropaic, by requesting that God grant the presence of the Holy Spirit wherever the solution might be sprinkled. Expulsion of evil influences, then, appears as a sort of necessary preamble to the fuller realization of divine power—and a striking demonstration of the priestly *munus* (office/duty) of sanctifying.

Note that this prayer implores God that evil spirits may flee and God's Spirit may dwell "wherever" the solution is sprinkled. The previous prayer, over the water alone, more specifically refers to the homes and places of the faithful. In this way the Order for Blessing Water indicates a primary use to which this holy water was expected to be put: the lay faithful would take it for sprinkling their homes, barns, fields, shops, etc. This was an eminent mode of actual or active participation in the blessings of the Middle Ages and the Tridentine era, even though some might characterize it as private devotion. The use of the same holy water in every other blessing, as well as at the beginning of the Mass, kept it firmly within the framework of liturgy. Thus, in a remarkable way, holy water linked the official public worship of the Church with the daily lives of the faithful.

BLESSINGS IN ROMAN LITURGICAL BOOKS
AFTER THE SECOND VATICAN COUNCIL

The fathers of the Second Vatican Council, considering blessings under the category of sacramentals, commanded that they undergo a revision aimed above all at fostering intelligent, actual, and easy participation on the part of the faithful (". . . conscia, actuosa et facili participatione fidelium"). They also ordered that the reserved blessings should be reduced to only a few, and that limited provision be made for the administration of some sacramentals at the hands of qualified lay persons.[19] In 1965, the Sacred Congregation of Rites allowed all priests to bestow the majority of blessings, thereby implementing one of the council's mandates by quickly eliminating the reservation of certain blessings to particular religious orders and congregations.[20] The work of actually revising the texts of the blessings was entrusted to Study Group (*Coetus*) 23 of the *Consilium* for Implementing the Constitution on the Sacred Liturgy, headed by Pierre-Marie Gy, OP.[21]

Commentators divide the subsequent process of revising the blessings into two phases.[22] The first, extending from 1970 to

---

19   Second Vatican Council, Constitution on the Sacred Liturgy *Sacrosanctum Concilium*, (4 December 1963) no. 79: "The sacramentals are to undergo a revision which takes into account the primary principle of enabling the faithful to participate intelligently, actively and easily; the circumstances of our own days must also be considered. When rituals are revised, as laid down in Art. 63, new sacramentals may also be added as the need for these becomes apparent. Reserved blessings shall be very few; reservations shall be in favor of bishops or ordinaries. Let provision be made that some sacramentals, at least in special circumstances and at the discretion of the ordinary, may be administered by qualified lay persons."

20   Sacred Congregation for Rites, Instruction on the Orderly Carrying Out of the Constitution on the Liturgy *Inter Oecumenici* (26 September 1964), in *Documents on the Liturgy 1963–1979: Conciliar, Papal, and Curial Texts* (Collegeville, MN: Liturgical Press, 1982) no. 77 (p. 105): "The blessings in the *Rituale Romanum* tit. IX, cap. 9, 10, 11, hitherto reserved, may be given by any priest, except for: the blessing of a bell for the use of a blessed church or oratory (cap. 9, no. 11); the blessing of the cornerstone of a church (cap. 9, no. 16); the blessing of a new church or public oratory (cap. 9, no. 17); the blessing of an antemensium (cap. 9, no. 21); the blessing of a new cemetery (cap. 9, no. 22); papal blessings (cap. 10, nos. 1–3); the blessing and erection of the stations of the cross (cap. 11, no. 1), reserved to the bishop."

21   Annibale Bugnini, *The Reform of the Liturgy 1948–1975*, trans. Matthew J. O'Connell (Collegeville, MN: Liturgical Press, 1990) 570, n. 1: "Group 23 on the sacramentals: *relator*: P.-M. Gy; *secretary*: S. Mazzarello; *members*: J. Mejia, J. Rabau, J. Hofinger, F. Vandenbroucke, and D. Sicard. Subsequently added were A. Chavasse, B. Löwenberg, and K. Ritzer. Although the two groups [22 and 23] were distinct, they always worked together." Balthasar Fischer served as *relator* or chair of the Study Group 22, the other *coetus* charged with revising the rites of the Ritual.

22   Mario Lessi-Ariosto, "Linee interpretative dell'iter redazionale del *De Benedictionibus*," in *Rivista liturgica* 73 (1986) 214–230; Enzo Lodi, "Le bénédictionnel romain pour la sanctification de la vie: sources et contenus," in *Les bénédictions et les sacra-*

1974, was preparatory. During this phase, the doctrinal and practical principles that would guide the actual revision of the texts of the blessings were set forth.[23] In addition to the concerns specifically noted in *Sacrosanctum Concilium*, three more of these principles proved particularly momentous. First, the Study Group defined blessing primarily as thanksgiving and praise, as is evident in an internal communication of the Sacred Congregation for Divine Worship dated 23 February 1972:

> Blessings . . . have, above all and perhaps in the first place, an element of thanksgiving and of blessing towards God, a very beautiful example of which is found in the formulae over the bread and wine at the offertory of the restored rite of the Mass: "Blessed are you Lord God of the universe, because from your goodness we have received bread . . . wine. . . ." The special theological importance of blessing rests in this, that it recognizes and proclaims the goodness of creation and the providence of the Creator. In the various circumstances of his life, man, made to the image of God, giving thanks recognizes and confesses that all created things come forth from the hands of God.[24]

---

mentaux dans la liturgie: Conférences Saint-Serge, XXXIVᵉ Semaine d'Etudes Liturgiques, Paris 1987, ed. Achille M. Triacca and Alessandro Pistoia, Bibliotheca Ephemerides Liturgicae Subsidia 44 (Rome: C.L.V.-Edizioni Liturgiche, 1988) 181–206; Bugnini, *Reform of the Liturgy*, 778–783; for a brief summary of the process of revision citing the relevant official texts, see "De Benedictionibus," in *Notitiae* 19 (1983) 320–322.

23   For three distinct but closely related listings of these norms, see Lessi-Ariosto, "Linee interpretative," 217–219; Lodi, "Le bénédictionnel romain," 182–183; and Bugnini, *Reform of the Liturgy*, 778–780.

24   Sacred Congregation for Divine Worship, Letter, "De benedictionibus," 23 Feb 1972, courtesy of the University of Notre Dame Archives, my translation: "Benedictiones . . . habent insuper, et forsitan primo loco, elementum gratiarum actionis et benedictionis erga Deum, cuius perpulchrum exemplum invenitur in formulis super panem et vinum ad offertorium ritus Missae instaurati: 'Benedictus es Domine Deus universi, quia de tua largitate accepimus panem . . . vinum. . . .' Praecipuum momentum theologicum benedictionis in eo consistit quod agnoscit et proclamat bonitatem creaturarum et providentiam Creatoris. In variis circumstantiis vitae suae homo, ad imaginem Dei factus, gratias agens agnoscit et confitetur omnes res creatas provenire e manibus Dei." See also "Labores coetuum a studiis: De benedictionibus," in *Notitiae* 6 (1970) 245; and "Labores coetuum a studiis: De benedictionibus," in *Notitiae* 7 (1971) 126, 128.

From this perspective, blessing serves primarily as a sort of creedal statement on God's creative activity. As in this passage, influential liturgists of the post-conciliar period frequently claim that the Eucharist provides a model for prayers of blessing, often relying heavily upon the evidence offered by the problematic ancient Christian text known as the *Apostolic Tradition*.[25] As a second momentous working principle, the Study Group posited that blessings are invoked primarily on people and their activity, and only secondarily on the things and places that they use. This stress on the primacy of human thanksgiving and praise towards God is also evident throughout the writings of Catholic theologians who worked on blessings in the post-Vatican II period.[26] In light of the final product of the Study Group's work,

---

25   For a recent overview demonstrating how complicated it is to interpret the *Apostolic Tradition*, see Paul F. Bradshaw, Maxwell E. Johnson, and L. Edward Phillips, *The Apostolic Tradition: A Commentary* (Minneapolis: Fortress Press, 2002) 1–17. For examples of scholars who invoke the Eucharist as a model for blessings, see André Gignac, "Les bénédictions: sous le signe de la création et de l'espérance évangélique," in *Dans vos assemblées: Sens et pratique de la célébration liturgique*, vol. 2, ed. Joseph Gelineau et al. (Paris: Desclée, 1971) 579–596, at 583–586; Enrico Mazza, "I *Praenotanda generalia* del rituale romano: De Benedictionibus," in *Rivista liturgica* 73 (1986) 231–250, at 239–240; Jounel, "Le livre de bénédictions," esp. 29–30, 33, and 43. This claim is tied up with the wording of Eucharistic prayers in such sources as the *Apostolic Tradition* and ubiquitous theories regarding the evolution of the Eucharistic prayer from Jewish modes of blessing, thanksgiving, and praise—particularly the *berakoth*—as expressed for example in Louis Bouyer, *Eucharist: Theology and Spirituality of the Eucharistic Prayer*, trans. Charles Underhill Quinn (Notre Dame: University of Notre Dame Press, 1968); and Robert Cabié, *The Church At Prayer: An Introduction to the Liturgy, Vol. 2: The Eucharist*, trans. Matthew J. O'Connell (Collegeville, MN: Liturgical Press, 1986) 20–35. Not yet fully appreciated are the criticisms in Paul F. Bradshaw, *The Search for the Origins of Christian Worship: Sources and Methods for the Study of Early Liturgy*, 2nd ed. (Oxford: Oxford University Press, 2002) 139: he argues that among the three "main obstacles to real progress in the search for the origins and development of early Christian eucharistic practices" is "a widespread belief that it is necessary to trace both the overall pattern of the rite and the prayer used in it back to a standard, fixed Jewish liturgy."

26   Marcel Metzger, "Les bénédictions des personnes et des éléments dans les *Constitutions apostoliques*," in *Les bénédictions et les sacramentaux dans les liturgie*, 207–224, at 207: speaking at a conference sponsored by the Holy See in 1987, Metzger

one can summarize these principles by describing rites of blessing as opportunities to help the faithful, particularly through their activity in the world, give thanksgiving and praise to God for the goods of creation.

The Study Group's final principle is expressed as follows: "in blessings the element of invocation against diabolic powers can be allowed: nevertheless, vigilance is necessary lest blessings become just as 'amulets' or 'talismans'. . . ."[27] Apotropaic invocations or prayers aimed at counteracting diabolic influence, then, are dispensable if they conflict with the overriding demand to discourage superstition. Exorcisms, if only by omission, do not appear to be allowed at all: they are addressed to the demon or to the creature and so cannot be qualified as invocations, which are addressed to God. This third principle, however timidly expressed, could potentially justify—as the finished product of the Study Group's labors attests—the complete elimination of a predominant feature of pre-Vatican II blessings.

The second phase began at the end of 1974 with the constitution of a second Study Group, which was subsequently dissolved and whose work was then taken up by a third Study Group.[28] The

---

began his paper as follows: "Si on étend le mot bénédiction à toutes les prières de louange et d'action de grâces, éléments fondamentaux des liturgies juive et chrétienne. . .;" my translation: "If one extends the word benediction to all prayers of praise and thanksgiving, fundamental elements of Jewish and Christian liturgies. . . ." This understanding arises from a certain reading of the Hebrew word for blessing and the *Apostolic Tradition* which can be seen, for example, in Thomas G. Simons, *Blessings: A Reappraisal of their Nature, Purpose, and Celebration* (Saratoga, CA: Resource Publications, 1981) 33–48. The biography on the back cover of the book says that Simons "is a member of the International Committee for English in the Liturgy (ICEL) and serves in the Study Group on Blessings." See also Mazza, "I *Praenotanda generalia*," 241.

27   "Labores coetuum a studiis: De benedictionibus," in *Notitiae* 6 (1970) 245–246, at 246: "in benedictionibus admitti potest elementum invocationis contra potestates diabolicas: attamen invigilandum est ne benedictiones fiant quasi 'amuleta' seu 'talismana'. . . ." See also "Labores coetuum a studiis: de benedictionibus," in *Notitiae* 7 (1971) 123–132, at 129; and Mazza, "I *Praenotanda generalia*," 249–250.

28   "Adunationes apud S. C. pro Cultu Divino," in *Notitiae* 10 (1974) 347; "Adunatio consultorum sectionis pro cultu divino," in *Notitiae* 14 (1978) 73.

new book of blessings was not completed until Pope John Paul II promulgated it under the title *De Benedictionibus* on 31 May 1984. This current book of blessings contains a "General Introduction" (*Praenotanda generalia*) providing a theological explanation of blessings along with practical norms for their celebration. The introduction stresses that blessings, as part of the Church's liturgy, should be celebrated communally.[29] It then indicates that the typical rite of blessing is comprised of two parts: first, the proclamation of the word of God; second, praise of divine goodness and petition for heavenly help.[30] The first part can contain several elements, including introductory rites (song, sign of the cross, greeting, along with an introductory instruction to explain the meaning of the blessing), a reading from scripture, and intercessions. While other elements of the blessing may be omitted, the reading from scripture, which is considered fundamental, may not be. The second part of the typical current rite of blessing is limited to the formula of blessing or the prayer itself, along with any sign belonging to the rite—such as the sign of the cross or a sprinkling with water, which appears in several of the rites.[31]

One immediately notes a radical change in the structure of blessings. First, a "liturgy of the word" has been added to the prayer of blessing that constituted the fundamental core of most blessings in the previous Roman Ritual. Second, holy water is no longer central to the rites of blessing. Accordingly, the Order for Blessing Water, that once occupied the place of honor, now occupies the relative obscurity of chapter 33.

In 1987, ICEL completed its translation and adaptation of *De Benedictionibus*, entitled *Book of Blessings*, "for study and comment"

---

29   *Rituale Romanum ex decreto Oecumenici Concilii Vaticani II instauratum auctoritate Ioannis Pauli II promulgatum: De Benedictionibus*, Editio typica (Vatican City: Libreria Editrice Vaticana, 1984, reprint 1993) Praenotanda, no. 16.

30   *De Benedictionibus*, Praenotanda, no. 20. See Julian Lopez Martin, "Las orientaciones generales del bendicional," in *Phase* 157 (1987) 45–57, at 50–51: Martin properly notes that the typical structure is an imitation of the liturgical structure of the revised sacraments.

31   *De Benedictionibus*, Praenotanda, no. 22.

as well as "for interim use."[32] The Holy See approved the *Book of Blessings* on 27 January 1989, for use in the United States *ad interim*.[33] From 3 December 1989, the First Sunday of Advent, the National Conference of Catholic Bishops (NCCB) declared, "the use of the *Book of Blessings* is mandatory in the dioceses of the United States of America. From that day forward no other English version may be used."[34] The *Book of Blessings* contains translations of orders and prayers of blessing from *De Benedictionibus*, along with 42 orders and prayers composed by the NCCB's Committee on the Liturgy or added from other liturgical books. The numbering and ordering of material differs from that of the Latin typical edition.

Chapter 41 of the *Book of Blessings* contains the "Order for the Blessing of Holy Water Outside Mass." It can be characterized as a translation of *De Benedictionibus* chapter 33. Nonetheless the typical edition *De Benedictionibus* provides the sole basis for the analysis that follows. The translations, which are my own, strive for a literal rendering of the original Latin.

THE PRESENT ORDER

The current Order for Blessing Water Outside the Celebration of Mass (*Ordo ad faciendam aquam benedictam extra missae celebrationem*) is reserved for the clergy—whether bishop, priest or deacon. This Order is, by virtue of its context, the immediate successor of the Order for Blessing Water in the pre-Vatican II Ritual. The previous Order was never used within the Mass, but rather

---

32   *Book of Blessings: For Study and Comment by the Bishops of the Member and Associate Member Conferences of the International Commission on English in the Liturgy* (Washington, DC: International Commission on English in the Liturgy, 1987). On the adaptation of the typical edition for local use, see Jounel, "Le livre des bénédictions," 45–46, and 52.

33   Congregation for Divine Worship, "Decree," in *Book of Blessings*, prepared by International Commission on English in the Liturgy (Collegeville, MN: Liturgical Press, 1989) vi.

34   NCCB, "Decree," in *Book of Blessings* 1989, v.

in the sacristy or in the church before Mass began. The current Missal contains a distinct Order for Blessing Water within the Mass, which may be used in lieu of the penitential rite, but that shall be discussed briefly for comparative purposes only. The Order for Blessing Water outside the Celebration of Mass in *De Benedictionibus* of 1984 begins with the sign of the cross in the name of the Father, Son, and Holy Spirit. The introductory rites continue as the celebrant greets those gathered for the blessing with the following words, or with other suitable words from Scripture: "May God, who from water and the Holy Spirit has regenerated us in Christ, be with all."[35] This constitutes a kind of versicle, to which all are to reply, "And with your spirit," or some other suitable response. Then the celebrant, if it is appropriate (*pro opportunitate*), prepares those gathered for the celebration of the blessing with the following words, or something similar:

> With this blessing of water, we recall Christ the living water and the sacrament of baptism, in which we have been reborn in water and the Holy Spirit. Whenever, therefore, we are sprinkled with this water, or upon entering a church or staying at home we use it with the sign of the cross, we will give thanks to God for his indescribable gift, and implore his help, in order that we might by living hold on to what we have received by faith.[36]

---

35   *De Benedictionibus*, no. 1089: "Deus, qui ex aqua et Spiritu Sancto / nos regeneravit in Christo, / sit cum omnibus."

36   *De Benedictionibus*, no. 1090: "Hac aquae benedictione, Christum aquam vivam ac Baptismatis recolimus sacramentum, in quo ex aqua et Spiritu Sancto renati sumus. Quoties ergo hac aqua aspergemur, vel ea tum intrantes in ecclesiam tum domi manentes cum signo crucis utemur, gratias Deo agemus pro inenarrabili dono eius, eiusque implorabimus auxilium, ut sacramentum vivendo teneamus, quod fide percepimus." See Lodi, "Le bénédictionnel romain," 193: "Il s'agit ici d'un emprunt à la collecte du lundi de l'octave pascale, qui remonte au sacramentaire Grégorien-Paduensis, dans la monition introductive;" my translation: "What we have here is a borrowing from the collect of Monday of the Paschal Octave, which goes back to the Gregorian-Paduense Sacramentary, in the introductory remark." I have checked the Paduense, and am unable to verify any resemblance between it and the introductory remark in *De Benedictionibus*.

The use of water assumed by the rites is twofold: it is sprinkled on "us"—that is, we who are present for the celebration—or we sign ourselves with it upon entering a church or even at home. By using it in these ways, we recall Christ and our baptism, give thanks to God, and implore his aid in living the sacrament that we have received in faith. At the outset, then, the Order is framed as a memorial of the participants' baptism marked by thanksgiving.

The reading from scripture follows. The Order provides the full text of John 7:37-39, and then indicates six other possible scriptural readings.[37]

The prayer of blessing comes next. Here there are three options, but no indication that the celebrant can use "similar words." The celebrant chooses from one of the three, reciting it with hands outstretched. The first follows:

> Blessed are you, Lord, all-powerful God,
> who (*qui*) in Christ, the living water of our salvation,
> have deigned to bless and inwardly reform us:
> grant that we who by the sprinkling of this water
> or by its use are strengthened
> may, with renewed youth of the soul
> through the power of the Holy Spirit,
> continually walk in newness of life.
> Through Christ our Lord.
> R. Amen.[38]

The *qui* clause characterizes God as having reformed us inwardly by baptism. The petition seeks that we might be helped by the sprinkling or use of this water, in order to walk continually in newness of life. The prayer requests the renewal of "us" who are

---

37   *De Benedictionibus*, nos. 1091–1092: Is 12:1–6; Is 55:1–11; Sir 15:1–6; 1 Jn 5:1–6; Rv 7:13–17; Rv 22:1–5; Jn 13:3–15.

38   *De Benedictionibus*, no. 1093: "Benedictus es, Domine, Deus omnipotens, / qui nos in Christo, aqua viva salutis nostrae, / benedicere dignatus es et intus reformare: / concede ut qui huius aquae aspersione / vel usu munimur, / renovata animae iuventute / per virtutem Sancti Spiritus / in novitate vitae iugiter ambulemus. / Per Christum Dominum nostrum. / R. Amen."

present for the celebration. It does not allow that any thing or place might benefit from the water. Furthermore, the prayer neither blesses nor exorcizes the water. In fact, the status of the water does not appear to change at all. These same comments stand for the second oration provided in the current Order:

> Lord, holy Father,
> look upon us,
> who (*qui*), redeemed by your Son,
> have been reborn through Baptism
> in water and the Holy Spirit:
> grant, we beseech you,
> that those who will be sprinkled with this water,
> may be renewed in body and in mind
> and may render pure service to you.
> Through Christ our Lord.
> R. Amen.[39]

This formula invokes renewal in body and mind upon those who will be sprinkled with this water, in order that they may render pure service to the Father. In this case the *qui* clause does not describe God, but "us" who have been redeemed and reborn in baptism. Once again baptism is recalled, and the water itself is not actually blessed—only the people to be sprinkled with it. The third and final option for a prayer of blessing also brings to mind the sacrament of baptism. Threefold in structure, each part attributes a specific act to one Person in the Trinity by means of a *qui* clause, and asks that Person to bless and purify the Church:

> God creator of all things, who (*qui*) in water and the Spirit
> have given form and image to man and to the universe.
> R. Bless and purify your Church.

---

39   *De Benedictionibus*, no. 1094: "Domine, sancte Pater, / respice super nos, / qui per Filium tuum redempti, / ex aqua et Spiritu Sancto / per Baptismum sumus renati: / praesta, quaesumus, / ut qui hac aqua fuerint aspersi, / corpore et mente renoventur / et puram tibi exhibeant servitutem. / Per Christum Dominum nostrum. / R. Amen."

Christ, who (*qui*) from the side pierced on the cross
have made the sacraments of salvation flow forth.
R. Bless and purify your Church.

Holy Spirit, who (*qui*) from the baptismal bosom of the Church,
in the bath of regeneration,
have made us new creatures.
R. Bless and purify your Church.[40]

This blessing refers to the water of creation, the water that flowed
from Christ's side, and the water of baptism. The water of the
Order, however, is not specifically mentioned. So while this formula presents a tidy summary of water's role in salvation history,
it does not request that the water of the Order be blessed. The
petition, contained in the response of the congregation, asks
instead that the Church be blessed and purified.

At the end of the Order, the celebrant sprinkles those present
with holy water and says the following: "May this water be a
memorial of baptism received, and may it recall Christ, who has
redeemed us by his Passion and Resurrection. R. Amen." When
appropriate (*pro opportunitate*), those present sing a fitting song.[41]
Thus the theme of baptism opens the Order, closes it, and is
prominent throughout. The fundamental point of the Order is to
aid the faithful in recalling their baptism and the work of Christ
in the economy of salvation.

At this point numerous theological questions arise. For
instance, at the completion of this Order, is the water used therein
blessed? Does it differ from any other water? Can one answer "yes"
to these questions when the Ordo itself provides no justification

---

40   *De Benedictionibus*, no. 1095: "Omnium creator Deus, qui ex aqua et Spiritu
/ formam dedisti atque imaginem homini et universo. / R. Ecclesiam tuam benedic
atque emunda. / Christe, qui de rescisso in cruce latere / Sacramenta salutis scatere
fecisti. / R. Ecclesiam tuam benedic atque emunda. / Sancte Spiritus, qui e baptismali
Ecclesiae gremio, / in regenerationis lavacro, / novas nos constituisti creaturas. / R.
Ecclesiam tuam benedic atque emunda."

41   *De Benedictionibus*, no. 1096: "Sit haec aqua suscepti Baptismatis memoria,
/ et Christum recolat, / qui Passione et Resurrectione sua nos redemit. / R. Amen."

for an affirmative answer? Are the members of Christ's faithful deceived who believe the water in their churches' fonts is blessed? Will the farmer who sprinkles such water on his failing crops only benefit to the extent that it helps him recall his salvation? If a mother sprinkles it on her sick infant, does the infant who has not yet the use of reason—and so cannot "recall Christ"—benefit? For whom is the blessing intended—the mother or the infant? Indeed, if the purpose of blessing is primarily praise and thanksgiving, can anyone who is absent from the liturgical celebration of the Order participate in the blessing? The implications of this radical shift in the euchology of blessings have yet to be considered.

A radical shift it is. The above analysis demonstrates that the present Order is in no way derived from the previous Order; it is not a revision, but an entirely new work. This is in fact typical of the current *De Benedictionibus*. Only five of the more than 100 formulae that appear in the book are directly inspired by the Ritual of 1952. Nor are the prayers drawn from ancient liturgical books, as is the case with many orations in the revised Missal.[42] Pierre Jounel explains the grounds for constructing the blessings of the Ritual *ex nihilo* as follows: "The Eucharistic conception of blessing having been lost since the distant times of the *Apostolic Constitutions*, the medieval sacramentaries and more recent rituals could not be of any great help."[43] With this statement, Jounel effectively tosses the Church's entire patrimony of blessings into the trash bin. Moreover, his reference to such an ancient and obscure text betrays the extent to which the work of revising the blessings was dependent upon a particular interpretation of the history of blessings—an interpretation which smacks of archeologism and might not withstand critical examination.

---

42   Lodi, "Le bénédictionnel romain," 194–195, demonstrates that at least a few turns of phrase in the various formulae of blessing are drawn from orations in the Roman Missal of 1970.

43   Jounel, "Le livre des bénédictions," 49–50, my translation: "La conception eucharistique de la bénédiction ayant été oubliée depuis les temps lointains des *Constitutions apostoliques*, les sacramentaires médiévaux et les rituels plus récents ne pouvaient pas être d'un grand secours."

By contrast, the 1952 Order for Blessing Water descended directly from a tradition that can be definitively traced to the origins of liturgical books. The Romano-Germanic Pontifical, compiled at Mainz in the mid-tenth century, contains the very same exorcisms and prayers of blessing for both salt and water that are found in the Ritual of 1952.[44] Earlier still, they are found in their integrity in the Gregorian Sacramentary.[45] In turn, the redactor of the Gregorian Sacramentary adapted, with only a few minor variations, the prayer over the water in the Blessing of Water to be Sprinkled in a Home (*Benedictio aquae spargendae in domo*) found in the Old Gelasian Sacramentary. The Gelasian is, due to its antiquity and the completeness of the manuscript, a privileged witness of early Roman liturgy; copied at Chelles around 750, the manuscript contains earlier material originally compiled in southern Italy.[46] A number of verbal parallels also link the exorcisms of salt and water in the Gelasian with those in the Gregorian, and therefore with the Order for Blessing Water found in the 1952 Roman Ritual.[47]

---

44   *Le pontifical romano-germanique du dixième siècle: Le texte II (NN. XCIX-CCLVIII)*, ed. Cyrille Vogel and Reinhard Elze, Studi e Testi 227 (Vatican City: Biblioteca Apostolica Vaticana, 1963) 152–154. Only a few minor variations can be found, although the formula for mixing the salt with the water differs significantly: "In nomine pa+tris et fi+lii et spiritus + sancti, benedicatur haec commixtio salis et aquae."

45   Jean Deshusses, *Le sacramentaire grégorien: ses principales formes d'après les plus anciens manuscrits*, vol. 1, 3rd ed. (Fribourg: Éditions Universitaires, 1992) nos. 1451–1455 (pp. 472–475). See also Adolph Franz, *Die kirchlichen Benediktionen im Mittelalter* (Graz: Akademische Druck- und Verlagsanstalt, 1960) 148–149: Franz argues that the redactor of the Gregorian formulae for blessing water made use of the Gelasian formulae, although which other sources he used, or how much he himself composed, cannot be determined.

46   Matthieu Smyth, *La liturgie oubliée: La prière eucharistique en Gaule antique et dans l'Occident non romain* (Paris: Cerf, 2003) 126–314.

47   *Liber Sacramentorum Romanae Aeclesiae Ordinis Anni Circuli (Cod. Vat. Reg. lat. 316/Paris Bibl. Nat. 7193, 41/56) (Sacramentarium Gelasianum)*, ed. Leo Cunibert Mohlberg, OSB, Rerum Ecclesiasticarum Documenta, Series Maior, Fontes V, 3rd ed. (Rome: Casa Editrice Herder, 1981) III,lxxv–lxxvi (pp. 225–226); for a facsimile of the original manuscript, see *Sacramentarium Gelasianum e codice Vaticano Reginensi Latino 316* (Vatican City: n.p., 1975) 220r–222r.

Another contrast is evident in the Order for Blessing Water within Mass, which constitutes the second appendix of the latest Roman Missal. This Order offers three prayers of blessing which are more continuous with the tradition of blessing water in several ways.[48] First, they in fact beseech God to bless the water. Second, they mention apotropaic effects of the holy water—even if that reference is somewhat muted and the ancient enemy is not named. Third, they at least allow, where it is customary, the mixing of the water with salt. Striking in their absence from *De Benedictionibus*, the presence of these elements in the Missal betrays some theological disparity between those responsible for the respective liturgical books.

WHY THE CONTRAST?

The above examination of the differences between the previous and the present Order for Blessing Water Outside of Mass provides a vivid illustration of the fact that the *De Benedictionibus* promulgated in 1984 is no mere revision of the blessings from the pre-Vatican II Roman Ritual. It is rather a completely different work, which appears to be undergirded by a radically different understanding of the nature of blessing and exorcism, an understanding that is in part characterized by the practical principles of revision set forth by Study Group 23 and discussed above.

What theological shifts, it may be asked, led to the new understanding that entailed the wholesale re-writing of the Ritual's blessings? David Stosur reasons that, in the absence of sustained

---

48   The first option, here provided as an example, is found in *Missale Romanum ex decreto Sacrosancti Oecumenici Concilii Vaticani II instauratum auctoritate Pauli PP. VI promulgatum Ioannis Pauli PP. II cura recognitum*, Editio typica tertia (Vatican City: Typis Vaticanis, 2002) no. 1249: "Omnipotens sempiterne Deus, qui voluisti ut per aquam, fontem vitae ac purificationis principium, etiam animae mundarentur aeternaeque vitae munus exciperent, dignare, quaesumus, hanc aquam benedicere, qua volumus hac die tua, Domine, communiri. Fontem vivum in nobis tuae gratiae renovari et ab omni malo spiritus et corporis per ipsam nos defendi concedas, ut mundis tibi cordibus propinquare tuamque digne salutem valeamus accipere. Per Christum Dominum nostrum. R. Amen."

attention given to blessings in and of themselves, "a contemporary theology of blessings . . . must simply be extrapolated from approaches that theologians since Vatican II have taken to the sacraments and to the liturgy in general."[49] He proceeds to do this, appealing particularly to reflections on the liturgy by Otto Semmelroth, Edward Schillebeeckx, and Karl Rahner. Particularly worthy of note is the following passage, in which Stosur weaves together some of Rahner's comments on the liturgy:

> The very "conceptual model" of sacramentality therefore shifts according to the way God's relationship to the world is understood—in Rahner's terms, from one "based on the implicit assumption that grace can be an unmerited gift of God only if it becomes present in a secular and sinful world to which it is mostly denied," to one which "starts out from the assumption that the secular world from the outset is always encompassed and permeated with the grace of the divine self-communication:" "The sacraments accordingly are not really to be understood as successive individual incursions of God into a secular world, but as 'outbursts' . . . of the innermost, ever present gracious endowment of the world with God himself into history. The material things of creation, as necessary components of the "liturgy of the world," are by that very fact valuable. The value of material creation is in turn understood and acknowledged in sacramental celebrations, where these things are utilized for the purpose of symbolizing this "primordial" liturgy.[50]

This notion of the "liturgy of the world," whether rightly or wrongly attributed to Rahner,[51] could go a long way towards explaining why the current Order for Blessing Water Outside of Mass does not explicitly bless or exorcize the water, and moreover,

---

49   David A. Stosur, "The Theology of Liturgical Blessing in the Book of Blessings: A Phenomenologico-theological Investigation of a Liturgical Book" (Ph.D. diss., University of Notre Dame, 1994) 8.

50   Stosur, "The Theology of Liturgical Blessing," 15–16.

51   For an example of an application of this notion by an influential figure, see Nathan Mitchell, "Who is at the Table? Reclaiming Real Presence," in *Commonweal* (27 January 1995) 15.

why things (rather than people) generally are not blessed or exorcized in *De Benedictionibus*. Although the specific notion is specifically invoked rather infrequently, the "liturgy of the world" could shed light on the general consensus articulated by many theologians writing on blessings in the post-conciliar period: God's creatures are blessed from their creation; liturgical blessings are opportunities to praise and thank God for this, and, from the pastoral perspective, to edify those present by recalling it.[52]

One scholar of holy water, writing before Vatican II, expressed quite a different view of the state of creation in the following passage: "By the fall of our first parents, the spirit of evil obtained influence not only over man, but also over inanimate nature, whence he is called in Scripture 'the prince of this world'" (Jn 12:31, 14:30, 16:11). For this reason, when the Church exorcizes something, "the curse put upon it is removed, and Satan's power over it either destroyed entirely, or at least diminished."[53] The same commentator articulated what he claimed to be the consensus regarding holy water as follows:

> Nearly all theologians teach that Holy Water, used with the proper intention and disposition, confers actual graces, remits venial sin, restrains the power of Satan, and secures temporal blessings, for example, bodily health and protection against temporal evils. When preparing Holy Water, the officiating minister in the name of the whole Church prays for these divine favors in particular. Surely, then, the pious use of this "permanent sacramental" is a most helpful means of salvation.[54]

---

52   For a representative example, consider Reiner Kaczynski, "Blessings in Rome and the Non-Roman West," in *Handbook for Liturgical Studies*, vol. 4: *Sacraments and Sacramentals*, ed. Anscar J. Chupungco (Collegeville, MN: Liturgical Press, 2000) 393–410, at 393–394: "Every blessing is, first of all, thankful praise of God, the origin and giver of every blessing . . . the Church gratefully remembers the fact that human beings and things are already blessed by creation and redemption and it thanks God for this."

53   Houck, *Fountains of Joy*, 123.

54   Ibid., 122; for a similar but more detailed description of the effects of holy water, see Joseph Gaume, *L'eau bénite au dix-neuvième siècle*, 3rd ed. (Paris: Gaume Frères et J. Duprey, 1866) 262–279 and 295–315.

Hence blessing or consecrating a thing in general or water in particular entailed breaking Satan's influence over it, so that it could
no longer serve as an instrument of his hate.[55] Then, by the power
of Christ entrusted to the Church, the thing blessed could be used
as an efficacious instrument for good—assuming the proper disposition of the person who benefits from the use of the item.[56] This
type of exorcism is frequently found in ancient rituals, including,
for example, rites of baptism.[57] It is prefatory in nature; if something
or someone is to become an instrument of blessing, then, logically,
that person or thing must be free from demonic influence. Such
prefatory exorcisms do not indicate that the devil possesses the
thing or person in the sense of indwelling, but in the sense of having some claim, jurisdiction, or power over it by virtue of the Fall.

Such a view is, perhaps, somewhat pessimistic regarding the
state of creation after the Fall.[58] Yet it is in keeping with a biblical

55   Gaume, *L'eau bénite*, 103: "En effet, sanctifier une chose, c'est la soustraire à
l'influence du démon, la purifier des souillures dont il l'a salie et la rendre à sa pureté
native. Que par suite de sa victoire sur le Roi de la création, le démon ait fait des créatures
ses esclaves et les instruments de sa haine, aussi bien dans l'ordre physique que dans l'ordre moral, c'est le grand fait sur lequel pose tout l'histoire de l'humanité;" my translation: "In effect, to sanctify a thing is to remove it from the influence of the demon, to
cleanse it of the impurities with which he had soiled it and to return it to its native
purity. In consequence of his victory over the king of creation, the demon had made
some creatures his slaves and the instruments of his hate, both in the physical order as
well as in the moral; this is the grand reality on which all of human history stands."
56   Gaume, *L'eau bénite*, 106; Theiler, *Holy Water*, 23.
57   *De baptismo adultorum*, nos. 8–9, in *The Roman Ritual in Latin and English
with Rubrics and Planechant* [sic] *Notation, Vol. 1: The Sacraments and Processions*, ed.
Philip T. Weller (Milwaukee: Bruce Publishing Co., 1950) 70. In the Tridentine baptismal rite, the power of the evil spirit was cast out before the Holy Spirit was invoked
to take up its dwelling in the catechumen. The priest was directed to exsufflate (*exsufflat*) or blow three times into the face of the catechumen—whether an infant or an
adult—and command, "Go out from him (her) unclean spirit, and make way for the
Holy Spirit the Paraclete." This was immediately followed by an insufflation with
obvious epicletic force: "Here in the form of a cross he breathes (*halat*) in his face, and
says: N., receive the good Spirit through this insufflation (*insufflationem*), and the
blessing of God."
58   Gignac, "Les bénédictions," 588–589; Kaczynski, "Blessings in Rome," 400;
Lessi-Ariosto, "Linee Interpretative," 224: "L'eredità liturgica del titolo IX del *Rituale*

understanding of the state of creation, as indicated for example in Romans 8:19–21: "For creation awaits with eager expectation the revelation of the children of God; for creation was subject to futility . . . in hope that creation itself would be set free from slavery to corruption and share in the glorious freedom of the children of God." On the other hand, any view that discounts the influence of evil in favor of an insistence on the goodness of creation can be accused of an optimism that verges on naïveté.[59] Perhaps such optimistic views betray a privileged first-world bias in their facile dismissal of the radical consequences of sin on the created world: "Cursed be the ground because of you! In toil shall you eat its yield all the days of your life" (Gen 3:17). Certainly God created all things good; but we no longer live in the Garden of Eden.

Nevertheless, such optimistic views culminate in a reinterpretation of exorcism, which exerts considerable influence over the current Order for Blessing Water. Achille M. Triacca articulates a new understanding that justifies the transformation evident in the blessings of the Ritual. In his view, "the most authentic" (*le plus authentique*) liturgical and ecclesiastical view of exorcism is characterized by "the optimistic vision" (*la vision optimiste*) that encompasses all of salvation history and the orientation of all creation towards redemption. Hence Triacca highlights the importance of anamnesis (understood as a memorial of salvation history) in the euchology of exorcisms. He goes on to argue that in its most authentic form, exorcism is nothing other than an epiclesis of the

---

Romanum, De benedictionibus, dal 1614 in poi, nonostante la purificazione operata in rapporto a collezioni di benedizioni medievali, era infatti ancora troppo tributaria di una visuale pessimistica della realtà che portava più alla tendenza invocativo-impetrativo-esorcistica e insieme a quella consacratorio-sacralizzante come controparte positiva;" my translation: "The liturgical inheritance of Title IX of the *Rituale Romanum, De benedictionibus*, from 1614 on, despite the purification effected with relation to collections of medieval blessings, was in fact still too indebted to a pessimistic view of reality that inclined more toward the invocative-imperative-exorcistic tendency, and at the same time toward the consecratory-sacralizing as its positive counterpoint."

59   For an example of such an overly optimistic view, see Lessi-Ariosto, "Linee Interpretative," 225.

Holy Spirit.[60] Triacca's criteria for authenticity are somewhat obscure, as is the logic of his argument. As noted in the above discussion of the previous Order, the expulsion of evil influences appeared as a prerequisite for the fuller realization of divine power in the object to be blessed, rather than as an end in itself. Yet by no means should exorcism be conflated with epiclesis.

Nonetheless, each of the three formulae of blessing in the present Order for Blessing Water Outside of Mass mentions the Holy Spirit, and anamnesis or remembrance of salvation history—especially of one's own baptismal entrance into the economy of salvation—is the dominant theme. For those who see the connection, these elements are all that remain of the apotropaic themes that predominated in the previous Order for Blessing Water. Those who cannot admit that anamnesis and epiclesis are equivalent to exorcism, or that praise, thanksgiving, and recollection of one's baptism are equivalent to blessing water, may wonder if the radical changes in the Church's blessings faithfully reflect the Second Vatican Council's mandate that *sacramentalia recognoscantur*, that is, that the sacramentals simply be "revised."[61]

---

60   Achille M. Triacca, "Exorcisme: un sacramental en question: quelques pistes de réflexion pour des recherches 'Exorcizo te' ou 'Benedico te'?" in *Les bénédictions et les sacramentaux dans la liturgie*, 269–284, at 281–283.

61   *Sacrosanctum Concilium*, no. 79.

Very Members Incorporate: Reflections on the Sacral Language of *Divine Worship*

CLINTON ALLEN BRAND

A mong the first fruits of the liturgical provision according to the Apostolic Constitution *Anglicanorum Coetibus*, the recently promulgated Missal for Ordinariate usage, under the title *Divine Worship*, represents a momentous development in the history of Catholic worship: for the first time, the Catholic Church has officially recognized, blessed, approved, and made her own in a sustained and permanent fashion a collection of liturgical texts that found voice and developed outside the bounds of her visible communion.[1] *Divine Worship: The Missal* is noteworthy for many reasons, not least of which is its consistent use of a traditional idiom of liturgical English derived from the classic Books of Common Prayer. The Vatican commission *Anglicanae Traditiones* (advisory to the Congregation for the Doctrine of the Faith and the Congregation for Divine Worship and the Discipline of the Sacraments) had the task of assessing the wide variety of "liturgical books proper to the Anglican tradition" in order to discern, winnow, and harmonize a unified body of liturgical "patrimony" amenable to Catholic worship and duly conformed to Catholic doctrinal and sacramental norms, including the careful evaluation of linguistic register.[2] That the Holy See has defini-

---

1   The liturgical text approved for the Pastoral Provision parishes in the United States, *The Book of Divine Worship* (Mt. Pocono, PA: Newman House Press, 2003) merits mention as an important precedent and prefiguration, albeit one limited in scope and somewhat tentative in context, certainly in comparison with *Divine Worship*.

2   See Steven J. Lopes, "A Missal for the Ordinariates: The Work of the *Anglicanae Traditiones* Interdicasterial Commission," in *Antiphon* 19 (2015) 116–131, and

tively identified texts in traditional rather than contemporary English for such liturgical repatriation, in order to authenticate for the Ordinariates a "precious gift nourishing the faith" and "a treasure to be shared,"[3] deserves some comment and explanation. To some, it may seem intriguing or perplexing that the Catholic Church in the twenty-first century has been moved to reclaim a liturgical corpus and an idiom of prayer stemming from the Reformation, expressed in a hieratic dialect forged in the sixteenth century, and shaped over nearly five-hundred years of continuous, if checkered, public worship.

Hence, in these pages, I mean to explore the distinctive sacral language of *Divine Worship* as exemplified in the newly approved *Missal* (2015) and in *Occasional Services* (2014) with its rites for baptism, confirmation, matrimony, and funerals. This language, though unabashedly old-fashioned and sometimes slightly archaic without being obsolete, has proven itself over the centuries remarkably conducive to the active participation of the faithful and remains in its own way richly intelligible, even as it now finds a new place "meet and right" in union with the Catholic Church to serve the Ordinariates' "bounden duty" and mission. Accordingly, I would like also to discuss the function of liturgical language itself, in the ecclesial context of Catholic communion, and to consider both the promise and some of the perils of this special liturgical dialect, particularly as the Ordinariate faithful think about the pastoral stewardship of worshipping the Lord "in the beauty of holiness" by way of the traditional, hieratic vernacular best called "Prayer Book English." Thus I invite reflection on an idiom of worship that is familiar, formative, and beloved to many in the Ordinariates (but not everyone),

---

his "The Liturgy of the Ordinariates for Former Anglicans," in *Origins: CNS Documentary Service* 42 (2013) 579–583 (originally delivered as an address at the symposium on the Mission of the Ordinariates at St. Mary's Seminary in Houston, Texas, 2 February 2013).

3   Quotations from Pope Benedict XVI, Apostolic Constitution Providing for Personal Ordinariates for Anglicans Entering into Full Communion with the Catholic Church *Anglicanorum Coetibus* (4 November 2009) art. III.

and a style of liturgical prayer with roots deep in the English tradition, now renewed by authority of the Holy See, and yet awaiting the prospect of evangelizing new generations of Catholic faithful.

THE ECCLESIAL CONTEXT

In *Tract 90*, John Henry Newman wrote, "our Prayer Book is acknowledged on all hands to be of Catholic origin."[4] Thus Newman, a few years before his conversion, staked the claims of the Oxford Movement on the Catholic sources and the enduring Catholic character of the *Book of Common Prayer*, and he did so notwithstanding its excisions and occasional ambiguities and despite certain problematic formulations in the Thirty-Nine Articles, whose doctrinal difficulties famously would help deliver him into the communion of the Catholic Church. In suggesting that the English Prayer Book had the potential to serve as a vehicle for "Catholic" worship, Newman anticipated, at least implicitly, a possibility that would not come to fruition until the next century with the Second Vatican Council and its Constitution on the Sacred Liturgy, namely, that worship in the Roman Rite could find voice in a noble vernacular idiom. He foreshadowed, as well, in his witness of continuity between his Anglican formation and its Catholic fulfillment, the promise confirmed in *Anglicanorum Coetibus* that the Anglican tradition has managed to retain and convey "elements of sanctification and truth," as "forces impelling towards Catholic unity" and "as gifts properly belonging to the Church of Christ."[5] For Newman, this witness was forged, at least in part, by his abiding "affection and reverence" for the very words and rhythms of the Prayer Book, as much as his regard for its doc-

---

4   John Henry Newman, "Tract 90," in id., *The Via Media of the Anglican Church Illustrated in Lectures, Letters, and Tracts Written between 1830 and 1841*, vol. 2 (London: Longmans, 1914) 271.

5   Benedict XVI, *Anglicanorum Coetibus,* Introduction, para. 4, quoting Second Vatican Council, Dogmatic Constitution on the Church *Lumen Gentium* (21 November 1964) 8.

trinal content.[6] This attachment was something he shared with
many other converts, including G. K. Chesterton who, well after
he entered the Church, praised the Catholic resonance and special
linguistic vigor of the Prayer Book in "the music and magic of the
great sixteenth-century style," shaped by the "speech of men still
by instinct and habit of mind Catholic. . . . It is the one positive
possession and attraction; the one magnet and talisman for people
even outside the Anglican Church."[7] For Newman and Chesterton, as for many others who have followed in their steps, the standard for assessing the Prayer Book's language and content is the
measure of Catholic tradition and truth as supervised in every age
by the authority of the magisterial *Ecclesia docens*. What they could
not have imagined, from the vantage point of their own conversions, is the advent of a remarkable ecclesial context in which their
voices and those of many others have formed a chorus for the pastoral ears of *Ecclesia audiens* and come together with a set of liturgical developments and convergences in the Roman Rite itself to
make possible the formal validation of their experience and its
extension as part of the Church's evangelizing mission.

Some of the best resources and most cogent arguments, I have
discovered, for understanding the rationale, both theological and
sociolinguistic, for a sacral or hieratic liturgical vernacular in English come not from Anglican apologists for the old Prayer Book,
nor even from the testimony of converts, but from various discussions of *Liturgiam Authenticam* (2001), the Fifth Instruction for the
Right Implementation of *Sacrosanctum Concilium*, together with
the resultant 2010 revised English translation of the *Roman Missal*
in its Third Typical Edition. *Liturgiam Authenticam* calls for the
"development, in each vernacular, of a sacred style that will come
to be recognized as proper to liturgical language (*sermo proprie*

---

6   See Newman's sermon, "The Liturgy Public: Its Three Peculiar Uses" (7
February 1830), in *John Henry Newman Sermons 1824-1843, Vol. 1: Sermons on the
Liturgy and Sacraments and on Christ the Mediator*, ed. Placid Murray (Oxford: Clarendon Press, 1991) 73–74.
7   G. K. Chesterton, "My Six Conversions: IV. The Prayer-Book Problem,"
in id., *The Well and the Shallows* (London: Sheed & Ward, 1935) 46–47, 50.

liturgicus)."⁸ The instruction thereby signals a shift away from a principle of liturgical translation based on "dynamic equivalence," aimed at elusive goals of contemporary "relevance" and "accessibility," toward one based more on "formal equivalence," directed at accuracy, fidelity to the original Latin texts, and measured emulation of their stylistic features within the capacity of each vernacular language.⁹ Citing the example of the Eastern Catholic Rites and their venerable tradition of worship according to highly stylized, somewhat archaic forms of the liturgical vernacular, *Liturgiam Authenticam* thus recommends a comparable, albeit authentic, "inculturation" of the Latin Rite whereby the distinctive vocabulary, syntax, and grammar proper to divine worship and characteristic of the Latin tradition might be captured with dignity and stability and mediated through the historical resources and native genius of diverse peoples and tongues, all "to prepare for a new era of liturgical renewal."¹⁰

As Msgr. Andrew Burnham has pointed out, in the Anglophone context, the norms of *Liturgiam Authenticam* had the effect of complicating the ecumenical sharing of common texts reflective of modern Anglican liturgical revision in contemporary English.¹¹ At the same time, however, these norms auspiciously prepared the ground for another kind of ecumenical convergence, one that has now borne fruit through *Anglicanorum Coetibus*: in the sacral language of the traditional Books of Common Prayer, we find a ready-made, time-tested, carefully honed dialect of worship that, *mutatis mutandis*, with only a few adjustments, admirably answers to the promise of *Sacrosanctum Concilium* and the requirements of *Liturgiam Authenticam*. Though *Liturgiam Authenticam* and *Anglicanorum Coetibus* are circumstantially quite distinct, and while the new English translation of the *Roman Missal* and the texts of *Divine Worship* are rather differ-

---

8   Congregation for Divine Worship and the Discipline of the Sacraments, Fifth Instruction for the Right Implementation of the Constitution on the Sacred Liturgy *Liturgiam Authenticam* (28 March 2001) no. 27.

9   Ibid.; see also nos. 20, 23, 47, 49, 57, 59.

10   Ibid., no. 7; see also nos. 4, 5, 32, 47.

11   See Andrew Burnham, *Heaven and Earth in Little Space: The Re-enchantment of Liturgy* (Norwich: Canterbury Press, 2010) 37–39.

ent in style and some content, all of these works of the Church represent a striking, perhaps providential, convergence of concerns with shared roots in Vatican II, its Decree on Ecumenism, and its Constitution on the Sacred Liturgy. It may be tempting to set the linguistic register of *Divine Worship* and the new *Roman Missal* in contrast, but both are complementary fruits of the same tree with a similar capacity for feeding the faithful in our own age.

To specify this ecclesial context a bit more, I would suggest that this alignment of influences could be understood in relation to a "hermeneutic of renewal in continuity" (a phrase which is not just the slogan of a single pontificate but a key to the Church's own self-understanding through the ages, with an emphasis upon "renewal" as much as "continuity").[12] And I would suggest too that the liturgical results of this convergence are best grasped with reference to principles of "organic development" that have shaped the evolution and growth of Catholic liturgy over the centuries, often by fits-and-starts and sometimes with notable "course-corrections" steered by the authority of the Apostolic See, yet keeping by-and-large to the path of the Church's pilgrimage through history.[13]

---

12   Benedict XVI, *Christmas Address to the Members of the Roman Curia* (22 December 2005): ". . . there is the 'hermeneutic of reform,' of renewal in the continuity of the one subject-Church which the Lord has given to us. She is a subject which increases in time and develops, yet always remaining the same, the one subject of the journeying People of God."

13   For a sound characterization of the meaning of "organic development," see Alcuin Reid, *The Organic Development of the Liturgy: The Principles of the Liturgical Reform and their Relation to the Twentieth-Century Liturgical Movement Prior to the Second Vatican Council*, 2nd ed. (San Francisco: Ignatius Press, 2005) 308: "Organic development holds openness to growth (prompted by pastoral needs) and continuity with Tradition in due proportion. It listens to scholarly desiderata and considers anew the values of practices lost in the passage of time, drawing upon them to improve liturgical Tradition gradually, only if and when this is truly necessary. Ecclesiastical authority supervises this growth, at times making prudential judgments about what is appropriate in the light of the needs of different ages, but always taking care that liturgical Tradition is never impoverished and that what is handed on is truly that precious heritage received from our fathers, perhaps judiciously pruned and carefully augmented (but not wholly reconstructed), according to the circumstances of the Church in each age, ensuring continuity of belief and practice."

But to some, no doubt, this application of standards of continuity and organic development to a liturgical tradition that began in manifest rupture from Catholic truth (in politically motivated schism, issuing in heresy) may seem problematic. Yet the pastoral generosity of Pope Benedict's Apostolic Constitution is premised on the studied acknowledgement that, despite the historical reality of rupture, the Anglican liturgical tradition managed to preserve and then subsequently revive and develop much that is indisputably Catholic in expression and content, affording a stream, so to speak, of residual and prevenient grace nourishing aspirations to restored ecclesial unity, at least for those properly disposed to drink of the waters.[14] To shift the metaphor a bit, through *Anglicanorum Coetibus* the pastoral solicitude of the Church has performed something of the Father's role as "vinedresser" (Jn 15:1), tending the vineyard of Christ to assure continued and wider fruitfulness, and, in the particular case of reclaiming Anglican liturgical patrimony, to graft selected growths, proven scions of Anglican provenance, back on the durable rootstalk of the Roman Rite.

Before turning to the particular claims and properties of Prayer Book English in the Ordinariate Missal, I think this ecclesial context is an important point of departure, especially as full communion in the Catholic Church, while allowing diversity of expression in the unity of the faith, entails full integration with the magisterial authority governing Catholic worship. This context is also important lest we think of *Divine Worship* only as the permissive indulgence of praying in a comfortable Anglican accent. While *Divine Worship* may be a pastoral *accommodation* of a certain, proven style of worship and though it may be a special kind of ecumenical *inculturation*,[15] it is also a more challenging *incorporation* of select

---

14   See Benedict XVI, *Anglicanorum Coetibus*, Introduction, para. 1. See also Michael Rear, "This Offer Was 400 Years in the Making," in *The Catholic Herald* (6 November 2009).

15   On *Divine Worship* as an example of legitimate liturgical "inculturation," see Hans-Jürgen Feulner, "'Anglican Use of the Roman Rite'? The Unity of the Liturgy in the Diversity of Its Rites and Forms," in *Antiphon* 17 (2013) 31–72, esp. 49–52.

Anglican patrimony into the saving, sanctifying work of the
Roman Rite itself.

THE FUNCTION OF LITURGICAL LANGUAGE AND
THE PROBLEM OF PERSONAL TASTE

But quite aside from the context of ecclesial sanction and the
attendant evangelizing responsibility, it may also be important to
recognize that not everyone will immediately like or appreciate the
language of *Divine Worship*, and some (including members of the
Ordinariates coming from different liturgical backgrounds and
accustomed to more contemporary language) may at first feel uneasy
with the Ordinariate Missal's consistent, uncompromising preference
for a style of traditional, liturgical English derived from the classic
Prayer Books. Some might question the pastoral effectiveness of such
a hieratic liturgical dialect in the twenty-first century, and certain
skeptics might dismiss *Divine Worship* as a "Tudorbethan fantasy,"
"an exercise in mock-Tudor nostalgia," or "a Cranmerian pastiche
with limited appeal." Even though it is anticipated that *Divine Worship* will be welcomed by the faithful of the Ordinariates, a measure
of criticism is to be expected and is in fact quite understandable. But
I would suggest that such misgivings can be an occasion to rediscover and rethink the evangelizing potential of Catholic worship in
a sacral idiom that is distinct from, yet complementary with, that of
the new English translation of the *Roman Missal*.

There is no accounting for taste, as they say, but it is a reality
of the last fifty years of experimentation with vernacular liturgical
language that viewpoints are many and fractured, in both Catholic
and Anglican quarters. As Msgr. Kevin Irwin once quipped, in
discussing styles of liturgical translations, "when two or three are
gathered together, there's sure to be at least four or five opinions."[16] David Crystal, the accomplished and prolific English lin-

---

16   Kevin W. Irwin, "Liturgy as Mediated Immediacy: Sacramentality and
Enacted Words" (for the USCCB series *The Intellectual Tasks of the New Evangelization*), at http://usccb.org/about/doctrine/intellectual-tasks/upload/intellectual-tasks-
of-the-new-evangelization-irwin.pdf.

guist, who has written widely on vernacular liturgical dialects, observes, however, that personal predilections about language are "relatively useless," apart from an informed analysis and understanding of what liturgical language *is* and what liturgical language *does* in the context of public worship viewed from both diachronic and synchronic perspectives.[17] Liturgy, of its very nature, as the public worship of God and the recollected enactment of divine mysteries, requires a language set apart from everyday communication, description, and commerce. Historically liturgical language, even when it aims at intelligibility and engaged participation in the vernacular, is inevitably, to one degree or another, a specialized idiom (a *Sondersprache*), a register of language purposefully situated and one that takes its place as an integral component in the overall *Gestalt* of enacted praise, thanksgiving, penitence, supplication, and sacramental participation.[18] Liturgical language in the Catholic tradition is the verbal cognate of the stylized gestures, ritual actions, vestments, candlesticks, and architectural ordering of the sanctuary, themselves hearkening back to the historical character of ancient cultural forms and all of

---

17   David Crystal, "A Liturgical Language in a Sociolinguistic Perspective," in *Language and the Worship of the Church*, ed. R. C. D. Jasper (New York: St. Martin's Press, 1990) 120–146, esp. 144–146; see also, "Language and Religion," in *Twentieth-Century Catholicism*, A Periodic Supplement to the Twentieth Century Encyclopedia of Catholicism 3, ed. Lancelot C. Sheppard (New York: Hawthorn Books, 1966) 11–28; "Linguistics and Liturgy," in *The Church Quarterly* 2 (1969) 23–30; and "A Liturgical Language in a Linguistic Perspective," in *New Blackfriars* 46 (1964) 148–156; together with chapter 11, "Language and the Liturgy: The Principles of a Liturgical Language," in id., *Linguistics, Language, and Religion* (New York: Hawthorn Books, 1965) 149–156.

18   Crystal's functionalist analysis of liturgical language independently complements and corroborates Christine Mohrmann's important historical investigation of the stylized character of early liturgical Latin: as she argues, from the earliest experience of vernacular worship in the Roman world, the idiom of Christian liturgical prayer was distinct from the everyday language of commerce (*sermo utilis*), from the language of literary sophistication (*sermo urbanus*), and from the language of the illiterate (*sermo vulgaris*) to constitute instead the very kind of *Sondersprache* outlined in *Liturgiam Authenticam* as *sermo proprie liturgicus*. See Mohrmann, *Liturgical Latin: Its Origins and Character* (Washington, DC: Catholic University of America Press, 1957).

which work together with the dialect of proclaimed prayer to take
the worshiping congregation out of the profane world into a
sacred precinct for a dedicated and communal encounter with
God. Accordingly, notes Crystal, liturgical language fulfills its
proper function when it achieves qualities of dignity, stability, and
memorability, and it typically, historically, has served these ends
through the select retention of "archaisms, specialized vocabulary,
and formulaic diction," all to help transcend the inevitable flux and
contingency of linguistic change and to shape an enduring idiom
of public prayer.[19]

Even yet, the descriptive account of what liturgical language
is and the functional analysis of what it does must find their motive
and normative character in a properly theological rationale.
Supremely in the Holy Eucharist and more broadly throughout
all liturgical rites, it is the purpose of the language of Christian
worship to help effect, to incarnate, indeed to inculturate diversely
the one, originary and summative *anamnesis* (or actualizing
remembrance) of the Paschal Mystery of Christ's passion, death,
resurrection, ascension, and coming again, that we might be more
perfectly conformed here and now to this memory and to our
eschatological hope hereafter.[20] Liturgy is *anamnetic* both in the
specific sense of making present the Paschal Mystery but also in
the more diffuse sense of remembering the whole of sacred history
and the ongoing salvific experience of all those received and constituted in the universal Church by this one Eucharistic faith.[21]

---

19   Crystal, "A Liturgical Language in a Linguistic Perspective," 151–152.
When Crystal goes on here to describe these linguistic features in detail, characterizing
them as *generally* representative of Christian liturgical languages across history and
cultures, his examples interestingly are taken from the traditional *Book of Common
Prayer*, as apt for an Anglophone readership, and this despite his being himself a
Catholic and a sometime consultor of ICEL.

20   See *Catechism of the Catholic Church*, 2nd ed. (Washington, DC: United
States Catholic Conference, 2000) nos. 1103, 1354, 1362.

21   See Joseph Ratzinger, *Principles of Catholic Theology: Building Stones for a
Fundamental Theology*, trans. Mary Frances McCarthy (San Francisco: Ignatius Press,
1987) 293.

Hence, insofar as language itself is the storehouse of sustaining
memory, one can say that the words of liturgical worship also
serve to recollect and evoke the ambient linguistic and historical
context in which that saving grace has been operative for pilgrim
peoples throughout the ages, for those scattered at Babel but now
gathered by the indwelling Spirit in the unity of the Church and
in the unifying culture of "the Church's own way of speaking"
(*ecclesiastica loquendi consuetudo*).[22] Accordingly, I would suggest
that the achievement of *Divine Worship* can be understood as a special application of this principle of linguistic *anamnesis* for the heal-
ing of schism, for the honor of a purified medium that nourished
aspirations to Catholic unity, and for the enfolding of a particular
liturgical patrimony that itself enfolds and contains in layered resonance the memory of salvation history in its Hebrew, Greek, and
Latin expressions, all mediated through an idiom of English going
back to the beginnings of our tongue's first sustained liturgical use
in the sixteenth century. The language of *Divine Worship*, including its characteristic archaisms, specialized vocabulary, and formulaic diction, with their roots in the historic Books of Common
Prayer, could be said, at least for a particular pastoral constituency
of converts in their ecclesial pilgrimage, to model and participate
in the typological and paschal pattern of *exitus* (going forth) and
reditus (coming home) with all the salient marks of the journey
preserved intact.[23]

Where the ecclesial context for appreciating the work of
Divine Worship, as issuing from the period between the Second
Vatican Council and *Liturgiam Authenticam* and into the pontificate of Benedict XVI, may help allay possible misgivings about
the venture, the wider discussion of liturgical theology in recent
decades also provides an important orientation for understanding
how and why the Holy See judged this body of liturgical patri-

---

22   St. Augustine of Hippo, *Enarrationes in Psalmos* 93,3 (CCL 39:1303).
23   On the *exitus-reditus* schema in the context of sacred worship, see Joseph
Ratzinger, *The Spirit of the Liturgy*, trans. John Saward (San Francisco: Ignatius Press,
2000) 32–34.

mony and its particular expressive dialect worthy of repatriation into the Roman Rite. The measured, sometimes spirited, assessment of the liturgical reforms ushered in by Vatican II has seen its fair share of controversy, but it has also stimulated a deeper exploration of the challenges of vernacular liturgy in tandem with an enriched appreciation of the Catholic Church's own patrimony of Latin liturgical prayer to help condition the Holy See's newfound openness to the kind of hieratic dialect inscribed in *Divine Worship*. Before moving on to a brief overview of Prayer Book English, it may be helpful to distil a few points from this wider discussion by way of outlining some principles relevant for appreciating the sacral language of *Divine Worship*:[24]

1) Liturgical language is not so much a tool of edifying information as it is the simulacrum of divine encounter and revelation; it is not and has never been the diffuse idiom of everyday communication; rather it is the Church's focused, concentrated instrument of *mediation* to effect, to incarnate our *participation* in the saving mysteries of our faith and to immerse, to wash the faithful in the figural meanings of Holy Scripture.

2) Liturgical language is stylized, enacted speech with its own kind of mediated intelligibility, and far from excluding archaic elements it welcomes a modicum of traditional expressions and ritualized, formulaic conventions that "reach to the roots," resonate in the auditory memory, and habituate an experience of worship

---

24   The principles that follow claim no originality and are gleaned from the following, among others: Uwe Michael Lang, *The Voice of the Church at Prayer: Reflections on Liturgy and Language* (San Francisco: Ignatius Press, 2012); Kevin W. Irwin, *What We Have Done, What We Have Failed to Do: Assessing the Liturgical Reforms of Vatican II* (New York: Paulist Press, 2013); Aidan Nichols, *Looking at the Liturgy: A Critical View of Its Contemporary Form* (San Francisco: Ignatius Press, 1996); Jeremy Driscoll, "Conceiving the Translating Task: The Roman Missal and the Vernacular," in *The Voice of the Church: A Forum on Liturgical Translation* (Washington DC: United States Catholic Conference, 2001) 49–95; Bruce E. Harbert, "The Roman Rite and the English Language," in *Antiphon* 9 (2005) 16–29; and Daniel B. Gallagher, "What Has Language to do with Beauty? The Philosophical Foundations of Liturgical Translations," in *Benedict XVI and the Roman Missal*, Fota Liturgy Series 4, ed. Janet E. Rutherford and James O'Brien (Dublin: Four Courts Press, 2013) 226–244.

wider, deeper, older than ourselves, transcending the gathered congregation in time and space to represent and configure our *incorporation* into the Communion of the Saints.

3) Liturgical language is recursive and immersive; it bears and demands repetition, day by day, week by week, season by season, year by year, without ever exhausting its capacity to stimulate meditation and work ongoing *conversion* of life; its words are "poetic" in the sense of being athletic, even ascetic, by gently, insistently stretching the limits of expression in order to exercise, train, tune, and elevate our faculties that we might lift up our hearts to God and open out our lives in love and service.

Nonetheless, it needs emphasizing that liturgical speech by itself, even at its best and richest, cannot achieve these ends without the necessary structures of authority, authentic unity of intention, and manifest bonds of communion that are more than merely notional or aspirational, something more than wishful thinking. Words, of course, signify their meanings in context, by authority and intention, according to their arrangement, occasion, purpose, and the attitude of their utterance (*ad placitum ex suppositione* in the phrase of medieval grammarians). Many of the same words that the Catholic Church now annexes to the Roman Rite have been prayed by Anglicans of one stripe or another under the banner of Protestant Establishment, sometimes with a pointedly anti-Catholic animus, or as a kind soothing word-music detachable from real belief, or as a badge of belonging to a nation or class, as a marker of "tribal" identity, freighted with all manner of sentiment and nostalgia.[25] That such associations are rightly receding

---

25   Elements of the Protestant wing of Anglicanism retain a reverence for the old *Book of Common Prayer* read through the lens of Reformed theology and Evangelical commitments (witness the publications of the Latimer Trust, for instance). An essentially agnostic, literary humanist appreciation of the Prayer Book is exemplified in Matthew Arnold; see his "A Psychological Parallel," in *Matthew Arnold: Essays Religious and Mixed*, ed. Robert H. Super (Ann Arbor, MI: University of Michigan Press, 1972) 135–137. And for a soulful paean to the Prayer Book from the heart of certain kind of contemporary romantic Toryism, see Roger Scruton, *Our Church: A Personal History of the Church of England* (London: Atlantic Books, 2013) 96–100.

and can be yet overcome in the Catholic faith and in Catholic mission is, in some sense, the burden and the challenge of the liturgical provision for *Anglicanorum Coetibus*. Those from an Anglican background know that the rich words of the Prayer Book can fall flat and ring hollow when an otherwise lovely *lex orandi* is divorced from an authoritative *lex credendi* and leaves *lex vivendi* prey to the *zeitgeist* of "lifestyle politics," setting souls adrift.

What a difference it makes to be fully, unambiguously Catholic, to cleave to the rock of Peter, to subscribe to the Magisterium, and to trust the pastoral solicitude of Holy Mother Church! When the Ordinariate faithful recite the familiar words of the Nicene Creed, "I believe one holy Catholic and Apostolic Church," those words must mean something very different as Catholics than those same words once said as Anglicans. It makes a profound difference to pray the Mass with the Collect for Purity at the beginning and the Prayer of Thanksgiving at the end, clustered now *not* around an equivocal Prayer of Consecration (one not altogether clear about what exactly it is doing), but irradiating from the confidence of the Roman Canon and the power of the Holy Sacrifice. Such context can literally *transfigure* the significance of familiar words. To make good on the promise of *Divine Worship,* the ranks of erstwhile Anglicans who have become Ordinariate Catholics face the challenge of learning to read their Anglican history and to examine their habits and affections in a new key, a new context, not so much for the defensive retention of a "goodly heritage," but to discover in its resources a new impetus for *transfiguring* mission in the fullness of the faith.

PRAYER BOOK ENGLISH AND *DIVINE WORSHIP*

Liturgiam Authenticam sets out a striking challenge in assessing the suitability of liturgical language as a mode of missionizing inculturation: "liturgical prayer not only is formed by the genius of a culture, but itself contributes to the development of that culture."[26] In

---

26   *Liturgiam Authenticam,* no. 47.

cautioning against an "an overly servile adherence to prevailing modes of expression," the instruction notes that stable idioms of public worship can derive a certain vitality from the best, time-tested resources of each language: "works that are commonly considered 'classics' in a given vernacular language may prove useful in providing a suitable standard for its vocabulary and usage."[27] While these norms offered some important, though necessarily circumscribed, guidance for the new English translation of the *Roman Missal* (hammered out just in the last decade), they also speak significantly to the rationale and motive that led the Holy See to tap into the linguistic sources of the Anglican tradition in making liturgical provision for the evangelizing work of the Ordinariates.

Nearly everyone agrees with the eminent historical linguists David Crystal and Ian Robinson that an enduring vernacular "religious English" first emerged in the sixteenth and seventeenth centuries with the *Book of Common Prayer* (BCP) and the so-called Authorized Version (AV) or King James Version of the Bible.[28] These two books gave the English language a distinctive Christian voice, shaped the subsequent development of English prose, and have exerted a wide influence far beyond the ranks of practicing Christians.[29] Everyone agrees on that, but a regrettable imprecision creeps into common knowledge with the loose habit of characterizing the style of this religious vernacular as somehow typically

---

27   bid., no. 32.

28   See Ian Robinson, "Religious English," in id., *The Survival of English: Essays in Criticism of Language* (Cambridge: Cambridge University Press, 1973) 22–65; also his "The Prose and Poetry of the Book of Common Prayer," in *The Book of Common Prayer: Past, Present & Future*, ed. Prudence Dailey (London: Continuum Books, 2011) 70–81; and David Crystal, *The Stories of English* (London: Allen Lane, 2004) 237–241, 278–279; together with his *Begat: The King James Bible and the English Language* (Oxford: Oxford University Press, 2010).

29   On the literary and cultural influence of the *Book of Common Prayer*, see James Wood, "God Talk: The Book of Common Prayer at Three Hundred and Fifty," in *The New Yorker* (22 October 2012), at http://www.newyorker.com/magazine/2012/10/22/god-talk. See also Paul G. Stanwood, "The Prayer Book as Literature," in *The Oxford Guide to the Book of Common Prayer*, ed. Charles Hefling and Cynthia Shattuck (New York: Oxford University Press, 2006) 140–149.

"Tudor" or worse "Elizabethan," and worse yet "Shakespearean." The adjective "Tudor" and that clever compound "Tudorbethan" are valid only as the vaguest historical shorthand for describing a linguistic register that actually stands in striking contrast to the common vernaculars of early modern England.[30] It is true that the first two editions of the BCP took shape in the Tudor reign of Edward VI, with few substantial revisions thereafter until the Stuart reign of Charles II in 1662. The King James Bible, of course, takes its name from the first Stuart monarch in 1611. Notably, the reign of Elizabeth I, in the period that gave us Shakespeare, contributed almost nothing significant to the dialect of "religious English," at a time when the language was changing rapidly (probably more rapidly than today) with the fairly recent advent of mechanical printing and well before English grammar found the stability and standardization it was to acquire only in the latter part of the seventeenth century. On the contrary, the "golden age" sixteenth-century English literature did not so much contribute to as rather draw from this sacral vernacular which had been forged in the first half of the century and which would receive with the AV its biblical crystallization at the beginning of the seventeenth century.[31] The point to grasp here is that the first BCPs and the original AV did not arise in a linguistic vacuum, but neither did they merely *reflect* or *imitate* a given, preexisting English vernacular, certainly not everyday speech; rather

---

30   On the many varieties of spoken and written English in the sixteenth century, see Charles Barber, *Early Modern English* (London: Andre Deutsch, 1976) 13–64.

31   In his *English Literature in the Sixteenth Century: Excluding Drama*, Oxford History of English Literature 3 (Oxford: Clarendon Press, 1954) 204–221, C. S. Lewis notes that the biblical translations of Tyndale and Coverdale, together with the distinctive style of the first Prayer Book (1549), emerged out of what he calls "the drab age" of English prose to fertilize and stimulate the flowering of literature that would issue in the expressive power of Shakespeare and his contemporaries. Ian Robinson, in *The Establishment of Modern English Prose in the Reformation and the Enlightenment* (Cambridge: Cambridge University Press, 1998), credits Cranmer's translations and adaptations of the Latin Missal's collects for the discovery and the veritable invention of coherent English syntax in the composition of the unified sentences: "So the well-formed sentence was developed in English not as a result of the activities of the Royal Society, to purify the language and make it fit for science, but to approach God" (103).

these books served to *create* and *forge* what would become its own
stable, enduring religious language, one that underwent a very slow,
at times almost imperceptible, conservative, organic development
in the centuries to follow, up to and including *Divine Worship,* not
to mention the Revised Standard Version of the Bible in its Catholic
Edition, itself heavily indebted and impressively faithful to the
cadences of the King James Bible and now approved for liturgical
use in the Ordinariates.[32]
  Yet the first BCP in 1549 and the AV in 1611 *already* sounded
old-fashioned, even slightly archaic, when they were first published, and they did so deliberately in order to capture with the
native resources of the English tongue the feel, the *gravitas,* the
"givenness," of much older texts.[33] The King James Bible, building
upon yet improving Tyndale, Coverdale, and the Rheims New
Testament (1582), shaped a new English prose precisely in simu-
lating the stylistic features of the ancient Hebrew and Greek Scriptures, together with the Latin Vulgate. The first *Book of Common
Prayer,* "understanded of the people,"[34] yet more exalted, more stylized than their everyday speech, left behind the quaintly wooden
cadences of late medieval English vernacular lay primers in order
to adopt, adapt, and to stretch out in a new kind of English the distinctive rhythms, richness, and density of the Sarum Missal in Latin
with its own roots in the ancient Roman sacramentaries. Tapping
the wellsprings of the native voice with Anglo-Saxon origins
together with the distinctive rhetoric of early Christian Latin, this
supple language managed to sound vital and fresh by virtue of hearkening back to something ancient and venerable. This language is

---

32   A three-volume edition of this *Lectionary* was published "for use of the Holy
See and the Dioceses of the Bishops' Conferences of Botswana, Ghana, Kenya,
Lesotho, Nigeria, South Africa, Swaziland, Zimbabwe and of those countries where
the Bishops have given approval" (San Francisco: Ignatius Press, 2012).

33   See Stella Brook, *The Language of the Book of Common Prayer* (New York:
Oxford University Press, 1965) 36–90, 106–108.

34   In the phrase of Article XXIV of the Thirty-Nine Articles; see *Documents
of the English Reformation 1526–1701,* ed. Gerald Bray, Corrected reprint (Cambridge:
James Clarke & Co., 2004) 298.

important for us today because it has proved itself enduring and fruitful and also because this dialect, including its stylized grammar and archaic expressions, is itself an example of those "elements of sanctification and truth" mentioned in *Anglicanorum Coetibus*— they are seeds of life which may have germinated outside the visible communion of the Catholic Church but which the same Church now plants in her own good soil to promote future growth.

The word "Tudorbethan," then, is not the most accurate name for the linguistic register of the historical Books of Common Prayer, now renewed in *Divine Worship*. Rather, this special mode of liturgical prayer is better termed "Prayer Book English," for it held on beyond its "Tudor" origins to grow through many successive editions of the Prayer Book and to undergo over four centuries much adaptation, augmentation, and diffusion throughout the English-speaking world.[35] The later national Prayer Books changed over time (the long-winded exhortations and biddings of 1549 gradually fell away, the Eucharistic rite was restructured several times, and many new prayers were added, even as others were gently pruned, adjusted, and corrected), but what persisted and what came to characterize the distinctive Anglican way of praying was the tenacious retention of this august, rich, and rolling style. The style endured and endures, notwithstanding the fitful abandonment of traditional liturgical English in the worship books of the Anglican Communion beginning around 1971 with the Church of England's *Alternative Services Series 3*.[36] The newer

---

35   On the incremental development of Prayer Book English beyond its "Tudor" origins into the twentieth century, see Brook, *The Language of the Book of Common Prayer*, 192–219.

36   For some diverse and critical perspectives on the rationale and results of modern liturgical revision and contemporary language worship in the Anglican Communion, see Daniel B. Stevick, *Language in Worship: Reflections on a Crisis* (New York: Seabury Press, 1970); Barry Spurr, *The Word in the Desert: Anglican and Roman Catholic Reactions to Liturgical Reform* (Cambridge: Lutterworth Press, 1995); and Peter Nicholas Davies, *Alien Rites? A Critical Examination of Contemporary English in Anglican Liturgies* (Aldershot: Ashgate, 2005). See also chapter 2, "Worship," in Edward Norman, *Anglican Difficulties: A New Syllabus of Errors* (London: Morehouse, 2004) 16–28.

prayers added to the classic Prayer Book repertory, before the vogue for contemporary language, are sometimes derided as "mock-Tudor," and one must admit that they are not all equal in quality or dignity (Cranmer's own prayers were not all equally good either). But most of them successfully, seamlessly take their place to exemplify the *same* language, just as recently composed Latin orations fit into the modern *Missale Romanum* side-by-side with intact prayers dating back to the seventh-century Gelasian Sacramentary. The Ordinariate Missal features new collects for Pope St. John Paul II and Blessed John Henry Newman, among others, all in Prayer Book English, carefully "retro-fitted" for style with reference to the Latin texts and their modern English translations, but they are none the worse for that, and manage to speak in the same sacral accent that characterizes the rest of *Divine Worship*. But "style," as here understood, is not just the particular linguistic properties of this or that prayer, but rather a function of the larger, sustained, recursive experience of liturgical worship, the orchestration and harmonization of the parts to the whole in a unified rite with its own integrity, continuity, and pastoral utility.

Yet the work of this style in the aggregate depends upon the local effects of its grammar, syntax, morphology, and vocabulary. A detailed survey of such linguistic features is not necessary here, but I will offer just a few observations on the special properties of Prayer Book English, most of which are familiar in operation and whose workings tend to function subliminally, irrespective of our technical grammatical knowledge. In addition to the aural qualities of dignity, sobriety, sonority, and balance, the Prayer Book's sentences are famous for exhibiting the quality that C. S. Lewis called "pithiness."[37] Like the ancient Roman collects that are their models, these sentences are like coiled springs compressing much expressive energy in little space. But to modern ears these same sentences often feel "spacious." Both "pithy" and "spacious" at once, this special dialect takes voice in rich periodic sentences, built on patterns of subordination (with many relative clauses) and coordination

---

37   Lewis, *English Literature in the Sixteenth Century*, 217–220.

(with frequent use of synonymous constructions and parataxis in doublets and triplets): "meek heart and due reverence;" "rest and quietness;" "all holy desires, all good counsels, and all just works." The native English habit of using two words to express a single multivalent idea (a convention going back to Anglo-Saxon times) also serves in Prayer Book English to illuminate the sense of specialized Latin loan-words through their coupling with common English equivalents, thereby enriching the meanings of both: "remission and forgiveness;" "love and charity;" "regenerate and born anew."[38] The result is never amplitude for its own sake, but rather such expressions serve as the sinews of a uniquely powerful tool of accumulative mediation, constantly shuttling between and bridging time and eternity, earth and heaven, sin and grace, the here-and-now with salvation history, while connecting, as well, the homely and the supernal, and linking the earthy coziness of simple English words with the lofty abstractions of Latin theology.

One familiar example will have to suffice. In the Prayer of Thanksgiving after Communion, the faithful give thanks that by virtue of the sacrament, "we are very members incorporate in the mystical body of thy Son, the blessed company of all faithful people, and are also heirs through hope of thy everlasting kingdom." Notice how the somewhat heavy and abstract Latinate phrase, slightly archaic on its own, "very members incorporate," finds humble explication in the simple phrase, "the blessed company of all faithful people," and then reaches for precise application from our hopeful inheritance of heavenly beatitude to the assurance of grace here and now "to continue in that holy fellowship and do all such works as thou hast prepared for us to walk in." The passage, in context, is not so much *descriptive* as *demonstrative*—it enacts what it says even as it summons the faithful to participate in a like enactment; it lifts us to heaven and then brings us back to earth, changed and equipped, perhaps even *transfigured* in a pledge taken on trust to live out the efficacy of the sacrament. This kind of "performative speech," I think, is one of the keys to understand-

---

38   See Brook, *The Language of the Book of Common Prayer*, 133.

ing how the Prayer Book has managed to instill and nourish a deeply sacramental worldview.[39]

Much has been written on how Prayer Book English affords a resonant sounding-board for mediating and appropriating the language of Holy Scripture.[40] The Bible, of course, is thickly woven into the very fabric of the Prayer Book's cadences, and it is thus knit not as a source of "proof-texts" or an historical-critical dataset or as therapeutic didacticism, but as the very poetry of God's presence and action among us, unfolded in all its typological and figural richness. It is no accident that sensibilities shaped by the old Prayer Books take so readily to the biblical poetics of the early Church fathers.[41] Though liturgical language should evince a certain consistency of register, the language of worship welcomes some stylistic variation, like Scripture itself, in its parts and their different functions. *Divine Worship* displays a graduated modulation of styles of traditional English: the readings (largely instructional and edifying) show the lucid intelligibility and accuracy of the RSV

---

39   See John Shoulson, *Newman and the Common Tradition: A Study in the Language of Church and Society* (Oxford: Clarendon Press, 1970), for an account of the *fiduciary* functions of religious language in a sacramental economy: "In religion, as in poetry, we are required to make a complex act of inference and assent, and we begin by taking on *trust* expressions which are usually in analogical, metaphorical, or symbolic form, and by acting out the claims they make" (4).

40   See, for examples, *The Bible in the Book of Common Prayer, 1662 & 1928* (London: SPCK, 1940); Henry Ives Bailey, *The Liturgy Compared with the Bible* (London: Rivingtons, 1833). The standard Prayer Book commentaries are useful for excavating the many embedded scriptural allusions: Charles Neil and James Mason Willoughby, *The Tutorial Prayer Book* (London: Harrison Trust, 1913); Francis Procter and Walter Howard Frere, *A New History of the Book of Common Prayer* (London: Macmillan, 1955); Massey Hamilton Shepherd, *The Oxford American Prayer Book Commentary* (New York: Oxford University Press, 1950); and Marion J. Hatchett, *Commentary on the American Prayer Book* (New York: Seabury Press, 1981).

41   Illustrated in the seventeenth-century Caroline Divines, among others, this Anglican penchant for biblical figuralism is also exemplified in Edward Bouverie Pusey's 1836 *Lectures on Types and Prophecies* (attended by Newman). See Shoulson, *Newman and the Common Tradition*, 67–68. See also Geoffrey Rowell, "'Making the Church of England Poetical:' Ephraim and the Oxford Movement," in *Hugoye: Journal of Syriac Studies* 2 (1999) 111–129.

Bible in its Catholic Edition; the orations, next, speak clearly but with a measure of rhetorical figuration (like the Latin originals); while the Mass antiphons and psalm texts provide a more poetic counterpoint and hence exhibit a greater degree of archaic diction and stylized syntax. *Divine Worship* makes the most of this modulated scriptural resonance through a rich provision for minor propers, following not only the precedent of the *Roman Missal* but also the tradition of the so-called Anglican missals of weaving "devotional enrichments" into the unadorned *Book of Common Prayer*.

The place of the Coverdale Psalter in *Divine Worship*, as in the classic Prayer Books, deserves some special mention. Ever since its inclusion in the 1662 BCP, its lyrical rhythms have punctuated traditional Prayer Book Worship and inspired a rich body of music. Some biblical scholars might complain that the Coverdale Psalter is not the most slavishly accurate of translations from the Hebrew, but no other English rendering manages so effectively to convey the musical clausulae of ancient Jewish lyrical poetry and its constant change-ringing parallelism with a vocabulary in many cases that is more readily intelligible and certainly more suited to singing and oral proclamation than most modern translations of the psalms.[42]

Liturgiam Authenticam instructs scrupulous care in the vernacular translation of personal pronouns and the attendant inflection of verbs to convey accurately and precisely the sense of the original Latin liturgical texts.[43] The document has mainly in mind the dangers of so-called "gender-inclusive language." Happily, that is not a worry for *Divine Worship*. Fortuitously, though, *Liturgiam*

---

42   For a detailed stylistic analysis of the Prayer Book Psalter, and its differences both from Coverdale's original 1535 text and from the Authorized Version's Psalms, see Brook, *The Language of the Book of Common Prayer*, 148–171: she notes, *inter alia*, the Psalter's fidelity to the Vulgate and hence its retention of Septuagintal readings that are uniquely resonant in the Catholic liturgical tradition (150); the richly musical handling of parallelism (158–159); and the Psalter's contribution to the distinctive cadences of the Prayer Book "by a willingness to use very simple words, skillfully placed, and a willingness to repeat phrases" (170). See also David Daniell, *The Bible in English: Its History and Influence* (New Haven: Yale University Press, 2003) 181–183, 189.

43   *Liturgiam Authenticam*, nos. 30, 31.

Authenticam does imply a positive valuation of a rich and subtle resource of Prayer Book English preserved in *Divine Worship*—namely, the use of "thou" and "thee" to designate the second-person singular, in contrast to the second-person plural "you." This is the distinction between the Latin *tu* and *vos* as retained in many modern European languages but altogether lost in contemporary idiomatic English (except in parts of the American South where folks know to distinguish between "you," singular, and "y'all," plural). There is a popular misunderstanding that use of "thou" and "thee" is simply an exalted, honorific way of addressing God Almighty in His loftiness. But, in fact, the second-person singular "thou" also signifies the familiar, affectionate, and intimate form of address, as opposed to the more formal, more distant "you."[44] Interestingly, nearly all regular English-speaking Catholics to this day feel no distance at all from God in praying the *Our Father* and the *Hail Mary*, those most intimate and memorable of prayers, long hallowed with these same traditional hieratic pronouns. Yet at the same time, "thou" is still reverential and finds in Prayer Book English, as in *Divine Worship*, some special, limited application also to individual human persons in the unique intimacy of sacramental action: "I baptize thee in the Name of the Father and of the Son and of the Holy Spirit;" "The Body of our Lord Jesus Christ preserve thy body and soul unto everlasting life;" "With this ring I thee wed."[45] The use of "thou" and "thee," then, is not simply ornamental but rather functional in bearing witness to the intersubjective mystery of personhood, the I-Thou relationship so richly pondered in Martin Buber's famous book of that title.[46]

---

44   See Brook, *The Language of the Book of Common Prayer*, 53–56; Crystal, *The Stories of English*, 307–310; and Barber, *Early Modern English*, 208–210.

45   On the Prayer Book's delicately functional modulation between forms of the second-person singular pronoun, familiar ("thou") and formal ("you"), see Brook, *The Language of the Book of Common Prayer*, 54–55.

46   See Martin Buber, *I and Thou*, trans. Ronald Gregor Smith (Edinburgh: T&T Clark, 1937). For a Catholic personalist complement to Buber more immediately relevant to liturgical formation, see Dietrich von Hildebrand, *Liturgy and Personality* (New York: Longmans, Green & Co., 1943).

Mainly, though, we address God as "thou" because He is *one* God in the mystery of the holy Trinity, but we also address God as "thou" because He is closer, more intimate, to us than we are to our own selves. Not everyone will immediately or fully understand these distinctions, to be sure, but in the recursive, immersive experience of worship they can imperceptibly operate their subliminal effects all the same. These are nuances of Prayer Book English that work not only "above the measure" of everyday speech (in Tolkien's phrase)[47] but also "below the surface," so to speak, subtly to tune the ear, and to train the heart for a deeper apprehension of the Trinitarian theology of God's self-revelation *and* for the greater honor of human persons made and redeemed in His image and likeness.

Though tested and proven over nearly five hundred years, the sacral language of *Divine Worship* has yet to disclose the measure of its evangelizing and sanctifying potential in the fullness of Catholic communion. It has yet to demonstrate its capacity, as a pastoral variation of the Roman Rite, for making possible again in our own time and for new generations what Romano Guardini called "the liturgical act," a prospect perhaps more difficult today and more imperative than ever before the Church's history.[48] *Anglicanorum Coetibus* is an audacious venture in realized ecumenism, a daring pledge in the new evangelization, and its success will require more than a collection of liturgical texts. It will demand and hopefully call forth the right kind of catechesis and explanation; it will depend upon effective preaching, dedicated pastoral care, and a particular way of modeling parish life and the apostolate of the laity, all of which are equally valuable components of Anglican patrimony; and it will require singular confi-

---

47   *The Letters of J.R.R. Tolkien*, ed. Humphrey Carpenter (Boston: Houghton Mifflin, 2000) 298.

48   See Robert E. Barron's reflections on Guardini's 1964 letter *Der Kultakt und die gegenwärtige Aufgabe der liturgischen Bildung* in "The Liturgical Act and the Church of the Twenty-first Century," in *Bridging the Great Divide: Musings of a Post-Liberal, Post-Conservative Evangelical Catholic* (Lanham, MD: Rowman & Littlefield, 2004) 53–66.

dence, charity, and courtesy in living out a special liturgical charism, bravely yet humbly, as a natural, normal way of being Catholic in these challenging times. The clergy and faithful of the Ordinariates have the special responsibility of using their formative heritage in a new key—now indeed with the power of the keys— to form others for the future, that the good seed, which having in the past fallen among the stones or in shallow soil, may now find rich ground to bear fruit and yield a harvest hundredfold.

Notes on Contributors

Clinton Allen Brand holds a Ph.D. from Vanderbilt University, and is Associate Professor and Chair of the Department of English at the University of St. Thomas in Houston, Texas. His academic specialties and research interests include early modern religious culture and literature; seventeenth-century English poetry; Dante, Shakespeare, and Milton; together with the literary, cultural, and religious legacy of the Book of Common Prayer. His articles have appeared in *English Literary Renaissance, Reformation, Albion, Modern Age,* and *The John Donne Journal.* He also writes on residual and emergent strains of Catholic faith and practice in the Anglican tradition. From 2011 to 2015 he served the Holy See as a member of the interdicasterial commission *Anglicanae Traditiones.*

Michael P. Foley received a Ph.D. in systematic theology from Boston College and is an Associate Professor of Patristics in the Great Texts Program at Baylor University, Texas. He has published over 200 essays on topics ranging from St. Augustine to contemporary cultural issues and is the editor or author of several books, including Frank Sheed's translation of Augustine's *Confessions.* His commentary and translation of the *Cassiciacum Dialogues of St. Augustine* will be published in a four-volume series by Yale University Press in 2019–2020. He served as vice president/treasurer of the Society for Catholic Liturgy from 2011 to 2013 and as president from 2013 to 2015.

Sister **Madeleine Grace**, CVI, is a member of the Congregation of the Sisters of the Incarnate Word and Blessed Sacrament. She is an Associate Professor of Theology at the University of St. Thomas in Houston, Texas, where she has taught for over twenty-five years. She obtained a doctorate in historical theology from St. Louis University. Her area of specialization is historical theology coupled with a keen interest in spirituality. More recently, her research has focused on the early bishops of the diocese of Galveston, Texas. Her monograph *Yankee Bishop to Master Builder: The Life and Times of Nicholas Aloysius Gallagher, Third Bishop of Galveston (1882–1918)* will be published by Texas A&M University Press. She is currently exploring the episcopate of Bishop Christopher Byrne extending from 1918 to 1950.

Father **Uwe Michael Lang**, a priest of the Oratory of St Philip Neri in London, holds a D.Phil. in theology from the University of Oxford, and teaches Church History and Patristics at Allen Hall Seminary. He is a Visiting Fellow at St Mary's University, Twickenham, and an Associate Staff Member at the Maryvale Institute, Birmingham. He has published widely in patristic and liturgical studies, including the books *Turning Towards the Lord: Orientation in Liturgical Prayer* (Ignatius Press, 2nd ed. 2009), *The Voice of the Church at Prayer: Reflections on Liturgy and Language* (Ignatius Press, 2012), and *Signs of the Holy One: Liturgy, Ritual and Expression of the Sacred* (Ignatius Press, 2015). He is a Board Member of the Society for Catholic Liturgy and the Editor of *Antiphon: A Journal for Liturgical Renewal*.

Ryan J. Marr received a Ph.D. in historical theology from Saint Louis University, is the Director of the National Institute for Newman Studies in Pittsburgh and Associate Editor of the *Newman Studies Journal*. Before moving to Pittsburgh, he taught for at Mercy College of Health Sciences in Des Moines. His research interests include the life and writings of John Henry Newman, ecclesiology, and the reception of Vatican II. He is the author of *To Be Perfect Is to Have Changed Often: The Development of John Henry Newman's Ecclesiological Outlook, 1845–1877* (Rowman & Littlefield, 2018), and has also contributed essays to *Newman and Life in the Spirit* (Fortress Press, 2014); *Learning from All the Faithful* (Wipf and Stock, 2016); and *The Oxford Handbook of John Henry Newman* (Oxford University Press, 2018).

Dom **Alcuin Reid** is the founding Prior of the Monastère Saint-Benoît in the diocese of Fréjus-Toulon, France, and the International Coordinator of the *Sacra Liturgia* initiatives. After studies in Theology and in Education in Melbourne, Australia, he was awarded a PhD from King's College, University of London, for a thesis on twentieth-century liturgical reform (2002), which was subsequently published as *The Organic Development of the Liturgy*, with a preface by Joseph Cardinal Ratzinger (Ignatius Press, 2005). He has lectured internationally and has published extensively in the field of liturgical studies. He has recently edited the *T&T Clark Companion to Liturgy* (Bloomsbury, 2016). He is currently working on *Continuity or Rupture? A Study of the Second Vatican Council's Reform of the Liturgy*.

Daniel G. Van Slyke earned a Ph.D. from Saint Louis University, and a J.D. from Texas A&M University School of Law. He taught at several universities and seminaries, including the University of Dallas and the Liturgical Institute at Mundelein. As Dean of Online Learning at Holy Apostles College and Seminary, he was instrumental for the online program's growth during critical years. At present, he is on sabbatical from teaching while he works as an attorney in the litigation department of a Dallas law firm. His contributions to patristics, liturgical studies, and sacramental theology have appeared in academic journals such as *Dumbarton Oaks Papers*, *Ephemerides Liturgicae*, and *New Blackfriars*. For eight years he sat on the Board of the Society for Catholic Liturgy, and for five years he served on the editorial staff of *Antiphon: A Journal for Liturgical Renewal*.